$9.00

Educational Change:
A Humanistic Approach

Educational Change:
A Humanistic Approach

Edited by
Ray Eiben, Ph.D.
Illinois State University
and
Al Milliren, Ph.D.
Illinois State University

University Associates, Inc.
7596 Eads Avenue
La Jolla, California 92037

Preface

Humanistic education is individualistic in respect to both the teacher and the learner. It is the collection and integration of those elements that make each educator more fully capable of entering the lives of those with whom he has contact and significantly exciting them to learn more about themselves and of the vast knowledge available during the twentieth century.

Much has been written on the topic of humanistic education during the past few years; it is not difficult to develop extensive bibliographies or to purchase materials that purport to serve as a panacea for all that is wrong with education. One may, therefore, question the reason for another book on the same subject. One of the problems in humanizing education is that the concepts are elusive; humanistic teaching is an experience, rather than a well-defined theory. It is this uniqueness that motivated us to put together the following materials. These activities and concepts have meaning for us in terms of humanizing education. The dimensions included in this book are those that personal experience has indicated to us as making a difference, and a major premise on which this book is based is that what teachers are and what they do makes a difference. It is also assumed that specific techniques and approaches for increasing the effectiveness of the teaching-learning situation are identifiable and that these can be used as educational interventions by and for pre-service and in-service teachers.

What we have brought together will not be totally integrated into the style and philosophy of others. What we do hope, however, is that some of the articles and activities will make sense to the reader—enough sense that they will be tried and adapted to the reader's own work setting.

Ray Eiben
Al Milliren

Normal, Illinois
May, 1976

Table of Contents

Introduction

In an era when knowledge expands at a tremendous rate, attitudes about self, learning, and the content to be learned become as important as the information to be mastered. Brown (1971) defines the affective component of education as the feeling or emotional aspect of experience and learning. He suggests that how a child or adult feels about wanting to learn, how he feels while he is learning, and what he feels after he has learned it are all critical aspects of effective educational experience. Castillo (1974) outlines a model of education in which the cognitive domain, the affective domain, the learner's readiness/awareness, and the learner's ability to respond become the components of a total educational program. We do not wish to deny the importance of the cognitive or intellectual component of learning. What we do suggest, however, is that when educators say that "schools exist to help children learn" they are expanding the definition of education to include more than intellectual competence and the process of education to incorporate more than the functions of thinking and memorizing.

There is a saying on one of the currently popular posters: "When someone's talking, no one is learning." What this suggests is that the student must become personally involved in the learning process, and the teacher must have tools at her disposal to make this possible. Relating this to the purposes of this volume, we seek to provide techniques and interventions that will allow the educator to be more free to become a part of the learning experience of her students. We have attempted to provide certain tools within this volume so that the teacher can translate secrecy, authoritarianism, self-aggrandizement, and emphasis on the picayune into a truly humanistic environment for discovery and learning.

Impetus for humanizing education comes from many sources. Patterson (1973, p. 21) identifies four major problems facing people today:

> poverty, pollution, population, and personal (or interpersonal) relations. The classroom (school) environment exemplifies personal (interpersonal) relations at its deepest level. It is a training ground for life, a life which is intimately involved with interaction with others—family, community, and society at large.

Today's problems and concerns are primarily people problems and people concerns, and the classroom can serve as an ongoing laboratory for the exploration and experiencing of relationships with people. It is through these relationships that we gain the zest for living and the skills for coping with the demands of life.

Combs (1971) suggests five major categories into which the perceptions of an effective helper may be divided: his subject, what people are like, himself, purposes—society's and his own—and those perceptions related to his task. The Florida studies (Combs, 1971) showed that "effective helpers" tended to perceive people as able, friendly, worthy, internally motivated, dependable, and helpful. In addition, effective helpers were more freeing than controlling, could focus on large issues rather than small ones, were self-revealing rather than self-concealing, preferred involvement to alienation, focused on process rather than goals or outcomes, and were altruistic rather than narcissistic. Relating this list to the purposes of this volume, the materials we have included assume that the teacher/helper has characteristics similar to these that Combs has delineated.

Affective learning is of four types: (1) cognitive learning about affects—the areas termed psychodynamics and group dynamics; (2) cognitive learning about our own personal affects involving verbal and nonverbal, personal and interpersonal experiences; (3) affective learning about our own affects, i.e., awareness of our feelings resulting from learning experiences such as those in (2); and (4) growth toward more positive affective states—higher self-esteem, acceptance of basic impulses, a sense of integration and integrity, and a positive view of self (Ward, 1972). Any program of humanistic development must provide a means for the participants—teachers, administrators, counselors, students, and parents—to become actively involved in the learning process. The use of small groups, role playing, psychodrama, and affective techniques provides the vehicle for feelings to be identified, esteem to be enhanced, and interpersonal relationships to be characterized by a sense of oneness.

As the reader becomes acquainted with the interventions and activities included in this handbook, she may wish to relate to the following principles and beliefs, which underlie the authors' selection and inclusion of various strategies and techniques that can enhance the humanization of teaching.

1. Teaching is an intimate relationship between a teacher who cares about herself as a person and a student who can reciprocate in this relationship and is comfortable in an atmosphere where people are valued.

2. All individuals have a natural desire to learn, with the process of learning occurring in an infinite variety of ways.

3. Each individual learns best in his own way and at his own pace.

4. Effective learning requires the involvement of the whole person—his thoughts *and* his feelings *and* his actions.

5. Learning occurs best when the learner experiences the least amount of personal threat and fear of external evaluation.

6. The most significant learning occurs when the material and/or skill being learned is valued by the learner.

7. Most significant learning occurs through doing—when the learner becomes personally involved in the learning act.

8. Learning occurs best when the learner becomes responsible for his own learning.

9. Creative and self-reliant learners develop best in an atmosphere of responsible freedom wherein self-evaluation and self-criticism are fostered.

10. The most useful learning for an age of cultural change and "future shock" involves the development of: (a) learning competence, or learning how to learn; (b) openness to experience; and (c) acceptance of change as being central to life itself.

11. Learning is the acquisition of personal meaning; teaching is the process of facilitating that acquisition.

Words do not seem to be sufficient to describe humanistic teaching and learning; action is necessary. With this credo, we offer this book as our unique contribution to humanistic learning. For the reader of this volume, the goal is to transcend the mere reading of the material. In order for what is included here to come alive, it must become an actual here-and-now experience for the user.

SOME CONCERNS

Many psychologists and educators have been highly critical of affective emphases that have become popular during the past few years. We feel that we would be remiss if we did not include a discussion of cautions and concerns. While we do not want to frighten educators away from participating in workshops and programs in the affective domain, it is, we feel, important that enthusiasm be tempered with an awareness of some of the possible pitfalls of involvement in programs that can be highly emotional. Careful selection of programs and leaders may serve to eliminate most of the concerns expressed in subsequent pages.

Much of the responsibility for assuring that educators participate in beneficial humanistic programs rests with the institutions and individuals who present various offerings. If presenters follow the ethical guidelines of their professional organizations, e.g., the American Psychological Association or the American Personnel and Guidance Association, few negative transactions will result from participation.

During the past few years it has become fashionable for educators to jump on many of the "humanistic" and interpersonal-development bandwagons. Disciples of communication skills (Ivey), values clarification

(Simon), body awareness (Gunther), responding behaviors (Carkhuff), Gestalt approaches (Perls), transactional analysis (Berne, Harris, James), reality therapy (Glasser), effectiveness training (Gordon), and achievement motivation (Hall) can be found in nearly every large community. Workshops relating to the approaches above are regularly offered and have many takers; many, it might be added, charge substantial fees for participation. In some cases, exponents of the various approaches create an enthusiasm little different from many religious cults.

We do not intend that the humanistic dimensions mentioned in this book be placed in a bag with the label "Do not touch, dangerous ingredients." What we do hope to convey is that there are a number of considerations that may help teachers experience lasting improvement in their interpersonal functioning.

I. Leaders of interpersonal-development programs that deal with psychological principles frequently do not make sure that the teacher-participants have enough background in the behavioral sciences to allow them to understand situations that may come up if they use the "growth" techniques in their own classes. This danger is especially prevalent in approaches where participants are asked to touch and feel each other, to engage in the development of fantasies, and to deal with aspects of their existence involving unresolved conflicts with parents, children, and significant other adults in their lives. Too often participants are encouraged to disclose and expose themselves with little, if any, follow-up.

II. Professional educators involved with various training programs do not always have their "own thing" together well enough to serve as appropriate models for clients whom they are hoping to change. Workshops and training programs are conducted under the pretense that an "expert" is able to help participants move in the direction of greater competency in their own lives and in dealing with others. Often, however, the expert's own effectiveness as a person is subject to question. This creates dissonance in the minds of the participants; a dissonance that can lead them to question the validity of an entire program which, were it not for facilitator inconsistencies, might have been of immense value to the participants. The editors remember attending a personal-growth workshop where the leader told the group how willing he was to really get close to the participants and how eager he was to get to know and help them. The problem of dissonance arose for one group member when she invited the leader to eat lunch with her, only to be told that he really didn't have time to spend with the group members "who were not where he was at."

III. Many programs having an interpersonal emphasis rely heavily on gimmicks, exercises, and techniques. It is our contention that approaches of short duration, with heavy emphasis on activities, create an illusion within the mind of the participant that all one needs to do to make people more human is to give them a few games to play. Changes of a long-lasting nature do not take place with gimmickry alone. Unfortunately, this precludes effectively implementing change through the use of similar activities when gimmickry has once been attempted within a school setting. Teachers who have been turned off by certain "groupie" activities may be resentful when similar group activities are used as part of a total program of planned change.

Many groups fail to indicate to the participants that "doing one's thing" is only a limited part of the growth process. One of our most frequent observations is that participation in interpersonal-development groups can lead to a state of "pseudo self-actualization" on the part of participants. In effect, they leave the group feeling justified for being themselves rather than examining their behavior and its consequences. All too often, participants develop feelings of self-satisfaction without the accompanying sensitivity to others, and/or they learn to be "free" without assuming responsibility for their behavior.

IV. Little attention may be given to processing or talking-through the activities of the typical program in interpersonal-skill development. For example, leaders often do not deal constructively with negative transactions, and participants are given little that can be used to guide their further development. (Processing should include a sharing of participants' thoughts and feelings, and suggested action responses to the materials presented.) Little attention may also be given to processing the activities in terms of specific ways in which the growth program can be related to the classroom. This lack of concern with processing carries over to the participants' use of specific approaches in their own school situations. What might have been a total, in-depth learning experience for the student can become only a shallow exposure to something "new" that the teacher has experienced.

V. Participants may be given little help in integrating their new interpersonal learnings within an environment that may be hostile when they attempt to implement different interactive modes. (The teacher is stimulated to be more free with students and to sit down and have real dialogues with them. This attempt at change is met by school administrators with expressions of concern and comments about the dangers inherent in using more permissive approaches with students.) It takes only slight resistance from the environment to block change when an individual has an incomplete integration of new knowledge within his own belief system and when he knows little about implementing change within a school. One of the editors' biggest frustrations has come from seeing teachers in in-service programs be really eager to try out new developments only to find a few weeks later that their attempts are stymied by a lack of acceptance within their own schools.

VI. In many cases, unique developmental needs of the individual are ignored. Many who espouse interpersonal affective approaches conduct programs in which the total group is everything and in which little opportunity exists for a participant to be able to ask such questions as "What does this new approach mean to me as an individual?" Such interpersonal techniques as nonverbal awareness, responding, and attending are applied with little attention being given to initial diagnosis or follow-up. In the area of interpersonal-skill development, it seems clear that meaningful change can come only with a long-term program of diagnosis, training, implementation, and feedback, with the entire cycle repeated to the point where the participant can decide whether he wants to integrate the new learnings into his total, responding self.

VII. There is, we feel, a danger in many interpersonal-skill programs that an awareness of certain behavioral phenomena is developed, but that the awareness does not transcend to a spontaneity of response and to an honesty in communication which are essential prerequisites to higher-level interpersonal functioning. Being able to respond with proper words but in a mechanical way is little better than having no response skills at all. As teachers acquire greater competency in interpersonal communication, they continually must be aware of the danger that those with whom they come in contact may be turned off by communication that is full of jargon or quite repetitive.

VIII. Commitment to a particular philosophy of dealing with people often does not become an integral part of the interpersonal-development program. The components remain merely parts and never come together as an integrated whole. The operational level becomes one of asking the question "Is this approach for me?" and never gets to the point where the statement becomes "Yes, this is the approach for me; now help me to make it a meaningful part of my total self." Our bias is that commitment must start with self; it is only then that commitment to a new approach of interacting with others can begin to make sense. Without integration, the person jumps from one innovative idea to another but remains basically the same individual. It does not take long for a student or a colleague to become disillusioned with the individual who is an adherent of meditation this week, Gestalt the next, and transactional analysis the third. New converts sometimes become bored and, in the long run, lose a potential for fostering rich human contact.

Fads and bandwagons have always plagued the sensibilities of educators. In fact, there have been few major breakthroughs in education that have not been overgeneralized into absurdity. Our concern is with those who join a bandwagon not because they care to be humanistic, but only because it seems to be the thing to do. The current period in education may ultimately be labeled "the era of the self" because so many are concerned with the development of human potential. Although human growth and self-development have always been primary goals of education, deep personal conviction on the part of the educator is required if they are to be effectively realized.

IX. Objectives of the programs may be ignored. With techniques and gimmicks freely available, it is easier to use them than it is to develop programs that make clear to participants where the facilitator hopes to take them and what the means will be to help them get there. It is our opinion that interpersonal-development programs wherein techniques and exercises are the sum total of the program provide more entertainment than they do growth. One of the advantages to a leader of short-term, gimmick-oriented programs is that, in this kind of approach, leaders can avoid having their ideas confronted. The participants are kept on edge by jumping them from game to game. What is even more deplorable, in our opinion, is the unwillingness of the program presenter to participate in any of the activities that are used as part of a particular approach. A willingness to truly become a participant should be a prerequisite for offering training programs with an interpersonal emphasis. Risk taking should be a mutual endeavor; the leaders risk having their ideals and beliefs challenged by the participants, the participants risk encountering experiences not previously a part of their existence.

There also appears to be a phenomenon of "designated growth"; this occurs when educators attempt to translate interpersonal growth workshops to their "back-home" school situations. The growth *objective* is often regarded as more important than the growth *process,* and programs and plans are designed that designate what "thou shalt become!" In many respects, this is a problem comparable to that of the "curricular imperative" wherein subject matter becomes important for its own sake rather than as an instrument for learning. If, in fact, the means for interpersonal growth are misconstrued as ends, and process is made into a requisite product, most attempts at programs of interpersonal development can achieve only minimal, if any, success.

We have no quarrel with those who are truly seeking to improve their interpersonal functioning. The human-potential movement can be a positive, contributing force in American education if it is viewed as a means of assisting individuals in increasing their interpersonal effectiveness. We are, however, concerned about those who seem to view humanism solely as a better or more subtle means for the manipulation or control of others.

In summary, there is an abundance of interpersonal- or growth-oriented programs available. We suggest that many of the criticisms of these programs are legitimate and that unless the leaders of these growth offerings face these concerns, the tremendous potential of this movement will never be realized. By carefully investigating the organization and the personnel offering the program and by comparing the program with the specific concerns mentioned here, it is hoped that teachers who wish to participate in

growth-oriented programs will be able to discern which of them offer important ingredients in the formula for successful teaching and living.

REFERENCES

Brown, G. I. *Human teaching for human learning.* New York: The Viking Press, 1971.

Castillo, G. A. *Left-handed teaching.* New York: Praeger, 1974.

Combs, A. W., Avila, D. L., & Purkey, W. W. *Helping relationships.* Boston: Allyn & Bacon, 1971.

Patterson, C. H. *Humanistic education.* Englewood Cliffs, N.J.: Prentice-Hall, 1973.

Ward, S. *Learning: Cognitive, affective, and psychomotor or the acquisition of coping skills.* Santa Barbara,
     Calif.: The Development of Research in Confluent Education, 1972.

Part One
Group Techniques

The use of small groups is as old as teaching; frequent use has been made of small groups to discuss important topics and to work on class-related projects. It may be questioned, however, whether the use of small groups in the typical classroom is as effective as it might be. Only within the last ten or fifteen years have affective goals become an important adjunct to the utilization of groups within the school setting. Rather than merely a focus on accomplishing a task, there has been an emphasis on the process that is going on in the group. Questions such as the following have been asked:

1. Who talks to whom?
2. Who are accepted as members of the group?
3. Who is in the position of leadership?
4. How is influence gained in the group?
5. What norms are part of the group's operation?

There has been an expansion, therefore, of the level of operation, from exclusive emphasis on the task level to the inclusion of group process and interpersonal levels.

A classroom group is assigned the task of listing and discussing the most critical needs of the community in which they live. At the task level a major question is "What are we supposed to be doing?" Frequently, there will be little movement in the direction of accomplishing the task. At this point the teacher needs to be aware of group process and how the process is affecting task-level accomplishment. At this level the teacher may ask the group, "What is happening?" "Is the absence of leadership preventing the task from being accomplished?" "Are the norms developed by the group getting in the way of listing the points appropriate to the task?" By sitting back for a few minutes and looking at what is happening in the group, the teacher may be able to eliminate major impediments to the group's achievement of its goals and allow the group to acquire the good feelings associated with successful task-level accomplishment.

On many occasions there may be an understanding of the task and a high level of operation at the group-process level, but still the existence of a climate of mistrust and low-level risk taking. There may be a need to focus on the interpersonal level, to ask questions about liking and trust and how these concepts are affecting the group's operation. If members of a group have a low level of trust and liking for each other, it may be difficult for them to work together on a task, even though the points mentioned may be significant ones and the elements related to group process are not posing any threat to the group's operation. It is at the interpersonal level that feelings are discussed and concerns are raised that relate to the interpersonal transactions occurring among group members. The risks of being involved with interpersonal processing are considerable, but the potential to check out interpersonal assumptions and move to a higher level of trust and caring is worth the risks involved.

An important question in the teacher's use of small groups is what her role is to be in facilitating these groups. Traditionally, the teacher has functioned as the leader or has decided who the leader would be. In the use of small groups within a humanistic framework, the teacher's role may be less authoritarian, placing a greater responsibility on the students to discover what the boundaries of the group are and what their role is in a situation where leadership is diffused to include all participants.

A tacit assumption in the use of small groups within a humanistic framework is that better relationships among students develop as does an improved rapport between teacher and students. As better relationships develop, improved self-understanding and an increased understanding of group process are important by-products. Associated with these ends are improved abilities in listening, responding, acting, and cooperating with others in developing an environment wherein the dignity of the individual person has a high priority.

Teachers need to have a basic understanding of structure, process, and content as it relates to group functioning. By structure we mean such components as time, setting, size, selection of members, frequency of meeting, duration, goals, and agenda. Process refers to the group action, the interaction among members, the transactions that can be observed, and the attitudes and relationships that develop during the life of the group. Content is the message of the group, the data resulting from the structure that has been developed, and the processes existing in a dynamic group.

In this section, the focus is on specific group techniques that can be used by the teacher as well as on ideas and suggestions related to leadership and other group topics. Hopefully, by using the suggestions and specific approaches identified in this section, the teacher will develop a thirst for additional information and expertise in the group-process area. This additional information and training can be obtained from the many excellent sources available to the practitioner.

Guidelines for Group Leadership

Ray Eiben

Although there are numerous approaches to group leadership (group centered, T-group, Gestalt, psychoanalytic, extensional, and so on), there are some common, key components of group leadership. This article outlines the minimum areas of expertise required of the individual who wants to work effectively as a group facilitator.

PREPARATION

Attention should be given to the physical surroundings in which the group activity is to take place. In an ideal situation, the room temperature is comfortable, the floor is carpeted (so that participants can sit or recline on it), the surroundings are free from distractions and external noise, and the furnishings are appropriate to the manner in which the group functions.

It is important that the size of the group is in accord with its function. If the tenor of the group is likely to be intense and emotional, eight to ten members is probably sufficient. Fourteen or fifteen participants is an acceptable number if the group is formed basically for discussion purposes. The leader should also take into account any subgrouping he may want to utilize as part of the group's operation. For example, if working in trios is to be an important adjunct to the functioning of the group, the total membership should be divisible by three.

The effective group leader defines the criteria for participation in the group and selects members accordingly. For example, because of the group's purpose, he may dictate that close friends are not to be in the same group. Or, if the group's focus is on personal problems or personal growth, the facilitator may screen out prospective members who are undergoing psychotherapy.

Participants should be informed early in the group's life of the general objectives of the group and the demands that will be made on group members. For example, if the self-disclosure of deeply personal information is a group requirement, members are made aware of this prior to or during the first meeting.

Temporal aspects of the group's life are defined so that members know the length of each meeting and date of termination of the group.

Any specific rules necessitated by the location of the meetings, by the orientation and personal philosophy of the leader, or by the demands of the agency sanctioning the group are also identified. For example: if smoking is forbidden in the room, members are informed of this; if the group is comprised of high school students, the members may have to be informed of school rules about leaving the group in the middle of a session; if the group leader has a particular orientation (Gestalt, etc.), he identifies the rules he proposes to follow that are consistent with his orientation (no use of "why" statements, say "I" when you mean "I," use of the "hot seat," etc.).

TUNING IN

The effective group leader shows that he is attending to what is happening by using eye contact, alert posture, appropriate gestures, and such other nonverbal cues as smiling and nodding.

Being "tuned in" means that the leader constantly monitors the group members so that he is always aware of the members' needs. For instance, he will know when someone wants to speak by the way in which the member leans forward, makes eye contact with the leader, moves in his seat, moves his lips in preparation to speak, etc.

The effective group leader allows time for silence and reflection. He does not feel obliged to talk whenever there is silence within the group.

Being an effective group leader involves making timely and appropriate interventions that help pinpoint and focus a particular issue or feeling. This means being able to identify, out of much extraneous verbal content, that which seems to be most significant to what the group (or individual) has determined to be its point of focus during that particular session. For example, if a group of children are talking about problems they have in communicating with their parents, and one group member inserts a comment about a problem he is having in school, the leader may want to make an intervention to get the group back on target.

The tuned-in group leader asks questions that help clarify what is unclear to members of the group. Cues to members' lack of understanding may be nonverbal (looking away from the member who is speaking, obvious boredom with what is taking place, etc.) or verbal (inappropriate responses, initiating side conversations, etc.).

The effective group leader avoids asking "why" questions and other questions that force the group member into a defensive or "because" response. In fact, the group leader should gradually eliminate all questions from his interventions because most questions seek answers that are already known. Generally, it is better to rephrase statements in such a way that they serve to clarify without questioning.

RECOGNIZING THE IMPORTANCE OF THE INDIVIDUAL

During every group session, the leader should make eye contact with each group member to indicate awareness of his presence. This communication may also be in the form of a pat on the back, a few words before or after a session, or an arm put around a group member.

Early in the life of the group, the leader learns each member's name and, subsequently, identifies each member by his first name when communicating with him. This behavior on the part of the leader serves as a model for group members in their responses to and expressions of concern for each other. In addition, the leader focuses on the individual by helping him to accept responsibility for saying "I" when he means himself rather than saying "us" or "we." (The latter terms are used only when summarizing a group vote or when making clear the position of the total group.)

The leader recognizes the contributions made by group members by appropriate verbal and nonverbal cues. For example, if a group member shows evidence of being helpful, the leader responds by saying such things as "Your response to Mary made it clear that you really understood what she was saying." This recognition of a member's expression is especially important if that member is seeking a level of involvement that includes new risk taking for him. For instance, if a group member who has been rather reticent shares some very personal feelings about a sister who is retarded, the leader may say something like "Jan, I feel that it is difficult for you to talk about these kinds of feelings, and I feel good that you trust us enough to share them with us."

The leader occasionally uses techniques such as "going around" to assist each group member to express feelings or ideas related to a particular situation. The leader needs to be aware of what effect this technique is having on the group; since it can become a tedious process, it probably should be used only when it is important to have all members of the group involved in a particular response.

If a group member does not speak during one or more sessions the group leader should utilize any opportunities that arise for assisting the member to speak, and should involve the silent member whenever it is possible to do so without discomfort. This might be done by discussing the norm of participation in the group and seeking the group members' feelings about different levels of participation. Another way to involve a quiet member of the group is to have him summarize what someone else in the group has said. The facilitator can also respond to nonverbal cues that can be interpreted with a fair degree of accuracy. For instance, the leader might say, "Even though you didn't say anything during this session, Bob, I could tell that you were really involved in what was going on." After a series of encounters that seem to represent the end of a phase of the group session, the leader might say, "So that we can all be on the same wavelength, Sally, I'm wondering if you would be willing to take a few minutes to share your perceptions of what has happened."

The use of occasional nonverbal, fantasy, or cognitive activities can provide a nonthreatening way for the shy group member to play a more active role in the group. Many ranking or consensus activities within subgroups can be used to involve reticent members. During the processing phase of these activities, the leader might mention how well everyone contributed within the small groups. Next he might try to get a commitment from each of the subgroup members to attempt this same level of involvement within the larger group.

The disrupter or overly vocal member may be confronted in a manner that will allow the group to deal with his behavior without humiliating him. One method might be to ask group members to spend some time talking about what qualities they think characterize an effective group member. This discussion could be followed by a discussion of actual group members in terms of how close they come to meeting these criteria.

Attention may be given to such aspects of group behavior as the fact that some group members always sit together. Pointing out this kind of behavior may lead to a discussion of group members' feelings of inclusion and exclusion and why members respond to one another differently.

CHECKING WHAT IS HAPPENING IN THE GROUP

The effective group leader, at crucial points during the session, asks the group to stop and take a look at where the group is "now" in relation to some of the goals and expectations that have previously been identified. He may say to the group, "Let's take a minute to go around the group and finish the sentence 'Right now I am feeling . . .' or 'Right now, in this group, what I see happening is . . . .'"

Rather than always assuming the responsibility for summarization and review, the effective group leader frequently asks group members to share their perceptions of the group process. After this sharing, the leader may say something like "Bill has given us a summary of what he feels is happening in the group. I'm wondering if there is anything anyone wants to add to Bill's comments."

If the discussion has digressed from the main topic, the leader may want to suggest (without criticizing any individual responsible for the digression) that the group move back to the focal point. He may say, for example, "I'm hearing what Jim has just been talking about, but I'm wondering if the group wants to continue with his point or go back to what I felt was left incomplete."

To be aware of what is happening in a group, the leader must respond to nonverbal as well as verbal cues. Although nonverbal cues can be misread, it is well worth any risk the leader must take to develop his skills in this area. Such feelings as boredom, physical withdrawal from the group, anger, and extreme anxiety or unhappiness must be responded to so that the behaviors can be used in learning experiences for the entire group.

As a preliminary to having members assume leadership functions, the task of summarizing at the end-of-group sessions may be rotated among all members of the group. It is important to make sure that the end-of-session comments are not always made by the same individual.

In summarizing at the beginning and at the end of a session, the leader should attempt to relate the session to previous ones and to give the members a sense of direction for future meetings. An appropriate beginning comment might be "We've talked about problems of getting along with teachers during the past three sessions; let's do some thinking today and this week about where we want to go with this topic." An appropriate end-of-session comment might be "We've been talking about the kinds of problems you are having in getting along with your teachers. Perhaps next time we might talk about how these problems relate to some of the problems we have had here in the group in getting to know one another and in getting along with one another."

Appropriate beginning statements can accomplish two things: (1) refresh the members' memories as to what has happened in the group during previous sessions, and (2) encourage the group members to talk about whatever has a high priority for them at that particular time.

Happenings within the group may be checked against a model of group progress such as Gibb's TORI[1] (Trust, Openness, Realization, and Interdependence) Model.

Part of the leader's responsibility is to constantly check with the group to determine whether the group is moving toward the achievement of norms that are indicative of an effective group. He may use activities to

---

[1]See J. William Pfeiffer and John E. Jones (Eds.), *The 1972 Annual Handbook for Group Facilitators,* La Jolla, Calif.: University Associates, 1972, pp. 157-162.

determine the trust level within the group; in one such activity, members write on cards two or three things about themselves that they do not often share with other people. The leader would then suggest that the members talk about the extent to which they feel free to share this information, rather than about the nature of the information.

FOCUSING ON FEELINGS

The effective leader is constantly aware of the adage that feelings are everything, that the expression of feelings is the *sine qua non* of the group's existence. If free expression of feelings does not exist in the group, the whole purpose of the group may be questioned.

To keep the focus on feeling states, the effective leader may interject such questions as "How did you feel when that happened?" or "You mentioned being made fun of on the playground; how did that make you feel?" or "You talked about your parents telling you how well they thought you had done; how did that make you feel?"

The leader must be aware of the feeling reactions members have to one another and point these out if it appears that a focusing comment will facilitate the group's functioning. "A minute ago I noticed that Sara disagreed pretty strongly with what Jim said. Does anyone have any comments about Sara's expression of anger?"

Other ways in which the leader may keep the group's focus on feelings include such comments as "I had the feeling the group was really with you," or "I'm not getting much of a reaction from the group. It's almost like the group felt a little detached from what you were talking about," or "Since the other group members haven't experienced what you have, perhaps they are having difficulty giving you much of a feeling reaction." The leader should avoid labeling any feelings as "good" or "bad."

The leader should make clear the distinction between feelings, thoughts, and ideas. In other words, if a statement begins with the term "I feel" and what is being expressed is really a thought or idea, the leader should point out the discrepancy in the communication.

It is the responsibility of the group leader to be aware of the ability of each group member to handle the type and intensity of feelings being expressed. If, for example, a lot of anger is directed toward one group member, and it is becoming clear that the member is showing excessive anxiety, the leader should intervene in order to put the member on safer ground. Such a situation, however, should not be passed up in terms of the learning that might develop from it. Processing the situation and talking about ways of dealing with anger may be profitable for the entire group.

An ever-present danger in focusing on feelings is that they may escalate beyond the province of the group. It is often necessary to avoid the temptation to make an interpretation of a member's feelings after they have been expressed. For example, if a counselor or teacher is involved in a career-development group he may ask group members to develop a fantasy relating to their ideal job or to an ideal day. It may turn out that the fantasy of one of the group members revolves around the absence of certain significant others in his life. The highly charged nature of this disclosure precludes interpretation within the context of this career-development group. If any interpretation is to be made, the member expressing the feeling or describing the situation should be the one to make it.

Gestalt Rules and Games in Education

Gerhard Kohn

INTRODUCTION

Gestalt Therapy is an existential technique stressing the "here" and "now" as well as the "I" and "thou." It is not intended to face a student with a dogmatic list of do's and don'ts. Rules are offered in a spirit of experimentation. The student may perform these experimental situations. The techniques of Gestalt Therapy will often point up the many ways in which he prevents himself from being successful as well as the "holes" he has in his personality. The essence of this technique is in the perspective which the student attains in viewing his behavior.

RULES

The rules of Gestalt Therapy are few, but are invoked by the counselor stringently.

Rule 1. *The communication between counselor and student remains in the "now."*

Communication in the present tense is encouraged and the emphasis is on what is happening now. What does the student feel at this moment? In the communication, intellectualized "about-ism" is avoided and when the student refers to events of the past, he is asked to be in the past in fantasy and to reenact the event in the present.

Rule 2. *Rule of the "I" and "thou."*

Reproduced by permission of Gerhard Kohn, Ph.D., Director, Gestalt Training Institute, Orange County, California. From two papers presented at the 1972 Conference of the California Psychological Association.

Students often speak about others and even more often communicate as though their words were aimed at no one in particular. The counselor redirects communication, asking, "to whom are you saying this?" and helping the student make a distinction between "talking to" and "talking at" the listener.

Rule 3. *The use of the word "I."*

Frequently the student distantiates himself from his behavior by using the third person, the "it." This affords him the opportunity to avoid responsibility and involvement. Changing the "it" to "I," the student is led to assume a greater degree of responsibility for his behavior.

Rule. 4. *Developing awareness and the "what" and "how" instead of pursuing the "why."*

Guiding the student away from the "why" and toward the "what" and "how" of his behavior leads him to the here and now of his experiences and away from the endless explanations, speculations, and interpretations. The counselor will ask the student, "What are you aware of now?" "How do you experience what you have just done?" "What do you experience this very moment as we talk about your behavior?" As the counselor helps the student to rely on his senses (Dr. Perls frequently says: "lose your mind and come to your senses"), the student is helped to distinguish between the realities out there and the fantasies which he creates in his own mind.

Rule 5. *No gossiping.*

Speaking about other people, particularly those not present, is a frequently used way to avoid realities. In the Gestalt technique, the "no gossiping" rule is invoked even though the individual talked about may be present in the room. The student then is asked to actually address the other person directly rather than talking to the counselor about him. No gossiping rules promote feelings and prevent avoidance of same.

Rule 6. *Changing questions into statements.*

Dr. Perls observes that the questioner oftentimes does not really seek information and that the question frequently is not a "true" question. He will ask that such a question be changed into a statement. He makes the distinction between genuine and hypocritical questions, the latter being manipulative.

GAMES

In Gestalt technique, Dr. Perls requires the use of "games." He does not, as other existential therapists do, discourage any use of games, but enables his patients to be aware of the "games" played and to substitute desirable for undesirable games. Certain games are an integral part of the Gestalt Therapy techniques.

1. *The Dialogue Game*

Most notable among games that Dr. Perls finds useful is the game in which two parts of a manifested personality develop a dialogue between one another. It may be his so-called top dog (the top dog moralizes, condemns, is bossy, and proclaims all the "shoulds") and the so-called bottom dog game (the bottom dog makes excuses, rationalizes, and is passively resistant). Using an empty chair, the student is then asked to develop a dialogue between the two splits (personalities), placing the top dog in one chair and the bottom dog in the other. A similar split is found among students who have difficulties integrating the "good boy" personality with the "bad boy" personality or the "masculine" personality with the "feminine" personality. Dr. Perls also applies this dialogue game to various body parts such as the right hand versus the left hand. Such dialogue can also be developed between the student and some significant person in his environment, simply addressing this significant person as if he were actually in the room.

2. *Making the Rounds Game*

Students will frequently say "I can't stand anyone in this school," "no one likes me here," or "everyone is against me." The student is then asked to make a round, stopping in front of every other person in the group and saying to each person some remark pertaining to his feeling about each person. The student might also be asked to stand in front of everyone in this group and say to him, "I can't stand you" or "you don't like me." "You hate me."

3. *Completing Unfinished Business*

Whenever the student presents to the counselor some indications of unresolved feelings to which Dr. Perls refers as unfinished business, the counselor may then ask the student to "finish this business" (oftentimes this unfinished business may relate to the realm of interpersonal relationships with teachers, siblings, friends, or parents).

4. *I Take Responsibility*

Many students who are seen by counselors are relating experiences for which they would find it extremely hard to assume responsibility if they were asked to do so. The student is then asked with each statement he makes to use the phrase "and I take responsibility for it." By adding this phrase, he becomes aware more and more of the foolishness of his behavior and the inability to justify the behavior for which he is attempting to find justification.

5. *I Have a Secret Game*

The student who feels guilt and shame and is coming to the counselor with seemingly well guarded personal secrets may be instructed not to share the secret itself, but imagine how he feels others would react to it, and then relate this reaction to the counselor. The student may then find out that others would not react as horribly toward him, knowing the secret which he is guarding, and the student may be willing to share it more readily.

6. *Playing the Projection*

Some students come to the counselor indicating that they can't trust him, he is just doing this for a living, and he is not really interested in the student. The student may then be asked to play the role of an untrustworthy person or he may be asked to enact this very attitude, after which he might find that he is projecting on the counselor a trait which he possesses himself.

7. *Reversals*

The student who comes into the counselor's office oftentimes with a chip on his shoulder, suffering from a feeling of being rejected by everyone is asked to play the opposite role, the role of one who is liked by everyone, who is completely open without a chip on his shoulder. This might help the student realize that his overt behavior represents frequently a reversal of underlying impulses.

8. *Exaggeration Game*

The exaggeration game is played by Dr. Perls with a patient quite frequently. Oftentimes, Dr. Perls himself will exaggerate a patient's movement or his motion or his statement, repeating movement or statement in exaggeration and then asking the patient to exaggerate his own movement or his own expression.

The student may simply be asked to repeat an important statement which he has just made two, three, four, five, or six times, requesting of him that he say it again but louder and louder, or the student may be asked to repeat a gesture or facial grimace, requesting of him that he exaggerate this gesture or grimace as much as he can.

Using Encounter Group Principles
in Teaching

Albert E. Roark

The demands of the current world situation are such that the scientist, of whatever stature or field of specialization, cannot ignore his fellow man. And it is fair to say that today every man is to some extent a technologist if not a true scientist. Our ecological problems have been generally exacerbated if not created through the careless use of scientific and technological advances. Indeed, the very existence of human life as we know it now is threatened by scientifically created weapons, waste, and consumption. If we stipulate that this bent toward self-destruction is not purposeful, then how can we account for man's lemming-like behavior in the use of scientific and technical knowledge?

Man's current problems stem largely from estrangement. Briefly, the concept of estrangement being developed here is that humans possess the curious ability to act as if other humans were not also human; or to act as if they did not know better when it is obvious that they do. It is this ability which allows one human to harm another without remorse because he simply does not see the kinship between himself and the other person. This same ability allows a person to accumulate knowledge and then act as if he did not possess it because he does not feel a relationship between the knowledge he possesses and his situation. It is as if the person were able to place knowledge, understanding, and awareness in special compartments reserved for use in only very restricted circumstances—not necessarily those circumstances for which they have the most utility.

This condition, probably uniquely human, is fostered by the need to defend oneself against either psychological or physical attacks in which the defense is made much easier if one can assume that the assailant is a stranger who need not be given concern or credibility. It is also a result of a mind

Reprinted from the Earth Science Teacher Preparation Project *Newsletter*, September 1970. Used with permission of the author.

which can accumulate data much faster than it can see the relationships between these data. This results in the tragic condition of modern man who is on the one hand engulfed with knowledge which he only vaguely understands and which he is hard pressed to relate to his personal life except in the most transient of situations, and who is on the other hand tightly encased in an impenetrable cocoon of defenses, worries, and preoccupations. This cocoon serves as a protection against the real and the imagined assaults of the world, but it also keeps a person from being in tune with himself and seeing the relationship between himself, others, and his environment. In order for a person to learn, he must overcome the restricting influence of this cocoon and expand his awareness and experience while simultaneously developing an understanding of these experiences.

The task of education is to help people bring meaning and understanding into their lives and to determine the nature of their relationship to mankind. This view of education is in contrast to "training," which is seen as the development of skill and knowledge in a specific area for a specific purpose. Education in this context is a much broader and more difficult task, the outcomes of which are far less certain and specific than those of a training program. It is in the context of education—not training—that the application of encounter group procedures to the teaching of science is proposed. These procedures are proposed because they have been particularly effective in penetrating people's *cocoons* and allowing them to find meaning in life.

Encounter groups and the broader concept of sensitivity training have become household words in the last few years. Perhaps no other phenomenon has ever attracted public attention in such a dramatic fashion. It is not proposed here that every classroom be turned into an encounter group, but rather that encounter group principles be incorporated into everyday teaching practices. The encounter group principles which are particularly applicable are these:

1. The meaning which is important is the *personal meaning* of each person and *not* an abstract generalized meaning.

2. Statements, discussions and other interpersonal interaction should be in the *present* and not in the past or future.

3. The majority of all interaction should resolve around the *people in the group* and their experiences at the moment.

4. Statements are more valid if they are *personal responses* for which the speaker accepts responsibility and not references to authority, theory or abstractions.

The teacher should be aware that in approaching education from this perspective several assumptions are being made:

1. First of all, education is aimed at human effectiveness.

2. Personal meaning is more important in learning than objective or abstract meaning.

3. Total organismic reaction is more effective in learning than either an intellectual or affective reaction in isolation.

4. Human interaction is essential for complete human development.

5. The major task of teaching is to provide an opportunity to learn in a psychologically safe environment with suitable resources and *not* to provide information.

Different demands are placed on the teacher in this approach. He must be willing to be a person rather than a teacher or an authority. This means that he must learn to respond personally rather than abstractly to student questions and demands. The most difficult task of all involves allowing the students to be truly independent persons with independent views. There is no need, however, for a super person with no faults and a Ph.D. in psychology. Indeed, until the teacher can simply be himself with all his human foibles and greatness, this approach has not been fully implemented.

PROCEDURES

The implementation of this approach in teaching is much more difficult than it seems to the casual observer or to the person first contemplating doing so. The first problem is that most of us have been exposed only to models of education which rely on content as a unifying theme, and when we abandon this model we are lost. We have no way of knowing if the class is proceeding in the proper way or of measuring our effectiveness. Second, however good our intentions, it is next to impossible to escape the feeling that, personal meaning or not, there are some things that everybody should know and some things that are right and some that are wrong. And perhaps the most frightening thing of all is the feeling that you should be *doing* something; but if you can't lecture or assign work, what can you do? The following are techniques which have helped teachers implement the encounter group approach.

1. Allowing students to select their own subject matter and approach for study.

2. Allowing students to evaluate themselves or at least participate in their evaluation.

3. Making clear through both action and words that the student is responsible for what he learns and the teacher is responsible for providing the situation and resources.

4. Providing extensive opportunities for discussions (large and small groups) where students can see how their ideas compare with others and learn to express theirs. Brilhart, *Effective Group Discussion,* and Stanford and Stanford, *Learning Discussion Skills Through Games,* provide excellent guidelines to leading discussions.

5. Providing opportunities for students to work cooperatively in at least the same proportion as they work competitively.

6. Stressing that the classwork is being done for the present benefit of the students and not as preparation for the future.

7. Using simulation to recreate on a smaller scale the problems and situations in the world in which the students are interested. (Rogers, *Freedom to Learn,* is a good source of ideas.)

8. Role-playing either in conjunction with other techniques or alone for short periods of time. This is an excellent technique for helping students put themselves into other situations and see situations from other people's viewpoints.

9. Through "games" providing opportunities for students to learn more about themselves and others as they learn about subject matter. The teacher is urged to enroll in a small group-techniques class to learn how to apply these to the classroom. The following books will serve as an introduction to this area: Schutz, *Joy: Expanding Human Awareness;* Malamud and Machover, *Toward Self-Understanding: Group Techniques in Self-Confrontation;* and Stanford and Stanford, *Learning Discussion Skills Through Games.*

10. Inquiry or discovery approaches to teaching science. These approaches are compatible with the application of encounter group techniques.

The teacher should keep in mind, however, that the essence of this approach lies in the teacher-student relationship and not in any specific technique. If the relationship is based on open, direct, nondefensive communication of the person's total being at all times in a democratic atmosphere, then the basic requirements of an encounter group approach to education have been met. (Rogers, *Freedom to Learn,* can provide the philosophical and psychological rationale of this method.)

The outcomes of applying encounter group procedures to teaching lie in two distinct areas. First, the classroom atmosphere and procedures change dramatically. Students demonstrate an increased interest in learning and the subject matter. Excitement and involvement become common so that the end of the class period becomes more of a nuisance than a signal for termination. The diversity of activity increases, resulting in the opportunity for broader exposure to subject matter than usual. The question of relevancy ceases to exist since students have chosen relevant areas and means for study. Dramatic changes are seen in a second aspect of the classroom. A "we" feeling develops so that every student feels he belongs and is important. Feelings of caring and concern for each other develop among the students as they get to know and appreciate each other. Students develop stronger feelings of individuality through self-initiated activity as they develop a "we" feeling through the cooperative work.

Ultimately, this approach leads to increased human effectiveness through increases in clarity of perceptions; self-knowledge; environmental knowledge; and through awareness of self, others, environment, and their relationships. Intellectual beliefs and actions come closer together. Self-confidence and feelings of self-worth tend to increase. As the foregoing changes take place the student becomes more assertive and willing to stand up for his beliefs.

Even the partial accomplishment of these outcomes extends beyond the requirements of training and into the realm of education. In essence this approach strives for an enlightened "I-Thou" relationship between self, others, and the environment—a goal worthy of science or any other discipline.

REFERENCES

Brilhart, John K. *Effective group discussion* (2nd ed.). Dubuque, Iowa: W. C. Brown, 1974.

Malamud, Daniel I., & Machover, Solomon. *Toward self understanding: Group techniques in self-confrontation*. Springfield, Ill.: Charles C Thomas, 1965.

Rogers, Carl Ransom. *Freedom to learn*. Columbus, Ohio: Charles E. Merrill, 1969.

Schutz, William C. *Joy: Expanding human awareness*. New York: Grove Press, 1967.

Stanford, Gene, & Stanford, Barbara D. *Learning discussion skills through games*. New York: Citation Press, 1969.

Human Relations Training
in the Classroom

Gene Stanford

Schools are showing increased interest in the use of human relations training techniques, but until recently they have confined their applications to attempting to improve their staff, or, at best, teacher-student relations. Some schools have established T-groups as adjuncts to their counseling program, but few teachers have as yet seen the value of using laboratory methods as aids to teaching the subject matter of the course.

A notable exception was the Ford-Esalen Project in Affective Learning undertaken during the school year 1967-68 under the direction of George I. Brown of the Graduate School of Education of the University of California at Santa Barbara. Its goal was to develop and disseminate sample lessons combining affective learning with the traditional public school curriculum. Experienced teachers from a number of California school systems and with a wide range of subject-matter interest were involved. They devised activities that ranged from having all students in a high school English class answer the question, "It takes courage for me to . . . ," in conjunction with a study of the novel *Red Badge of Courage* to having first graders lie alone under sheets to experience isolation from the group.

The Human Relations Education Project of Western New York, under the direction of James J. Foley, has also had success in integrating training principles into the curriculum. The project includes all grades and encourages teachers to use inductive learning experiences in the affective domain to aid students' personal emotional development and improve interpersonal relations. For example, fourth graders are asked to keep an "All About Me" folder, to role-play racial conflicts, to talk about what kinds of people they like. High school math classes learn how to solve problems

Reproduced by special permission from *Human Relations Training News*, Vol. 14, No. 4, 1970, courtesy of Gene Stanford and the NTL Institute for Applied Behavioral Science.

through cooperative thinking. Social studies classes, in a study of stereo-typing, examine the ways in which members of their own group are both similar and unique.

In neither of these projects was an attempt made to measure the results in terms of changes in the students themselves. The Ford-Esalen project was by definition a survey of possible methods and relied only on "clinical" evaluation. The staff of the Human Relations Education Project discovered significant changes in teacher attitudes, but did not evaluate changes in the students. An occasional individual teacher who has had success with training techniques in the classroom has written enthusiastically about his experience, as in the case of David M. Litsey, whose "Small-Group Training and the English Classroom" appeared in a recent issue of *English Journal.* Rarely, however, have these individuals concerned themselves with careful measurement of results.

To test the impact of small group training when used as part of the curriculum, I undertook work with experimental English classes at Horton Watkins High School in suburban St. Louis, Missouri, during the school year 1969-70. With the cooperation of Dr. Gordon R. Garrett, the school's director of research, I used a variety of measures including questionnaires, direct observation, and video taping, to determine whether groups which experienced the activities described below changed in any significant way compared with control groups taught by traditional methods.

Analysis of the data indicates that experimental groups perceived themselves as becoming more socially sensitive and adept at leadership, while control groups did not change significantly. Experimental groups reported that they were better able to work together, and observation corroborated this finding, while students in control groups were tired and frustrated by the end of the semester. Experimental groups seemed to have a more positive attitude toward the subject matter. Moreover, experimental groups made at least as much scholastic progress—and in some cases more—than control groups with more time for cognitive learning.

Two pairs of groups in the experiment spent 18 weeks studying grammar and composition; two other pairs studied nonfiction and science fiction literature. The T-group activities were used in essentially the same way with both types of groups.

The sequence of activities outlined is similar to that used with the experimental groups and could be followed over the course of the year by any classroom teacher with adjustments for grade level and subject matter. The activities usually do not require the entire period, but can be used for the first part of a period, and followed by subject-matter work.

CLASSROOM ACTIVITIES

1. Each student introduces himself to the group, telling anything about himself that he feels will help others know him better.

2. Students write brief first impressions of others and turn them in to the teacher. They then share their first impressions orally.

3. Each student introduces himself again, giving his name and telling one thing that he likes.

4. Students take turns being "visiting celebrities." Other members of the group conduct interviews to find out as much as possible about the "celebrity."

5. Each student introduces himself again, telling one thing that he dislikes.

6. Using only eye contact, each student "chooses" a partner from across the room and maintains eye contact for 15 seconds. This exercise is repeated at frequent intervals, with explanation of why eye contact is essential for good communication.

7. Each student introduces himself, giving his name and telling how he feels at that moment.

8. Each student is given a clue to a mystery, and the group must work together to solve it. The teacher provides feedback on the group's effectiveness.

9. In a discussion of a question related to the subject matter of the course, each student must contribute once within the first 10 minutes.

10. Each student is asked to introduce another to the group, telling the group what sort of person he is.

11. In a discussion of a subject matter question, each student must contribute by responding to a previous contribution.

12. Using a subject matter question, each student is asked to summarize the differences in the contributions of two previous speakers.

13. Working in pairs, students practice drawing out the speaker by asking questions, displaying empathy, and showing support rather than arguing.

14. Working with the entire group, students practice drawing out the speaker.

15. After a brief description of roles possible in a group, each student is assigned a role to play during a subject matter discussion.

16. After a brief description of possible anti-group roles, each student is assigned a role and plays it during the subject matter discussion.

17. Students play the "Lost on the Moon" game to learn to arrive at consensus through compromise and careful listening to the arguments of others.

18. During a subject matter discussion, student observers sitting outside the group note the actions of participants and give them feedback.

19. Students fill out a questionnaire, containing such items as "Who in this group do you listen to most?," and results are distributed by the teacher at the next class.

20. The "metaphor game" is played to help students begin to express their reactions to others in the group. Each student secretly chooses another member of the class and tells the group what music, bird, animal, food, color, and weather that person reminds him of. The other students guess the identity of the person chosen.

21. During a subject matter discussion, each student pretends to be the person on his immediate right.

22. Each student describes how he thinks the group would react to the revelation of his most personal secret. (The secrets are not disclosed.)

23. Students write secrets in camouflaged handwriting on identical slips of paper which are then distributed at random. Other members read the secrets aloud as if they were their own.

24. Each student in turn is asked to answer a question about himself or his reaction to the group. One question is used at the beginning of each period. Questions include the following:

> How does each person here feel toward you?
> What would you change about the group's (an individual's) behavior toward you?
> If you could be anyone else in this group, who would it be?
> Who here is happier than you are?
> What is a question you would rather not be asked?
> What is one thing you would change about yourself if you could?
> In what way are you similar to each person here?
> Who in this group frightens you?
> What is the first impression you give other people?
> Who in this group are you most comfortable with?
> Who in this group likes you the least?
> Who in this group would you like to know more about? What would you like to know?
> Who in this group is most nearly like you?
> What misconceptions does this group have about you?
> How have you attempted to fool this group?
> Who in this group do you wish liked you better?

25. The teacher hands back the first impressions written earlier in the course. Students share them with one another and discuss how their impressions have changed.

NOTES ON THE ACTIVITIES

It should be noted that approximately the first third of the activities deal with getting acquainted. It takes students a surprisingly long time to learn one another's names, and even longer to feel comfortable together. The more information they can pick up about each other, the more quickly they will feel relaxed and comfortable. The teacher must not leave this process to chance. If he does, the quieter members will never provide others with information and will soon be ignored without having had a chance to be known.

The second set of activities deals primarily with increasing effective group work. These exercises promote careful listening and encourage all group members to contribute, to share leadership, and to build a group product.

Only toward the end of the training period are students really encouraged to talk about their emotional responses to one another. In a traditional school setting, where competition is keen and suspicion of others is high, the threat level will remain high longer than one might imagine. Seated in front of a teacher who is required by the school to evaluate him, confronted by peers on whom he depends for social support, a student is highly unlikely to feel free to talk about himself and his feelings about others. Only gradually can he be shown through experience that he can trust others in the class and can talk openly about himself without fear. Hence the usual "T-group questions" are postponed until an atmosphere of trust is well established.

As the teacher works with these activities, ways in which they can be related directly to subject matter will become apparent. For example, my science fiction classes were to study a story in which the chief character has prudently built a fallout shelter for his family and must decide which of his neighbors to admit when the sirens warn of an imminent attack. Before assigning the story, I asked students to imagine that they had built such shelters and were forced to decide which members of the class, if any, they would admit, knowing that their own chances for survival decreased with each person admitted. The results were twofold. Students began to notice their evaluations of others in the class, and when they read the story the next day their understanding of its conflicts was enhanced. Here's the way one student described the experience in her journal. "We were supposed to have read 'The Shelter' for today. It was the best thing I ever read!!! It's easier to understand and have feelings for certain things when you have first-hand evidence and experience."

One reason that the classroom is the ideal human relations laboratory is that as students go about their scholastic work a myriad of problems in interpersonal relations arise quite naturally. The teacher can make use of these problems to train students to deal more effectively with others. An experience I had with two students, Bob and Linda, illustrates this point. Each had complained to me about the other. Bob was the center of attention in every discussion and was well liked by almost all group members. Linda annoyed him; her contributions seemed "stupid" to him, and so he made frequent sarcastic comments to her. Mousy Linda resented his cutting remarks but didn't know how to fight back; she asked me to transfer her to another class. Other members felt Bob was being cruel in his treatment of Linda. Bob was embarrassed and hurt by these reactions.

Rather than counseling the two students separately in the hope of "working something out," I dealt with the conflict as a group problem for the entire class. With the consent of Bob and Linda, I told the group about the problem and asked them all to present their perceptions of what was going on. Each described the conflict from his point of view, some siding with Bob, some with Linda.

I then told Linda and Bob to voice all their resentments toward one another and to enumerate the changes each wanted the other to make. They were then able to work out a solution, face-saving to both, to assure their future comfort. Finally—in order to demonstrate that each was still important to and accepted by the group—I had each class member describe one quality of both Bob and Linda that he liked or appreciated.

The benefits of T-group experiences with the classroom and related to the cognitive goals of the course cannot be overrated. My experience has demonstrated that these methods can lead to improvement in cognitive learning as well as to significant affective growth. Although there is certainly value in special groups set up for the sole purpose of counseling, the classroom offers unique opportunities for human relations training because it provides real situations and problems to deal with.

Exploring Sex Roles

Sara K. Winter

When a woman begins to experiment with being strong, taking responsibility for her life, and showing anger directly, she pulls back in fear: "Women shouldn't behave like that." When a man cries, or reaches out for help, or shows weakness, he is pushing against all his past learning: "That's not acting like a man."

Teaching an experiential course at Wesleyan University, "Personality and Role: Male and Female Roles," Dr. Fredrik de Boer and I designed a series of exercises in which students could explore the ways that sex roles constrain their own behavior. Our underlying model was that being fully human means being more than "appropriately male" or "appropriately female"—it means being free to express your own individuality, whether or not this fits with the conventional behavior expected for your sex. This fits in with the increasing recognition within the women's liberation movement that *both* sexes, and not just women, are oppressed and limited by standards which say, "Men behave in only this way; women, in only that way." We assume that *both* men *and* women will be more whole as they discover the parts of themselves that have heretofore been denied as inappropriate for their own sex.

We worked with a group of 12 students, six women and six men, primarily college seniors. Only two of the students had acting experience, and only a few had been in encounter groups before. The class, cross-listed in Theater and Psychology, met for 2 one and one-half hour sessions weekly throughout the semester. We organized the course in three phases: (1) group-building, the creation of trust, and the development of improvisational theater skills; (2) exploration of the effects of sex roles, and (3) performance—communicating our experience to the campus as a whole. In

Reproduced by special permission from *Social Change*, Vol. 3, No. 3, 1973, courtesy of Sara K. Winter and the NTL Institute for Applied Behavioral Science.

this article I shall describe the specific exercises which we developed for the second phase. We explored sex roles in two ways: (a) by working with behavior or feelings usually labeled "male" or "female" in our culture; and (b) by asking students to reverse roles, with men acting as women, and women acting as men.

CONFRONTING FEAR

A note about defensiveness and fear is appropriate here. In all these exercises, students were asked to act in ways which had been labeled, all their lives, as absolutely *not* "the right thing to do." Any leader using exercises which challenge sex-role stereotypes can expect group members to be hesitant, self-conscious, or even terrified at the prospect of experimenting with "forbidden" behavior. We dealt with these feelings in several ways. Before introducing the sex-role exercises to the class, we used some conventional encounter-group trust exercises. We designed further exercises that encouraged body contact and discussed feelings and fears about touching and being touched by members of the same and the opposite sex. We played together, acted childish together. We used a "secret pooling" exercise in which students anonymously stated their worst fears of what could happen in the group. At several points we divided the group, allowing men and women to meet separately in order to increase solidarity and trust within each sex group. By the time the sex-role exercises were begun, students felt comfortable about appearing silly or strange or ridiculous in the presence of one another.

ROLES AND REALITY

Perhaps the most important vehicle for confronting defensiveness and fear, however, was our stress that these exercises involved *playing roles*. This approach was unfamiliar to me as an encounter-group leader; my focus in the past had been on encouraging group members to be "real," to confront hidden aspects of "themselves." In sharp contrast, we asked students in this course to play explicitly artificial roles—to "try something utterly unfamiliar."

With this set, students experienced the exercises as much less threatening. A male student, for example, might be reluctant to "show us your weak and dependent side." However, if asked to "act *like* a weak, dependent girl," he is embarrassed but gives it a try, and is able to put more and more of himself into his performance as he continues. A girl dissolves in embarrassment if asked to "be forceful." But when she is asked to "play a man telling off his wife," she finds that she does indeed have in her behavioral repertoire the material to play the role.

We discovered that once the student has actually *done* the supposedly threatening or impossible (even with a set of "just pretending"), she/he can readily own it as "part of the real self." In discussion after an exercise on dominating, for example, the girls openly discussed both their pleasure in dominating and their fears about being dominant in "real life." The initial instruction, "This isn't the real you, it's just a role," frees the student to try the behavior; having tried it, he/she can accept it as part of him/herself.

THE EXERCISES

Exercises on Sex-Role Stereotyped Behavior

In some of our exercises, we chose behavior generally regarded as "masculine" or "feminine" and asked both sexes to try it. All the exercises in this section were carried out with same-sex pairs and repeated with opposite-sex pairs, so the different experiences could be compared.

Being Strong, Dominant, and Assertive

Fighting. Two people first thumb-wrestle. Then they stand toe to toe, facing each other, with palms touching the other's palms; each tries to press forward to throw the other off balance. This is repeated with the two standing farther apart, so that more force is necessary.

Slow-motion wrestling. Pairs have a wrestling match, continuing until one "pins" the other, but in extremely slow motion. (The slow motion equalizes the pair in actual physical strength, since one person cannot pin the other without the other's acquiescence at every stage of the process.) The group watched pairs wrestle in turn; this was followed by a slow-motion "barroom brawl" with all participating.

Arm-wrestling tournament. Girls arm-wrestled girls, with the victors then arm-wrestling each other until the "girls' champion" emerged. A "men's champion" was similarly chosen. Then the male victor and the female victor arm-wrestled.

Dominance and submission. As a homework assignment, members were paired and asked to make an appointment to spend 35 minutes together at an arranged time and place. The written instructions for the exercise, opened when they arrived at the rendezvous, were: "(name) is to dominate totally; (other name) is to submit utterly, for a period of 35 minutes beginning now. Don't discuss the instructions; don't stop until the time is up. Rules: no sex, no violence, no public humiliation." Each student worked with one student of the same sex and one of the opposite sex, in two different appointments, once in the dominant role and once in the submissive role.

Playing children. One session was spent "being children together," in solitary and in social play, playing games together, and so on. Students were asked to act themselves as children, and then to role-play a type of child they might have liked to have been. We also asked them to explore being angry and assertive children.

In these exercises, women had profound experiences of realizing how they undercut their strength, feared assertion, and resisted being dominant, even within the structure of a brief exercise. Men found dominance more comfortable, but also were put in touch with ways they had felt pressured throughout their lives to be more assertive or dominant than they wished. Most men and women discovered that they felt different being strong with someone of the same sex than they did with someone of the opposite sex. Women explored their competitive feelings particularly with other women and their fears of demonstrating their strength with men. Many students discovered that as "children" they were able to act out their desires to be more (or less) aggressive than in their present lives.

Being Nurturant

Baby day. We provided pacifiers and baby bottles with orange juice and chocolate milk. First men "mothered" the women "babies," giving pacifiers and bottles. Further extensions included teaching baby to walk, disobedient baby, angry baby, spanking the baby. Then women "mothered" the male "babies."

Baby behavior in a bar. The group role-played a scene in a bar, with two students as bartenders, the rest as patrons. "Drinks" were the baby bottles. Students were asked to be adults in the bar, but to allow baby behavior to occur whenever they felt like it.

Feelings about a real baby. A young couple, the same age as the students, brought their three-month-old baby to class. Everyone held the baby, played with the baby, asked questions, talked about how he or she felt.

In these exercises, not surprisingly, most of the women were initially more comfortable than men with both the nurturing and the baby roles. Students of both sexes experienced feelings ranging from deep satisfaction to aversion and fear in relation to being helpless, being taken care of, asking for help, and giving help.

Exercises with Sex-Role Reversals

In a second series of exercises, we asked the sexes to reverse roles—to "play that you are the opposite sex." Beginning with less demanding exercises, we worked gradually toward full role reversals.

Panel discussion. Most of the group served as audience as three members began a discussion on a set topic. The three persons in the discussion were assigned fixed roles: one as a strong, dominant male; one as a helpless, unself-confident female; and one as an egalitarian person. As the discussion continued, members of the audience were free to go up and replace any of the participants, picking up the vacated role and continuing the talk. The exercise continued until all students had had a chance to rotate through all three roles.

A date for the junior prom. With the sexes reversed, "men" role-played calling on the telephone for a date, picking up the date, driving to the dance, talking, dancing, going out after the dance, and the goodnight scene. Couples interacted with one another at the dance.

Miss America and Mr. America contests. First, a Miss America contest was held, with men as the candidates and women playing a panel of male judges. The "girls" first paraded as if in bathing suits, then performed talent numbers, and then were asked questions by the judges for the "personality" competition. The judges then discussed the "girls" in their hearing, and awarded prizes. For the Mr. America contest, the situation was reversed: girls played the "men" competitors by showing off their physiques, role-playing weight-lifting, and answering the "personality" questions posed by the men, who played a panel of female judges.

Quarrels. Students were paired and again asked to play the role of the opposite sex. "You are in a serious relationship with this other person— going steady, engaged, or married—and tensions between you have been building up for some time. Right now you are beginning to talk about the problem, and all the difficulties are emerging into a real argument."

The cocktail party. Men and women brought extra clothes to class one day. Meeting separately, each sex tried on the clothes of the opposite sex, experimenting with different garments until each person had found a costume as a certain type of person of the opposite sex. Then the two groups met for a role-played cocktail party, taking opposite-sex roles. Social conversation took place between the sexes and among each sex, as it would have at a real party. Then students changed back into their own clothes to discuss the experience.

These exercises appeared to have a cumulative effect; students' experiences and insight deepened and became more subtle as they moved from the less demanding to the more demanding role-reversal tasks. Several themes consistently emerged in the discussions which followed each exercise: (1) *There were wide individual differences in what aspects of the traditional male and female roles were experienced in what ways.* Individuals found what they liked and disliked in the opposite sex role. They discovered that the roles were sometimes extremely constraining; at other times, extremely freeing and exhilarating.

(2) *Striking material emerged about each sex's stereotypes of the other.* At the cocktail party, for instance, the women playing men found that their conversation with the other "men" reflected their idea that men, alone with one another, concentrate on crude sexual remarks, politics, and sports. Corresponding male stereotypes of women emerged as the men, playing "girls"

at the junior prom, were prudish, superficial, and trivial in conversation. (3) *Many students had strong experiences of empathy for the opposite sex.* For example, in the cocktail party men experienced for the first time women's sense of being physically invaded by men's casual touch; women empathized with the stress men experience in having to take the initiative in making contacts. The Quarrel exercise was especially productive for empathy; many students had the experience of speaking lines that had actually been used against them in real-life arguments in the past, and understanding for the first time how the other person must have felt at the time.

Living a New Sex Role

One final exercise required students to experiment with changing their sex-typed behavior in "real life." Each person designed a role for him/herself and played it for one hour, without telling the other people in the real-life situation what was going on. A quiet girl, for instance, ate dinner in the college dining room as a dominant, sexy siren. One male experimented with giving up the initiative for one hour in the middle of a date. Subsequent discussion focused on the ease (for some) and difficulty (for others) of trying new behavior; the effects (or lack of effects) of the role on others; and feelings of pleasure or displeasure with the changed behavior.

GENERATING OPENNESS

To give some idea of the issues opened by these exercises and of the openness generated in the group by these methods, I report some of the content from a session near the end of the course. We asked students to pair with three different individuals in turn and to talk about "what is important for *you* about sex roles; what you know now." Important themes were then brought out in discussion with the group as a whole.

Issues discussed (all in very personal terms) included men's experiences with surrendering and being incompetent with women; aspects of traditional sex roles which different individuals still appreciated and found good; women's feeling of themselves as "feminine" or "unfeminine," and how they now felt about the criteria they had been using; homosexual feelings; men's experiences with and feelings about impotence; men's fears of women; women's guilt feelings when men are impotent with them; blatant and subtle aspects of one's own sexuality; men and women's experiences of faking or inauthenticity in sex; how the two sexes experience love-making differently; both sexes' feelings about their own and the other sex's bodies; men and women's similar and different fears about taking the initiative sexually.

As is apparent here, experiential work on sex *roles* focuses attention also on *sexuality*. The students themselves, as an outgrowth of their work with the sex-role exercises, moved naturally toward sharing very personal sexual experiences, questions, fears, and doubts. For most, this was the first experience of discussing such material in a mixed group. "Consciousness-raising" and the thoughtful sharing of deep personal experience in these areas—common in women's liberation groups and occasionally occuring in men's groups—was here taking place with both men and women present, to share and contrast their experiences and feelings.

SEX ROLES AND SOCIAL CHANGE

The exercises we designed to explore sex roles could be used in a wide variety of group settings. In personal growth groups, members could focus on parts of themselves that were being denied because of assumptions that they should be "masculine" or "feminine" in conventional ways. In married couples' groups, the focus could be on how each spouse expects him/herself and the other to feel and behave. In men's or women's groups, members could experiment collectively with behavior they had previously felt "belonged" to the other sex. In our course we found that these exercises enabled students to re-own denied parts of themselves, empathize more sensitively with the opposite sex, and expect and encourage change in others.

The distinction is often made between groups stressing "personal growth" goals and groups oriented toward organizational or social change. Though the focus in our course was on individual liberation from sex roles, I think it would be a mistake to view exercises such as these in the context of personal growth alone. Basic social institutions are grounded in the socialization of individuals to conventional sex-role standards. As sex roles change, institutions will change too. Our students, for example, generalized their experience in the course to many aspects of their life in the "real world"—questioning and changing their love relationships; their ideas about marriage, education, and child-rearing; their vocational goals. Organizational change and social change are inevitable long-range consequences of widespread "consciousness-raising" about sex roles in the lives of individuals.

A Parent-Youth Happening

Charles Ellzey

On both sides of the generation gap today are heard such complaints as "They won't listen," "They don't understand," and "They live in a different world." To facilitate bridge-building, I designed a two-hour laboratory for a Sunday afternoon with approximately 15 adults and their 15 teenagers.

The session was an outgrowth of two earlier ones, the first a day-and-a-half sensitivity training lab with about 30 members of a church youth group, the second a two-hour followup meeting which included interested parents. Several young people requested some kind of lab with their parents, and some parents likewise were interested.

We met in the church parlor two weeks after the parents' meeting. I made only one condition for attendance: no parent could come without a teenager and no teenager without at least one of his parents. As chance had it, an equal number of adults and youths, although not in every case an equal number from each family, were present. All the young people were to some extent acquainted; about half the parents knew one another, and about a third of the parents and young people were acquainted.

DESCRIPTION OF LABORATORY

Approximate Time	*Focus*
15 minutes	Informal introduction and refreshments period and orientation. Some input regarding the legitimacy of feelings and the importance of their expression and reception, of verbal and nonverbal communication, and of listening at both levels.

Reproduced by special permission from *Human Relations Training News*, Vol. 14, No. 1, 1970, courtesy of Charles H. Ellzey and the NTL Institute for Applied Behavioral Science.

20 minutes   Pairing of youths and adults who are unacquainted. Discuss "What it feels like to be what I am . . . (parent) (teenager)." After one partner expresses this, the listener checks his understanding by summarizing what he has heard and offering comments to indicate understanding. After 10 minutes the roles of speaker and listener are reversed.

5 minutes   Total group sharing of new ideas, insights, and feelings.

15 minutes   Pairing of different sets of youths and adults who are unacquainted. Discuss "What it must feel like to be what you are . . . (adult, parent) (teenager, boy or girl)." Each says what he imagines the other's situation feels like and checks the accuracy of his observations with the partner.

10 minutes   Total group sharing of ideas, insights, and feelings and discussion of implications of the two previous conversations.

10 minutes   New pairing of adults and teenagers who are unacquainted. Three-phase mirror exercise (nonverbal). Phase one: With hands not touching, one person moves hands, arms, or other parts of the body with the partner following; then they reverse roles. Phase two: One partner initiates movements; the other follows, and they exchange leadership without verbal cues. Phase three: The partners touch fingertips, again exchanging leadership. Changes from phase to phase and within phases are at my direction.

7 minutes   Talk about feelings and observations within the pair for a couple of minutes and then share with the total group.

5 minutes   Pairing as in mirroring. Slap hands exercise. Partner A holds hands with palms down or palms together; B tries to slap the outstretched hands before the other can withdraw them. Slapper role changes each time hands are slapped.

8 minutes   New pairing of unacquainted adults and teenagers. Blind-leading exercise (nonverbal). A, whose eyes are closed, leads B from place to place. They reverse roles at my direction.

15 minutes   The pairs talk about the exercise, then share with the total group. Talk about issues of trust, touching, leadership, authority, and control from the standpoints of both adults and teenagers.

55 minutes   Two families of parents and youths form a group. One family shares among its members its feelings and learnings, and discusses implications of the various exercises of the afternoon, addressing themselves to the statements, "What I would like to do differently in our family" or "In what way I intend to be different in our family." The other family acts as process observers and consultants, assisting the sharing family members

in communication, primarily with regard to hearing and interpreting correctly. At my direction after about 25 minutes the
two families reverse roles.

15 minutes Total group sharing of new feelings, ideas, insights, and
ramifications.

Most of the response to the various phases of the session were quite
positive. Typical comments were "I didn't know an adult had such feelings," "I found myself listening uncritically to my daughter for the first
time that I can remember," "I never knew before that adults had feelings
similar to mine," "It was nice to have an adult really listen to me," and "I
saw how I've shut out my son, even though I didn't intend to."

A few responses after the hand-slapping and blind-leading exercises
indicated some discomfort and embarrassment, and included the attitude,
"I don't see any point to it."

The general feeling was that the parents and their teenagers talked
together more freely in the final two-family exercise than they had been
able to do before. Obviously, the meat of the session was in the conversations within the families during this period. The previous encounters provided a warming-up process.

As is usually the case, this group was somewhat self-selected; those who
attended were inclined to want to improve their family relationships and
communications. Several of the adults were quite anxious before the session, and their attitudes as they arrived indicated family atmospheres of
considerable tension.

Progress was made on both sides toward the goals of openness, listening and hearing, and understanding of feelings. Some progress was observed in the last conversation toward identifying the communications and
relational problems as "ours" rather than "yours," toward sometimes saying
"my" fault instead of "yours." Yet understanding was also shown that this
one session did not solve all problems.

I would like to see this experience at the beginning of a longer lab.
We were just starting to develop the warmth and openness that build real
learning and behavioral change in parent-teenager relations. Progress of
only a tentative kind could be seen. Still, any achievement in helping parents and teenagers to talk openly appears to be worthwhile.

Leaderless Groups for High School Students

Irene G. Casper

The purpose of this paper is to describe the use of leaderless groups as a way of helping high school students communicate more effectively with each other.

An interested group of faculty members of the Greater Egg Harbor Regional High School District, New Jersey, realized that the opportunity for students to talk with each other is, to a large extent, limited to a few minutes during the lunch period. The school is in a rural area and the students are transported by bus.

In order to increase opportunity for student-to-student interaction, the faculty formed weekly discussion groups. These groups, which became known as Multi-Racial Discussion Groups, were composed of black and white students and one faculty member as discussion leader. However, student request to participate in the program was greater than the number of faculty who were interested in working with a group. As a result, those of us responsible for administering the program began to explore other ways of providing students with the possibility of participating in discussion groups.

We asked ourselves the question, "Can we reduce the student-faculty ratio and still provide the students with an opportunity for meaningful dialogue with each other?"

With this concern in mind, a public announcement was made requesting that all students interested in participating in the program on Communication Skill Sessions (as it was called) indicate this by signing their names on the appropriate list.

Reproduced by special permission from *Human Relations Training News*, Vol. 14, No. 4, 1970, courtesy of Irene G. Casper and the NTL Institute for Applied Behavioral Science.

Structurally, it was decided to form a maximum of six groups with eight students in each. Two adults (one a faculty member and the other the writer, a consultant to the school) were to work with all of the groups. Their role was to give instructions and rove among the groups to observe their functioning. Thus, each student group was defined as a "leaderless group" since there was not an assigned discussion leader.

The purpose for these groups was threefold: (1) to provide students with a chance to engage in meaningful dialogue; (2) to increase their effectiveness with specific communication skills; and (3) to see if these objectives (1 and 2) could be achieved with "roving" faculty rather than an adult working continually with one group. Sessions were held for one class period (42 minutes) a week for five weeks.

Each week the adult leaders presented the student groups with a specific task to provide them with a focus for that period. The first week a micro-lab type design was used in order to have students get to know as much as possible about each other in a short period of time and also as a "taster" of what was to come in the following weeks. Some examples of problems posed were "What are your expectations?," "What do you value most in life?," "Imagine you were an animal; what would you be?," and "How would you describe yourself and others in your group?"

Listening skills and perception of others were the major focus of the second session. Students were given pictures and diagrams and asked to discuss the differences in what they saw. They then related problems of perception and listening to their daily lives, at home and school.

The third session centered on the development of group problem-solving skills. They were given the "Bombshelter Task" to solve, within which they are to decide who the survivors would be in case of nuclear attack.

Up to this point the training sessions had focused primarily on the role of the individual. Thus it was decided that students would now be able to look at a group as a whole. Therefore, the fourth session involved using a "fish bowl" grouping design and the outside group was given specific observational tasks.

Then, since a major purpose for these sessions was to give students the opportunity to talk with each other, the final session provided them with time to look at their values and relationships with peers, teachers, and parents. The group members were posed with questions such as "What would you like to say to your parents?," "What do teachers do that 'bugs' you?," "What do you do that 'bugs' them?," "What would you like to do differently in your relationships with others?," and "What have you done today that made you proud to be you?"

A pencil questionnaire was distributed at the end of the final session in order to get some feedback from students concerning the effectiveness of the program.[1] In response to the question "What did you learn that you didn't know before?," the most frequently occurring comment was "how much people are alike and also different." Several students also indicated the following learnings: "no one can be seen as a stereotype," "needed to listen more," "respect for opinion of others," "could talk without fear of criticism," and "made new friends."

Answers to the question "What didn't you like about these sessions?" gave some ideas as to possible changes if this experiment of leaderless groups were to be tried again. Students indicated that they did not like the high noise level, that a larger room would help, that it was hard to open up and express what they thought in the formal classroom setting, that more people should participate, and that members of groups should mix more.

These sessions were held during regular class periods; thus the individual student was always faced with the decision as to whether he should attend the communication sessions or class. However, 38 of the original 48 participants attended at least three of the five sessions.

It would seem from these comments that the program was successful in bringing students together to talk with each other and increase their communication skills. The high noise level mentioned by some students as an aspect they disliked about the sessions is of concern to the persons directing the program. It is their opinion that some of the confusion was not task related, and a few students were having a good time getting out of regular class sessions; on the other hand, more space would also have reduced the noise level. Also, there was indication that students were not used to expressing their own opinions and felt awkward in doing so. If this is the case, then it would seem that a "lighthearted" phase is necessary for participants to experience before becoming task oriented.

As a result of this experience, our major concern at this point centers around this issue: if students have not been exposed to situations that allow them to engage in self-expression and interpersonal confrontation with others, should there be a phasing of activities directed toward increasing such freedom of interaction? If so, how? Or should the student be exposed to a completely instructional situation?

Also, we have developed a model which might be adapted by the classroom teacher who is interested in helping students express their thoughts and/or in obtaining feedback concerning his teaching-learning environment. It was shocking to hear from some of the students who participated in these discussion groups that they had never talked in small groups before or had never been asked to express their opinions! Think how much of our adult life is spent in small groups (committees, etc.). For what are we preparing our youth?

---

[1] Data for student evaluation was supplied by George Onufer, Coordinator of Group Dynamics, Program Guidance Counselor, Oakcrest High School.

The Bullring

A. J. Grainger

INTRODUCTION

What then is the Bullring that people should ask how it can operate in an ordinary school? It is most easily, though a little misleadingly, described as a free-discussion lesson; in it the children push the desks to one side, and, with the teacher, sit around in a circle facing one another. Their task is to study their behavior as it occurs and the teacher's task is to help them to do this. What, however, marks the Bullring off from an ordinary discussion period is the freedom; in the words of one 13-year-old girl, "you can say what you like and just about do what you like." She went on, "The Bullring is the nickname given to our discussions. This is so because the speaker and the person being spoken to are all alone, like the bull and the matador in a bullring." This nickname was invented by one of the children and no one found good cause to change it.

The Bullring started by accident in the sense that it developed out of an orthodox free-discussion period. It had been suggested to me that as a general principle children could learn very much more from each other—as opposed to learning from a teacher—than was generally recognized. However, when I watched my friend who advocated this, running one of his own groups, it seemed to me that he was still very much playing the role of the traditional guiding-hand and chairman. When, therefore, I came to run my discussion group, I decided to make as few comments as possible and, at least to begin with, not to answer questions. It seemed that in this way the children really would be forced to talk among themselves and not through the teacher. However, after the class had been talking in this way for 10 minutes or so, it occurred to me that what I was hearing above all

Reprinted from *The Bullring: A Classroom Experiment in Moral Education*, by A. J. Grainger. Oxford, England: Pergamon Press, 1970. Used with permission of the author.

—though in a symbolic and disguised form—was an expression of the difficulties they felt themselves to be facing in an unfamiliar situation. It seemed, therefore, more relevant at this point to attend to the latent content of the children's remarks than to make a contribution to what the discussion was apparently, or manifestly, about. How in fact one can follow the latent content of a discussion and what this involves in practice, I hope will become clear later on.

Although the Bullring takes freedom a step further forward than it is normally taken in schools, there are, of course, boundaries which must be observed, and children normally only had a Bullring once a week. If I took them for six periods a week, five would be ordinary English lessons and one would be a Bullring, or sometimes the ratio might be four to two.

NOTES FOR CHILDREN

The Aim

The aim is to give both children and adults an opportunity to increase their understanding of their own and other people's behaviour in the groups in which they find themselves. The increase in understanding aimed at can only be brought about by practical experience in group situations.

The Method

In order to provide a setting for this experience members of the group seat themselves in a circle so that equal opportunities to see and be seen, to hear and be heard, are offered to all. The *task* of each group is to study its own behaviour as it happens in "the here and now."

Freedom and the Rules

Complete freedom is neither possible nor desirable. Both teachers and children accept certain obligations and the following rules are laid down.

1. Damage must not be done to school or personal property.
2. There must be no excessive noise.
3. Acting in such a way as to cause physical harm is forbidden.
4. The meeting must stop if anyone enters the room and normal respect must be shown to teachers or children coming in on school business, etc.
5. Attendance is voluntary, but any child who wishes to be absent must inform the teacher on the school day before the next meeting.
6. The circle must not be broken. Visitors—either children or adults— may be admitted to the Bullring, but their task is the same as that of the permanent members.

Application of Learning

From time to time there will be ordinary lessons in which certain topics raised during the Bullrings will be discussed. An attempt will be made to link Bullring learning to other situations and some explanation will be given of the methods used in the interpretation and understanding of individual and group behaviour.

DIAGRAMS

The diagrams below, with the questions beneath them, were given to the children to discuss and write about in an ordinary lesson. The descriptions of group behavior "a" to "g" beneath the diagrams had to be assigned to the correct diagram as follows: (1) splitting into small groups; (2) splitting into two groups; (3) in "flight," running away; (4) following or attacking one leader; (5) action between most people; (6) action between two people only, "pairing"; (7) an ordinary class. The purpose of the questions was to draw attention to the appropriate behaviour for different occasions.

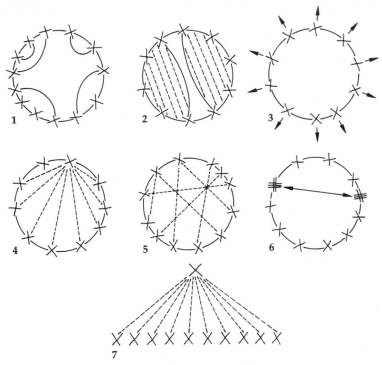

Diagrams Given to the Children

(a) Action between most people.
(b) An ordinary class.
(c) Following or attacking one leader.
(d) Splitting into small groups.
(e) In "flight," running away.
(f) Splitting into two groups.
(g) Action between two people only, "pairing."

1. Which of these groupings do you think is best in the Bullring? Say why.
2. Which of these groupings do you think is worst in the Bullring? Say why.
3. If you had to colour diagram No. 2 which colours would you choose? Say why.
4. Draw a diagram to show what you think has most often happened in the Bullring; it can be a mixture of more than one of the circles.

Which of the circles shows best how a group behaves in:
5. A game of football?
6. Class?
7. The playground?
8. Church?
9. A "General Excuse Me" dance?
10. A Last Waltz?
11. When might a group *need* to use No. 3?
12. Which of the diagrams best represent what happens in the cinema? It may be more than one.

Most, but not quite all of the children, felt that the "best" grouping for the Bullring was No. 5 "action between most people." Some preferred "following or attacking one leader," and this diagram, No. 4, most children recognized as being the same as No. 7 "an ordinary class." To prefer this to No. 5 indicated, I think, that the children felt bewildered by the freedom and wanted more control by the teacher, but even the 10 per cent to 15 per cent who favoured "following or attacking one leader" did not necessarily want the Bullrings to end. (Though I do not want to suggest that the American "T Group" courses are identical with the Bullring, since amongst other differences individual behaviour is commented on, a recent assessment of their effectiveness makes an interesting comparison. It was estimated that in America 20 per cent of those attending "T Group" courses "appear not to be helped at all," but that 80 per cent are "helped, and some very considerably."[1] My *impression* is that rather fewer than 20 per cent of the children appear not to be helped by the Bullring.)

The "worst" grouping for the Bullring was generally felt to be "split ting into small groups," and it is this to which the children refer when they complain about "the groups." The "groups" do, however, offer protection,

---

[1] Rose, B., "T-group?," *The* [London] *Times Educational Supplement*, 23 July, 1965.

and it is from a group of three or four individuals that a spokesman is sometimes found; having made his contribution, he then returns to the security
of his group, and whatever his public reception has been, he is usually sure
of being received back sympathetically by his friends. A notable exception
to this occurred when a boy stood up abruptly and asked, "What is the
meaning of life?" only to find himself on the floor when he sat down, since
someone had removed the chair from behind him! But the groups do interfere with learning if they become cliques for gossip; they are thus also
related to the idea of being "in flight" or running away (No. 3). Some children rated No. 3 as the "worst" grouping and few No. 2 or No. 6; groupings 2 and 6, splitting into two groups and "pairing," may be related if the
"pair" are acting on behalf of their respective "sides." Sometimes the whole
of one-half of the circle regards the whole of the other half as the "enemy"
with most children contributing in one way or another.

Children never have any difficulty in choosing colours for Diagram
No. 2, and the great majority select blue and red/pink, though there are
some who argue that black and white would be suitable as well; no other
alternatives were ever suggested. Answers to question 4 varied, but most
children used this as an opportunity to draw an elaborate and complicated
circle which showed all the possible alternatives taking place at once; some
had definite opinions that, for instance, "splitting into small groups" had
predominated, but most were reluctant to commit themselves to any one
particular grouping and wanted to represent all the possibilities.

The aim of these questions was to encourage the children to think
about different group formations and not necessarily to find a right or
wrong answer, though in practice there was normally a consensus. It is
appropriate—even essential—to take "sides" in a game of football (Q. 5).
Most ordinary classes in school follow or attack one leader, the teacher,
though this is not invariably true (Q. 6). Many children believed at first that
the playground grouping (Q. 7) represented "action between most people,"
though this was usually denied by a minority who insisted that this was
really splitting into small groups; again, usually, the majority came round
to the minority view, which seems nearer the truth. Church (Q. 8) was regarded as an example of following one leader, though as in answer to Question 6, about the ordinary classroom situation, there were references to individuals taking "flight" out of boredom.

Questions 9 and 10, based on dancing, were, admittedly, designed to
elicit the answers "action between most people" and "pairing" respec-
tively, although a General Excuse Me dance can only vaguely be said to
represent "action between most people," since, for though girls may dance
with girls, boys seldom dance with other boys. It would be more accurate
perhaps to regard this dance as an exercise in the frustrations of "pairing"
rather than genuine interaction. However, the children felt it exemplified

"action between most people" and were equally clear that the Last Waltz represented pairing. The symbolism of the dance is very potent and in some ways related to that of the Bullring—it makes use of the circle for instance—and it was partly this consideration, as well as the fact that the school Christmas dances were great occasions for everyone, that caused me to link the relatively positive aspects of "interaction" and "pairing" to dancing.

Many answers were offered to Question 11—escaping from fires, monsters, earthquakes, etc. Question 12 was designed as a talking-point; the children had to decide whether they went to the cinema to be "screen directed" and to follow the "leadership" of the film, or whether they went for the purpose of "action between two people only, 'pairing.'" It was often held that the appropriate behaviour was a mixture of the two, though some said that there was more "splitting into small groups" than anything else.

The preferred organization of the Bullring—"action between most people"—is not a fixed state in the sense that "following or attacking one leader" may be, but represents rather the group's ability to let the leadership role change appropriately—and generally quite rapidly. Once this has been experienced it is not difficult to see that it is qualitatively different both from the normal classroom situation and from group behaviour in the playground, the generally disliked "splitting into small groups."

These different groupings give some idea of the range of possibilities for action within any one group, and they provide some sort of scheme, not an exhaustive or an exclusive one, for studying group processes. The teacher in the Bullring does not say "I know," but "I think" or "I feel"; furthermore, what he thinks or feels is to some degree determined by the kind of person he is, and whether he likes it or not, he is affected by the group's behaviour. But his insights into the group's behaviour do become more accurate and less subjective as a result of his experience, though there is always the danger of becoming hardened in one's own misconceptions. For this reason it is helpful, particularly when the teacher is working with a large group of thirty or thirty-five children, to have a colleague with him who is able and willing to disagree.

How to Organize and Group Circles of Knowledge

Rita Dunn and Kenneth Dunn

No small-group instructional technique rivals a "circle of knowledge" as a reinforcement process. This teaching strategy permits students to:
1. Review previously learned information in an interesting way.
2. Focus their thinking on one major concept at a time.
3. Contribute to a group effort as part of a team.
4. Serve as catalysts for additional responses.
5. Develop ingenuity in helping team members to contribute.
6. Be exposed to and learn information without becoming bored.

Direct groups of between five and eight students to disperse evenly about the room (area, center) and form several small circles. Each group must have a recorder; again, the recorder may volunteer, be elected, be appointed by the group members or "take a turn." The teacher will either distribute a written question or problem which has *multiple* possible answers to the group or write one on a chalkboard or chart for all to see.

Each circle of knowledge will respond to the same question simultaneously (but quietly). A member in each group is designated as the first to begin, and the answers are then provided by one member at a time in clockwise (or counterclockwise) fashion. No member may skip his turn and no one may provide an answer until the person directly before him has delivered his; therefore, the answers stop while a member is "thinking" or groping for a possible response. No teammate may "give" an answer to another, but the group may "act out" or pantomime "hints" to help the person remember an item, an answer or a possible response.

From the book *Practical Approaches to Individualizing Instruction* by Rita Dunn and Kenneth Dunn, ©1972 by Parker Publishing Company, Inc., West Nyack, New York.

Only the recorder may write, and he jots down (in a phrase or two only) the suggestions (answers, responses, thoughts) of each participant as the circle of knowledge continues.

At the end of a predetermined amount of time, the teacher calls a halt to the "knowledge" sharing and all recorders must stop writing the groups' answers. The *number* of responses conjured up by each group is noted, but credit is not given for quantity alone.

The teacher then repeats the question that was posed to the entire group. In turn, a representative from each circle offers one of the answers suggested by that group. When an answer is provided, every recorder in the room looks at the list of answers developed by his/her group. If that answer is on his circle's list, he crosses it off, thus gradually decreasing the length of the list until only the answers that have not yet been reported to the group remain. This procedure continues until no circle has any remaining answers on its list.

The answers given by each circle of knowledge can be awarded points that are then recorded on the board to produce competition among the teams. The teacher might decide that each correct response will earn 10 points and that the circle achieving the most points will be the winner. Any time an answer is challenged by a rival circle, the teacher must decide whether it is right or wrong. If the answer is right and the challenger incorrect, the challenger's circle loses 5 points. If the answer is incorrect and the challenger was right, the circle who sponsored the answer loses 10 points and the challenger's circle gains 5 points.

The review provided by the intergroup discussion, the responses and the challengers make a "circle of knowledge" an effective technique for reinforcement through student participation.

Brainstorming

Sidney B. Simon, Leland W. Howe, and
Howard Kirschenbaum

PURPOSE

Brainstorming is a well-known, widely used problem solving tool. It encourages participants to use their imaginations and be creative. It helps elicit numerous solutions to any given problem, e.g. What shall we name this product? What should I do in this situation? How can we overcome this obstacle? In the area of values, it is very helpful in eliciting alternatives.

RULES FOR BRAINSTORMING[1]

1. No evaluation of any kind is allowed in a thinking-up session. If you judge and evaluate ideas as they are thought up, people tend to become more concerned with defending their ideas than with thinking up new and better ones. Evaluation must be ruled out.

2. Everyone is encouraged to think up as wild ideas as possible. It is easier to tame down a wild idea than to pep up a bland idea. In fact, if wild ideas are not forthcoming in a brainstorming session, it is usually evidence that the individual participants are censoring their own ideas. They are thinking twice before they spout out an idea for fear that they may come up with a silly one and sound foolish.

Reprinted by permission of Hart Publishing Company, Inc., from its copyrighted volume *Values Clarification: A Handbook of Practical Strategies for Teachers and Students,* by Sidney B. Simon, Leland W. Howe, and Howard Kirschenbaum.

[1]From an in-service training resource notebook for teachers of the gifted, put together by William M. Rogge.

3. Quantity is encouraged. Quantity eventually breeds quality. When a great number of ideas come pouring out in rapid succession, evaluation is generally ruled out. People are free to give their imaginations wide range, and good ideas result.

4. Everyone is encouraged to build upon or modify the ideas of others. Combining or modifying previously suggested ideas often leads to new ideas that are superior to those that sparked them.

TO THE TEACHER

Brainstorming can be used as an activity in and of itself, or it can be used in conjunction with some of the other strategies in this book. Here are some brainstorming topics—both serious and silly—that small groups in the class might work on.

1. How many ways can you think of to make this class a happier, more enjoyable place to be?

2. Your three-ton moving van, loaded with one million pipe cleaners (or balloons or chestnuts or brassieres) skids off the road, and gets stuck in the mud. How many ways can you think up for using your cargo to get your truck out of the mud?

3. What interesting, new subjects might we offer at our school next year?

4. Here is an object (give the group a mirror, a ruler, a wastepaper basket, etc.). Without using words, show as many funny ways as you can for using this object.

5. If our school were to change its name, what should the new name be?

Three Group Techniques

Ray Eiben

INNER-OUTER GROUP TECHNIQUE

Inner-Outer Group: Option One

Objectives

1. To provide a structure that facilitates feedback among group members.
2. To increase observer awareness of the processes of the inner group.

Procedure

The inner-outer group technique can be used in a number of ways. One approach is to divide a group of between sixteen and twenty members into two subgroups, one designated as the outer group and the other as the inner, or working group. The outer group is told that it is to observe the working group and make process comments subsequent to the completion of the activity. A list of questions to guide the outer group may be provided. Examples are:

1. Who assumed the leadership role?
2. How comfortable did members seem to be with the interactions that took place?
3. How did the group reach a decision?
4. Were some members excluded from the activity?
5. What kinds of norms were developed by the group?
6. Were members of the group free to express their opinions or did there seem to be a great deal of restraint?

The inner group is typically given a task activity to work on during a designated period of time, usually ten to fifteen minutes. After the inner group has used its allotted time, the groups are asked to switch positions and the new inner group is given ten to fifteen minutes to process the work of the preceding inner group. In this reversed situation, the inner group works on a task activity while the outer group observes them in preparation for their process session.

Activities

The following two activities can be used to demonstrate the inner-outer group technique when time is limited.

Dollar Bill Exercise. Any number of dollars are placed on the floor in the center of the inner group. The group is informed that they have no more than fifteen minutes to reach a decision as to who in the group is to receive the money. The group is apprised of the following rules:

1. No voting, drawing straws, flipping coins, etc., is allowed.

2. The decision is to be made by group consensus.

3. The leader will not take the money back at the end of the activity; if the group cannot reach a decision, the money will stay on the floor and the custodian can have it when he cleans the room.

4. The money is not to be spent on cooperative purposes; it is to go to the person who can articulate the best arguments for receiving it.

At the conclusion of the activity, the outer group processes the session using as a guide the list of questions under "Procedure" above. Questions related to the values of the group and how these values affected the deliberations can be added.

The Quarter Dilemma. When inner-outer techniques are used, it is feasible to give the two working groups similar tasks. The quarter dilemma is similar to the dollar exercise and leads to the expression of similar concerns and ideas. In this activity, quarters equal to the number of members of the inner group minus one are placed in a pile on the floor. The group is informed that it has fifteen minutes to decide who in the group will get the quarters. The quarters cannot be changed in any way (this precludes changing them into nickels or pennies in an attempt to divide the money equally). Nothing is said about one person receiving all the money. This gives the group an opportunity to establish norms regarding the division of the money. When this game follows the dollar game, comments are frequently withheld to determine what influence the previous group's deliberations have on the succeeding group. The activity is concluded with process comments made by the outer group.

Inner-Outer Group: Option Two

Objectives

1. To assist group members to define individual goals for group functioning.

2. To provide an opportunity for group members to participate in a dyadic encounter.

3. To initiate the process of giving feedback relating to individual functioning within a group.

Procedure

Members are asked to pair off with someone in the group whom they would like to know better. Following this, the pairs are asked to meet together for ten to fifteen minutes to discuss their responses to the following stimulus statements.

1. The ideal group member is _____.
2. In order for me to be a more effective group member, I need to

_____.

3. In the forthcoming group session, my goal will be to _____
_____. (Partners should agree on a response on this item.)

One representative from each dyad meets together in the inner-group setting and participates in a task-oriented activity. Other members position themselves so that they can hear and see their partners. At the end of the allotted time, dyads are asked to meet together again so that the observer can give the participant feedback on whether their goals were accomplished and on how the participant played his role during the session. As a guide to these feedback sessions, the facilitator may want to use a feedback checklist similar to the one following this section. After the ten- to fifteen-minute feedback session, the procedures are reversed; the working group is given a new activity, which is again followed by the feedback process.

FEEDBACK

With the increasing popularity of T-groups, encounter groups, personal-growth groups and humanistic education, the concept of feedback has become widely used and, consequently, is surrounded by much confusion. For our purpose, feedback is defined as a process of data sharing in which the prospective teacher receives information about her behavioral performance. In the school, children are taught that honesty is the best policy and that stealing, lying, and cheating are inappropriate behaviors. Yet, although these behaviors are denounced, teachers, administrators, and students are guilty of dishonesty in their interpersonal relationships. Feelings are not expressed and the potential for telling members of the educational community information about themselves that could be helpful remains unrealized. Feedback exercises are based on the assumption that personal growth occurs as individuals risk sharing data about the impact they feel they have on others and the impact that others have on them.

Feedback Procedure

In a group of from ten to fourteen members, the first procedure consists of each member giving positive feedback to each of the other group members. The suggested format is for one group member to volunteer to receive positive feedback and to have the other group members respond to him in this manner for a minute or two. After all group members have given feedback to the first member, a second member takes the spotlight and so on until all members have received positive feedback. To speed up the process, the group might be divided into two groups of from five to seven and the same procedures followed. If the facilitator feels that it would be helpful to follow the same general procedure with negative feedback, this would be a logical second step.

EMPTY-CHAIR TECHNIQUE

Objectives

1. To provide a way to share information without the confusion of having all members of a large group try to provide input simultaneously.

2. To provide group members the experience of reporting the results of a small-group session to the total group.

3. To enable members of a large group to view the decision-making process as well as to participate in it.

Time: Two hours

Number: Unlimited

Procedure

Groups of eight to ten members are formed prior to the session (groups that have been formed for other purposes can be retained). Group-forming activities such as nonverbal milling can be used.

Each of the small groups is asked to work on a particular task, e.g., pinpoint impediments to change or positive factors toward change within a particular organization; work on a particular task activity ("Lego Man,"[1] "Greeting Cards,"[2] plan for a particular meeting, establish a set of candidates for an election, develop an organization plan for an in-service week,

---

[1] In J. William Pfeiffer and John E. Jones (Eds.), *The 1972 Annual Handbook for Group Facilitators.* La Jolla, Calif.: University Associates, 1972, pp. 36–43.

[2] Ibid, pp. 44–50.

etc.). Each small group is asked to select a member who will report that group's findings when the total community meets back together.

The representatives from the small groups plus the group facilitators form a circle of chairs. One chair in the arrangement is left empty so that if a member of the larger group wants to make a comment, she can enter the circle, make the comment, and leave. Instructions are given that members on the outside may not speak unless they sit in the empty chair.

The empty chair is also an appropriate technique to use for sharing the processing of activities that have taken place within small groups.

Place a check in the column underneath the member's initials when his or her behavior corresponds to one of the following categories.

Categories	Member's Initials								
1. Uses group member's first name when giving feedback.									
2. Makes eye contact with member to whom he is giving feedback.									
3. Says "I" rather than "we" when he means "I."									
4. Feedback consists of two desired components: a. Recipients's behavior is described b. Feelings and reactions to behavior are stated clearly									
5. Exercise is performed with seriousness of purpose.									
6. Feedback deals with elements about which recipient can do something.									
7. Feedback is well timed, communicated at the earliest time after given behavior.									
8. The accuracy of feedback between individuals is checked out with other group members.									
9. Feedback is specific rather than general.									
10. Feedback is descriptive rather than evaluative and minimizes the need for the recipient to respond defensively.									

Figure 1. Feedback Checklist

Part Two
Psychodrama and Role Playing

Psychodrama and role playing are techniques used to teach participants to encounter difficult situations or the unknown in ways that reduce the threat of experiencing them directly. Before the teacher can deal with the data generated by specific situations, interactions must be spotlighted so that learning opportunities for both participants and observers can be enhanced. Psychodrama and role playing utilize the spontaneity and tendency to "act out" that are characteristic of youth in order to make them an important part of everyday teaching routine.

Interaction and involvement are important processes in the growth toward self-realization and acceptance of responsibility for one's own learning. Psychodrama and role playing are interventions that help bring out the feelings a student has about other people, his perceptions of how others feel about and behave toward him, and his feelings about himself derived from the data that is generated by the drama-like situation. As people relate to each other and their environment in structured ways, patterns of interaction and roles assumed can be looked at and discussed and feedback can be provided so that the growth cycle can continue.

Consideration of growth and change as a process implies that initial risks have to be taken and behavior from this risk taking responded to so that movement to the next higher level of growth can become reality. Psychodrama and role playing are ways of facilitating risk taking in order that the cycle of risk-feedback-change can continue to take place. By stepping into and acting out another's role, the person who takes risks becomes less threatened. Through the use of these techniques, the passivity and apathy characteristic of many classrooms can be reversed.

It can be hypothesized that many teachers do not use psychodrama and role playing extensively because of their fear of dealing with a situation over which they have minimal control. A teacher may argue that the consequences of an unrehearsed role-play drama can be negative and destructive to the participants. Affective learning entails taking certain risks, dealing with the ambiguity of situations that are unique, and movement beyond what is easy and routine. Another fear some teachers have in using psychodrama and role playing is that they deal with therapeutic-type data, which the teachers are ill-prepared to handle. There may be some truth to this argument, and precautions do need to be taken so that deeply personal concerns do not enter into the drama. A few rules can be stated prior to the psychodrama or role play that will eliminate a majority of these concerns. Suggesting to students that they not role play a situation in which they are personally involved or indicating that the teacher will stop the role play if it becomes potentially injurious to anyone will reduce the dangers. Knowing something about psychodrama and role playing (through reading the sections that follow or major books on the subjects such as Hawley (1973), Shaftel (1967), Epstein (1972), or Moreno (1946) will lessen these fears even more.

Psychodrama and role playing can be helpful as teaching interventions in:

1. Providing an avenue for the less verbal student to "loosen up" in a drama-like situation.

2. Inserting a bit of here-and-now realism into topics about which students do not have direct experience.

3. Making it possible for students to see that for certain problems there are a multitude of solutions.

4. Enhancing an understanding of those whose roles and backgrounds are different from those of the participants.

5. Developing the creative ability of students to pose different situations and roles related to particular topics.

6. Facilitating more open communication among students and between students and their teachers.

7. Making students more aware of their strengths and weaknesses in interactive situations.

8. Providing a more stimulating, exciting, classroom environment.

9. Determining responses to such emotions as anger, aggression, unhappiness, hostility, and love.

10. Enhancing the understanding of human relations and of developing skills that make the student more effectively capable of dealing with human relations situations outside the classroom.

In the section that follows, certain theoretical components of psychodrama and role playing are discussed and a sampling of activities is provided so that the reader can become aware of the tremendous possibilities in these two types of interventions. As is true with all the readings in this book, a great deal of responsibility is placed on the reader to use what is included herein as a springboard to developing his own activities and situations.

REFERENCES

Epstein, C. *Affective subjects in the classroom; Exploring race, sex, and drugs.* Scranton, Pa.: Intext Educational Publishers, 1972.

Hawley, R. C. *Value exploration through role-playing.* Amherst, Mass.: Education Research Associates, 1973.

Moreno, J. L. *Psychodrama* (Vols. 1, 2, 3). Beacon, N.Y.: Beacon House, 1946.

Shaftel, F. R., & Shaftel, G. *Role playing for social values: Decision making in the social studies.* Englewood Cliffs, N.J.: Prentice-Hall, 1967.

Psychodrama: An Underdeveloped Group Resource

James M. Sacks

HISTORY

In 1922 J. L. Moreno described his improvisational theater in Vienna devoted to the facilitation of spontaneity and creativity. Moreno, however, was not an impresario but a social psychiatrist. He soon developed a method for the diagnosis and measurement of group relationships which he called "sociometry" and a method of psychiatric treatment which he named "group psychotherapy." Years later he revived his interest in theatrical improvisation, combining it with group therapy in the form of "psychodrama." He founded the American Society of Group Psychotherapy and Psychodrama (1943) and the journals *Sociometry* (1937) and *Sociatry* (currently titled *Group Psychotherapy* and *Psychodrama*). He and others have written extensively on the subject, so that a thousand-item bibliography on psychodrama is now in publication (Greer and Sacks, 1972).

THE PSYCHODRAMA SESSION

The psychodrama group meets in a small theater-like room. The therapist or director begins with a "warmup"—a limited structuring of the session to reduce anxiety, build cohesion and to prepare the members for action. In the second phase of the session, the dramatic production, a protagonist is selected who enacts relevant scenes from his life. The "auxiliary egos" who play the complementary roles may be either group members or specially trained professionals. After the dramatic scenes have reached their natural climax, a final discussion is held.

Reprinted from *Educational Technology*, February 1973, by permission of Educational Technology Publications, Inc.

GOALS

Psychodrama corresponds in its goals to analytic psychotherapy insofar as it attempts to release repressed ideas or affects. In this sense psychodrama is essentially a subtractive method aimed at the removal of pathogenic complexes through insight. Psychodrama corresponds in its goals also to educational methods insofar as it attempts to expand the behavioral repertoire by teaching. In this sense psychodrama is additive, introducing new material into the psyche from without.

ACTION

Psychodrama's unique contributions to psychotherapy include the use of action, temporal flexibility and role flexibility. Physical acting out usually facilitates derepression more readily than verbal interpretation. The psychodrama protagonist who waves his arms and shouts angry words at his mother is more likely to experience hitherto repressed hostile feelings toward her than the analytic patient who only hears his analyst's interpretation that he bears unconscious resentment against her. Active involvement also helps develop interpersonal skills. Role rehearsal is an essential ingredient in the gaining of social skills just as practice is required in the development of any ability. It is a truism that one learns by doing.

TIME

The therapeutic mechanism of analysis relies on the revival of repressed memories of past experiences which have been producing deleterious influence in the present. In group therapy of the interpersonal school the past is essentially ignored. Current interpersonal behavior patterns within the group are observed and pointed out, but no attempt is made to explore the original cause. In psychodrama the here-and-now aspect of interpersonal psychotherapy is maintained while at the same time regression to pathogenic experience of the past is also employed. Traumatic memories of the past continue to be experienced in the unconscious as if they were still present. In psychodrama, therefore, the past is reenacted as present. The reliving of these experiences, as if they were still occurring, releases emotional catharsis more effectively than does the mere retelling of stories. Psychodrama also deals with future oriented states such as hope and fear. Aimless, indecisive or conflicted individuals may try various action possibilities just to see how they feel or a protagonist may be able to objectify the details of what he most fears by means of a psychodramatic scene.

ROLE

The psychodramatic protagonist has the option of changing identity or role from one person to another. Such changes introduce a myriad of psychodramatic techniques useful both in analytic psychodrama and role training. Typical variations are the following:

Monads: Scenes with One Role

1. *Soliloquy*—in which the protagonist speaks as himself.
2. *Individual role play*—in which the protagonist takes the role of another person speaking alone. He thus explores another person's view of the world.
3. *Mirror*—in which an auxiliary ego takes the protagonist's part. Here the protagonist is freed from the action entirely and is able to watch himself perform. Some protagonists who would be threatened by immediate involvement can use the mirror as a bridge to fuller participation later.
4. *Modeling*—in which an auxiliary ego demonstrates an alternative way of behaving for the benefit of the protagonist.

Dyads: Scenes with Two Roles

5. *Multiple-self*—in which the protagonist enacts ambivalence of self-confrontation by moving back and forth on the stage, alternating in role and personifying two different facets of himself.
6. *Monodrama*—in which the protagonist enacts a scene between himself and another person, again moving back and forth on the stage presenting the relationship by taking both roles.
7. *Double*—in which an auxiliary ego stations himself behind or beside the protagonist stimulating his productivity by adding occasional comments. The double may represent some latent or deeper self. The double may also move directly face-to-face with the protagonist for a scene of self-confrontation. The protagonist assumes the role of either of the two parts of himself by means of role reversal.
8. *Dialogue*—in which the protagonist as himself enacts a scene with an auxiliary ego who takes the role of another person. A life relationship is simulated but the substitution of the auxiliary ego for the real other frees the protagonist to discover where his actions and feelings will lead when the restrictions of real relationships are removed. The presence of the auxiliary ego as a flesh-and-blood human enables the relationship to develop through back-and-forth conversation.
9. *Objective monodrama*—in which the protagonist, by taking both roles alternately, illustrates interaction between other people. He might, for example, reenact a disturbing argument between his parents which he had observed.

10. *Objective double*—in which the protagonist takes the role of another person and, moving slightly to the side, also takes the role of this other person's double. He can then show both the manifest and latent levels, which he perceives in them.

11. *Role reversal*—in which a protagonist and auxiliary ego in dialogue exchange positions and see the world and themselves from the other's point of view. One advantage of role reversal in exploring a conflicted relationship is that each person finds it easier to see himself through the eyes of his opponent, knowing that his opponent is making the same momentary sacrifice of self-esteem.

12. *Patterning*—in which the protagonist adds an action dimension to the modeling situation. That is, he becomes the double of or a simultaneous copy of the one who is providing the role model.

13. *Objective dialogue*—in which the protagonist takes the role of a person other than himself, in dialogue with an auxiliary ego who is in the role of a third person. In this technique the protagonist avoids the inconvenience of the role shifting required in the objective monodrama.

14. *Multiple mirror monodrama*—in which an auxiliary ego presents two roles representing two parts of the protagonist's personality while the protagonist watches.

15. *Multiple mirror*—in which two auxiliaries illustrate various versions of the protagonist or enact their version of his inner conflicts while the protagonist watches.

16. *Mirror dialogue monodrama*—in which one auxiliary ego takes both parts in a dialogue between the protagonist and another person while the protagonist watches. In this way the auxiliary ego can demonstrate his perception of a protagonist's pattern of relating.

17. *Mirror dialogue*—in which two auxiliary egos demonstrate an interchange in which the protagonist is involved. This technique is frequently used by members of a therapy group to show the protagonist how he acts with another member. The dialogue form is necessary since the protagonist's pattern may not be clear from a single act but only from a pattern of interaction.

18. *Modeling double monodrama*—in which an auxiliary ego enacts two parts of the personality of a person significant to the protagonist, while the protagonist watches.

19. *Modeling dialogue monodrama*—in which an auxiliary ego taking both roles demonstrates a dialogue between two people significant to the protagonist while the protagonist watches.

20. *Modeling double*—in which two auxiliary egos enact two sides of the personality of someone significant to the protagonist, while the protagonist watches.

21. *Modeling dialogue*—in which two auxiliary egos enact a dialogue between two people significant to the protagonist while the protagonist watches.

Sixty-five further variations are possible as triads, such as the *dialogue with double,* in which the protagonist with a double at his side engages in conversation with an auxiliary ego. The protagonist's double throws in occasional comments which strike slightly beneath the surface of the protagonist's manifest role. It is an effective form of psychological interpretation which can take advantage of the heat of the moment.

PSYCHODRAMA IN AN EDUCATIONAL SETTING

The same basic laws of human psychology apply whether a person is considered as a psychotherapy patient or as a student. While therapeutic and educational goals differ, it would be surprising if there were not considerable overlap in methodology. Defenses against understanding of the world as well as defenses against understanding of self dissolve under analogous conditions. Psychodrama helps disarm the one as well as the other. Nor would it be correct to assume that the role of the educational institution must be confined to learning about the world or that insight has no place in the school. An atmosphere in which children are free to describe or enact their feelings is certainly conducive, even essential, to learning. Maximum absorption takes place with an optimal balance between intake and output. The child who is a passive sponge is both rare and deplorable.

While psychodrama can contribute to learning, its abuse can certainly frustrate that goal. Psychodrama is a tool for the use of the protagonist and never to be used as a device of psychological instruction. A probing atmosphere is anti-therapeutic in a clinical context and anti-educational in an academic context.

REFERENCES

Greer, Valerie U., & Sacks, James M. *Bibliography of psychodrama* (1972). Privately available: V. J. Greer, 505 West End Avenue, New York, New York.

Moreno, J. L. *Das Stegreiftheater*. Berlin: G. Kiepenheuer, 1923.

Moreno, J. L. Psychodrama and the psychopathology of interpersonal relations. *Psychodrama Monograph Number 16*. New York: Beacon House, 1945.

Moreno, J. L. *The first book on group psychotherapy*. New York: Beacon House, 1957.

Some Uses of Psychodrama in Education

Ella Mae Shearon and Wallace Shearon, Jr.

CONCEPTS PRESENTED IN INITIAL LECTURE AND DISCUSSION

The creative function of co-creators as Moreno has described in his concept of the psychodramatic community is one that could well be realized in the context of public or private elementary schools. Moreno has envisioned a society where all individuals belong not by consent but as initiators and co-creators. The school setting could provide an opportunity for self-realization and creative expansion of the role repertoire.

For decades Moreno has insightfully discerned that creativity is the problem of the universe and it is certainly the problem of the schools. In one speech he pointed out that the dinosaur perished because he extended the power of his organism in excess of its usefulness and that man may perish because of reducing the power of his organism by fabricating robots in excess of his control. Man has put a premium on power and efficiency and lost credence in spontaneity and creativity. The countermeasures of sociometric and sociatric approaches to group relationships as well as psychodramatic spontaneity training might well be man's answer to his actual survival—in order to survive man must be creative.

The school, functioning as a social agency has access to the main population and through the development of creativity, spontaneity and group work could provide preventive treatment as well as a self-actualizing environment and thereby create a totally new psychodrama community.

In Moreno's concept of creativity the individual would not simply adapt to situations but would *create* new situations and new roles. Children

Reprinted from *Group Psychotherapy and Psychodrama*, Vol. XXVI, 1973, J. L. Moreno, M.D., Editor, Beacon House Inc., Publisher. Originally from a paper presented at the Fifth International Congress of Group Psychotherapy, Zurich, Switzerland, August 19-25, 1973.

have long been observed as being natural auxiliary egos who engage in natural role playing, e.g., games of make believe; however, the educator's task could be to transform the natural role playing of make believe into *purposeful* role playing.

Moreno's concepts of (1) the warm up, (2) spontaneity and spontaneity training, (3) creativity, (4) tele, (5) sociometry, (6) social atom, (7) role reversal techniques in the teaching of academic subjects and better interpersonal relationships, could all be successfully utilized in the school setting.

The warm up allows for expression of roles which the individual rarely has the opportunity to play in daily life.

The warm up and spontaneity have a circular effect—one reinforces the other. Effectiveness in a specific act could be better realized with the benefit of an adequate warming up process. The warm up facilitates spontaneity which in turn is the chief catalyzer of creativity. Without spontaneity, which helps the individual to create new roles, one would be unable to develop through life a personality that would realize his highest potential.

In order to solve the problems of life one must be spontaneous, otherwise he may be trapped in a rigid, stereotyped cultural conserve role. This stereotyped behavior has a paralyzing effect on the personality. With the unpredictable future which looms ahead there is a necessity to provide flexibility for which spontaneity training allows. Spontaneity not only sets up the framework for an adequate solution to problems but also releases the latent genius in mankind.

The S factor would contain:
1. Appropriateness to the situation;
2. Degree of competencies for a solution to a situation;
3. Immediacy to the here-and-now situation.

The creativity/spontaneity principle enables one to be autonomous and free—free from any external influence and free from any internal influence which he cannot control.

Spontaneity might be conceived of as a freely produced experience and the self-initiated behavior of man. When spontaneity abounds man is thrown into action and "the moment is not a part of history but history becomes a part of the moment."

Moreno points out that creativity might not consist of an end product that is totally new and unique but that creativity could produce a *new relationship* which did not exist before.

Creativity factors lead one to respond constructively to new situations rather than merely adapting; in fact, it leads man to create situations. Moreno further concludes that robots, for example, merely react to situations but cannot create new situations. Robotism is the opposite of spontaneity.

Tele is another concept which could well be utilized in the school setting. Tele is the emotional tone between two human objects.

There is a flow of affection and disaffection between oneself and other individuals or groups. Tele becomes the "flow—to and fro—of affectivity between individuals." Man simply does not react with other human beings but he coacts as well.

Moreno explains tele as more than just reacting to other people—it is a built-in self-starter. He points out that there are self-energizing characteristics of tele which may initiate a feeling tone within the individual even before anything has happened to cause a reaction to another person. Moreno concludes, "Tele is the fundamental factor underlying our perception of others. We see them, not as they are, nor yet as we are, but as they are in relation to ourselves."

Tele is defined as "the simplest unit of feeling transmitted from one individual toward another." The key word is reciprocity. This concept is basic to Moreno's theory of personality as well as being the central theme of sociometry and an integral part of the social atom concept. The social atom deals with the type structure of one's phenomenological field and the human beings bring into that social structure feelings of attraction or repulsion to one another (telic relationship). This emotionally toned human interaction principle and the understanding of it has unlimited value in the school setting where telic relationships are so vital to self development.

The role reversal concept is a technique of socialization and self-integration and a requirement for establishing a psychodramatic community. It is a very effective teaching and learning device; in addition it can be used as a corrective for unsocial behavior. The concept of role reversal increases one's role perception and broadens the role repertoire. Moreno has discovered that the more roles the individual plays in life the greater his capacity is to reverse roles. Children frequently use their parents as natural untrained auxiliary ego objects in role reversal and this provides the child with a basic empathic viewpoint. They also employ the role reversal concept in the games of "playlike" and "make believe." They need specific teaching and training in order to acquire the technique of role reversal which must be mastered in order to benefit from the viewpoint of the other person. This technique involves sensitivity training in auxiliary ego concepts, and is applicable, for example, in the acquisition of understanding, insight, empathy, and identity into literature and literary characters.

The forementioned concepts of (1) warm up, (2) spontaneity and spontaneity training, (3) creativity, (4) tele, (5) sociometry, (6) social atom, and (7) role reversal techniques in the teaching of academic subjects and better interpersonal relationships could indeed revolutionize the entire school setting and gradually produce a creative psychodramatic community for co-creators to fulfill self-actualization and psycho-realization.

TECHNIQUES USED IN WORKSHOP TO ILLUSTRATE PSYCHODRAMATIC CONCEPTS

1. Various body movement warm ups.

2. Warm up to facilitate the understanding, empathy, and identity with literary characters. Group is in circle position facing outward and director warms group up by asking each group member to select a person from literature and to assume the role of that person. After a sufficient warm up to the selected role the circle turns around facing each other and each individual plays the literary role of his choice and acts out the role. Choice of role is, of course, significant and revealing. The director and group members may ask questions directed to each character presented.

The warm up leads to utilizing psychodramatic techniques (role reversal in particular) to explore Shakespeare's *Hamlet* from a psychodramatic viewpoint. Hamlet's social atom and conflicting selves (auxiliary egos) were enacted by group members and were warmed up to play these roles. A protagonist for Hamlet was chosen and the teaching of an art work was illustrated by the presentation of scenes which the protagonist was warmed up to do. Several insights were gained:

1. Hamlet in the original drama never really successfully role reversed with Claudius, his uncle, Gertrude, his mother, nor Ophelia, his lover. Had he done so the drama would have changed direction. Hamlet, locked into a cultural conserve and his own obsessive-compulsive thoughts, was lacking in spontaneity.

2. When the student who is studying Hamlet immerses himself into the role of Hamlet and plays him and then as that character (Hamlet) takes on a new role, e.g., in a role reversal process such as a scene with Hamlet's mother, Gertrude, then there is a different and perhaps more insightful experience than if the student simply initially played Gertrude. The taking on of a third role when assuming the character of a second role creates a totally new perspective.

3. The telic relationship between Hamlet and his mother, Gertrude the Queen, was explored. The protagonist, Hamlet, reported that he in the role of Gertrude gained an insight that he had never before realized as just a reader and a student of Hamlet. In the role of Gertrude the protagonist realized and experienced that Hamlet was a tremendous threat to Gertrude. The full impact of that was never before experienced by the protagonist as just a passive reader of the play as he mentally, but not psychodramatically identified with Hamlet. Also, the sexual vibes and ambivalent attraction and repulsion become more apparent and were more fully lived and experienced by the protagonist.

4. The auxiliary ego concept can be used to a great advantage in the teaching of literature. The literary character to be studied, e.g., Hamlet in this case, was presented as one person with varying conflicting selves,

moods, or roles that he played. Several auxiliary egos were successfully utilized to play the various Hamlets, e.g., the depressed and disappointed Hamlet who tends to be immobilized, the Hamlet with a strong superego who feels a responsibility to avenge his father's death, the Hamlet who feels a responsibility toward Ophelia, etc. These Hamlets were graphically embodied, thus psychodramatically illustrating the conflicts that existed within this particular literary character. This principle could well be applied in the teaching of other literature selections.

Using psychodramatic techniques in the teaching of musical concepts was explored by the workshop. Several musical psychodramatic warm ups were used that illustrated basic music principles:

1. Establishing concept of pitch;
2. Combining pitch to make chords;
3. Using rhythm to sing chords;
4. Clarity of interpretation by using role reversal.

Musical warm ups included:

1. Warming group up to be musical instrument of their choice.

2. Humming of buzzing bees' voices in order to establish the concept of pitch and chords. (Role reversal with bees enabling each individual to play a role which he does not usually experience in everyday life.)

3. Variety of songs played, e.g., marches and lyric melodies. Group members spontaneously became the music selection of their choice and acted out roles through body movement and dance.

4. Group was instructed to warm up to assuming the role of an animal and changed their identity from animal to animal whenever the music changed.

5. Establishing mood through piano music and assuming role to illustrate improvised music, e.g., mood of gaiety, etc. were acted out in dance.

Reference was made to an art work, Schubert's "Heidenröslein," and the concept of clarity of interpretation was illustrated by the role reversal between the rose bush and the boy. The singer of this art song acquired new insight and had a broader interpretation when the concept of role reversal between the rose bush and the boy is realized.

The workshop ended with a brief period for questions, discussion, and a final synthesis of the use of psychodrama in education.

APPENDIX: PSYCHODRAMATIC IDEAS THAT COULD BE SUCCESSFULLY UTILIZED IN THE SCHOOL SETTING

1. The spontaneity factor in teaching music.
2. Spontaneity tests as warm ups for creative writing and acting.
3. The Spontaneity Theory of Child Development.
4. Sociometry.

5. Social atom in art.
6. Psychodrama for kindergartners in fairy stories.
7. Psychodrama for kindergartners in puppet roles.
8. Puppets—dolls—projective situations.
9. Hypnosis in warm ups.
10. Act out fairy stories psychodramatically and change ending.
11. Act out characters from history, e.g., Columbus.
12. Be Queen—Elizabeth.
13. What are you experiencing?
14. Magic shop.
15. Magic carpet.
16. Be period of history.
17. Be mood.
18. Be strife in Civil War (either exemplify it yourself or use others and sculpt them).
19. Act out part that you have no empathy with—villain, ugly duckling.
20. Purposeful role playing for children rather than make believe (natural role playing).
21. Social Atom and its uses.
22. Social conflicts and psychodrama.
23. Acting out conflict situation between children.
24. Ethnic conflicts.

BIBLIOGRAPHY

Bischof, Ledford J. *Interpreting personality theories*. New York: Harper & Row, 1970.

Moreno, J. L. *Psychodrama*. (Vols. 1, 2, 3). Beacon, N.Y.: Beacon House, Inc., 1946.

Moreno, J. L. *Who shall survive*. Beacon, N.Y.: Beacon House, Inc., 1953.

Moreno, J. L. Spontaneity procedures in television broadcasting with special emphasis on interpersonal relation systems. *Sociometry*, Vol. 5, No. 1, 1942.

Moreno, J. L. *Sociometry and the science of man*. Beacon, N.Y.: Beacon House, Inc.

Role-Playing in Teacher Education

Leonard S. Kenworthy

Much has been recorded in recent years about the values of role-playing or sociodrama in social studies classes in elementary and in secondary schools. Almost nothing, however, has been said or written about the values of this method in the pre-service and in-service education of social studies teachers. After more than twenty years' experience with this method, the writer can say that role-playing has proved to be one of the most profitable, provocative, and productive methods in the education of social studies teachers.

SOME OF THE VALUES OF ROLE-PLAYING

The values of this method are many and varied. Of course all participants do not react favorably to it at first. Some are even threatened by it. This is especially true of persons who have become adept at reporting and/or discussing what they have read, or have won their way in schools through the use of words. But, after repeated experience with role-playing and discussion of it, almost all participants recognize its relevance. Instead of merely reading about situations in classrooms, hearing about them, or even seeing them, participants *experience* them in simulated situations. Such experiences often spark realistic analyses of theories.

By playing the roles of different types of pupils, participants almost always gain insight into the variety of behavior patterns one can find in typical classrooms and acquire an elementary understanding of some of those behavior patterns. They learn something about the role that feelings play in learning. Often they begin to realize for the first time the frustrations of slow students and why they escape into their shells, like turtles, or

---

Reprinted from *The Social Studies*, November 1973, with permission of Heldref Publications.

stick out their quills, like porcupines. And participants also learn through role-playing how dull many classrooms are for the gifted.

Many prospective and in-service teachers also gain a better understanding of themselves through role-playing and the subsequent analysis, in class or in private conferences, of the sociodramas in which they have taken part. Often they gain security through successful experiences the first time they play a role, or through the reenactment of a role after their initial failure has been discussed by their peers. Very often they learn to anticipate difficulties they will encounter in their own classes. Frequently they discover their own fears and shortcomings and begin to work on them.

Role-playing can also help a professor or a consultant to gain information on and insights into individuals and/or group needs and thereby help them grow in desirable directions. It is sometimes amazing how much an observer can learn about an individual or even a group in five to ten minute sociodramas. Through many such situations, he can, of course, learn much more. A dramatic example was the girl in one of my classes who always faced the chalkboard or stood looking out the window when she "taught" the class. This information, plus additional data, was used as evidence to support my recommendation that she not be encouraged to do her student teaching. Despite this recommendation, the girl was permitted to do so, but under another supervisor. Unfortunately she collapsed in her class and had to be removed from student teaching. Her inability to face groups, as revealed in role-playing, had provided an important clue to her personality, which, if utilized by the proper authorities, could have saved her an excruciating experience.

Of course role-playing is only one of many teaching techniques, albeit a highly-honed tool in the hands of a master craftsman. By taking part in sociodramas many times, under competent guidance, teachers and teachers-to-be can learn many skills needed for the successful use of this method. They can then use role-playing in their own classes advantageously and often.

Even if it is used only a few times, role-playing can add variety to a class at the college level or to a workshop; and variety usually adds to teaching and to learning.

Many or perhaps most college professors today need to be retrained in the art and science of teaching. They need to become coaches, on the sidelines, rather than quarterbacks, halfbacks, or linesmen. They need to become directors of stage productions rather than the stars in them. Role-playing is one excellent method of helping such persons to become facilitators of learning and observers of behavior rather than the central actors.

There are even some ways in which role-playing in college classes and in workshops is superior to student teaching or regular teaching. For example, it is possible in role-playing to enact a situation, then to discuss it, and to reenact it. That is not possible in a regular classroom situation. Likewise, a group can concentrate for a few minutes on a given problem and alternative solutions to it rather than devoting an entire period to this problem or situation. Ordinarily this is not possible in a regular classroom.

SOME SUGGESTIONS FOR USING ROLE-PLAYING

Space precludes a detailed account of how role-playing can be carried on most effectively with social studies teachers. Readers can find a wealth of suggestions in the general references on role-playing at the end of this article. However, there are a few hints which can be highlighted here on the effective use of role-playing with social studies teachers or teachers-to-be.

Of prime importance is the climate of the classroom or workshop. Role-playing will succeed only if an atmosphere of spontaneity, reality, frankness, kindness, and mutual aid is created. This can be accomplished in part by the willingness of the director to "let his hair down" and to play roles himself, setting the stage for similar spontaneity by the others involved. Not every college professor or workshop director will be able to be so flexible. If you are not willing to become a "ham" yourself, you had better not use this method.

Likewise, the director must set the stage for a frank and realistic discussion of the roles played. But frankness needs to be mixed generously with kindness. It has been my practice, for example, to preface negative comments on role-playing with complimentary remarks, even if I had to strain sometimes to do this. And I have insisted on this procedure with participants. Most harsh criticisms need to be saved by the director for personal conferences outside of class rather than being discussed in class, especially at the outset of role-playing. Directors of sociodramas may be tempted at times to go beyond their depth in counselling. Few of us are psychiatrists or even psychologists. We need, therefore, to post a sign in our minds, warning us to "Proceed with Caution," in our counselling.

As preparation for role-playing, a potential director should have seen sociodramas enacted and have taken part in them. He should have read some of the literature on this strategy or method. He may want to ask a master of this method to come to his class or workshop to work with his students or to serve as an observer, making suggestions to the class and/or to the director.

Almost all future participants in role-playing need some preparation, too. They should have a brief presentation of its methods and values and have done a little reading on it. If they can observe a role-playing session, so much the better. And there needs to be some discussion of this strategy before they take part in it, clarifying what their roles are to be. However, much more realistic discussions will take place *after* initial attempts have been made to use this method.

My own preference for the opening role-playing situations is to have the group select a problem or topic and then to become the teacher myself. The participants are then assigned roles of pupils or asked to pick their own roles. This puts the burden of proof on the usefulness of this method on me. These opening sociodramas can be brief, allowing time for the participants to evaluate the role of the teacher. Very soon they can be asked how *they* felt (as slow learners or fast learners or as other pupils).

It has been my practice to select the first students who will play the roles of teachers, usually asking them outside of class if they are willing to assume such roles. I have not introduced role-playing until I knew the participants fairly well and could hazard a guess as to who could play such roles successfully. This means deciding in advance who are the most mature, flexible individuals in the class and the least sensitive to criticisms. With such persons little advance preparation outside of class is necessary.

With participants who are more hesitant to play the role of teacher in front of their peers, I have usually suggested that they pick a situation which they wanted to act out.

By asking the participants to play the roles of pupils in a class, two objectives are sought. One is to get them to think in terms of how pupils react to classroom situations and teaching. The other is to encourage them to "loosen up" as individuals and to learn to take part in role-playing as individuals instead of merely being observers. From the very first sociodrama, we begin to talk about how the pupils feel, as well as how the teacher performed.

In almost every group in which I have conducted sociodramas, some participants have found it difficult to play the roles of pupils. At first they tend to be observers of the professor or consultant and to be highly amused at what he is doing. Usually a few participants will start laughing or create a disciplinary situation where it is not really warranted. This possible reaction needs to be discussed before the role-playing starts. If it takes place, I always stop the role-playing to encourage the group to react realistically, or even to warn them not to act as adults. Firmness at this point will pay rich dividends; laxness will probably ruin the simulations. If the participants do create disturbances merely to test the reaction of the teacher, I stop and discuss why they have done this. Usually it is because they are afraid of disciplinary situations. Therefore the role-playing has uncovered one of their basic fears and it is time to discuss this openly with them. These are cries for help—and a need to be honored. Sometimes the situation has called for such reactions; usually it has not. So we have a good opportunity to suggest situations where disciplinary troubles are likely to arise, and how to deal with them or avert them, and to role-play such situations.

Ordinarily five to ten minutes are enough for the initial sessions. The person playing the role of teacher has already revealed much about himself or herself. Comments can then be made about the person teaching—his voice, his bearing, his ability to involve the pupils immediately, his vocabulary, his use of concrete illustrations, etc.

Most participants playing the role of teacher will resent the fact that the role-playing has been stopped so soon. They will protest that they have merely gotten started. Sometimes that is a valid objection. But usually they have no idea how much they have already revealed about themselves as teachers. In a discussion of their performance, they will soon learn how much the class had learned about them. If they want, then, to continue, they are usually encouraged to do so.

In many instances they are willing, and sometimes eager, to replay the situation after discussion has taken place. This is a highly productive aspect of role-playing and they should be encouraged to do so, especially where their initial effort was not too good. In other cases they are ready to watch someone else replay the situation, learning by their observation of a peer. Whenever possible, the original role-player should be encouraged eventually to replay a bad situation in order to have a successful experience and to profit from his mistakes.

Whenever possible the participants are encouraged to criticize what has transpired because we learn better in most instances from our peers than from a college professor or workshop director. From the very first, however, participants are encouraged to make positive as well as negative remarks about what has taken place. This is important to preserve the ego of the person who has played the leading role—and it is an important lesson for teachers and teachers-to-be to learn as guides to younger people.

As the group becomes more adept at role-playing, I have sometimes stopped one person and asked another individual if he would be willing to proceed from where the original teacher left off. For some this can be a threatening experience. Therefore the choice of a person to play the role of a teacher on the spur-of-the-moment must be carefully considered—and that person given a chance to say "No." However, this is a wonderful way in which to evaluate the flexibility of participants. Some persons even find this easier than knowing in advance that they are to be "on the spot"; they have less time to worry about how they will perform.

Some participants who have worked closely with pupils and know how they tend to react, maintain that participants in college classes or workshops do not replicate the reactions of pupils. Often these critics are correct in their criticisms. However, this does not give us a chance to discuss how pupils *do* react and to begin to realize that all groups do not react in the same way even to similar situations. Moreover, perfect simulations are not necessary for learning to take place.

Role-playing has many possibilities in the realistic education of social studies teachers as well as in learning situations with pupils. Have you given it a try? Should you? If you have used this method, could you use it more and/or better? Good luck in your efforts. It can be fun as well as good learning.

A BRIEF BIBLIOGRAPHY ON ROLE-PLAYING AS A GENERAL METHOD

Chesler, Mark, & Fox, Robert. *Role-playing methods in the classroom.* Chicago: Science Research Associates, 1966, 86 pp.

Herman, Wayne L., Jr. Sociodrama: How it works, how you can use it. *Grade Teacher,* September, 1964, pp. 84, 86, 153.

Nichols, Hildred, & Williams, Lois. *Learning about role-playing for children and teachers.* Washington, D.C.: Association for Childhood Education International, 1960, 40 pp.

Shaftel, Fannie R. & Shaftel, George. *Building intelligent concern for others through role-playing.* New York: National Conference of Christians and Jews, 1967, 74 pp.

Shaftel, Fannie R. & Shaftel, George. *Role-playing for social values: Decision-making in the social studies.* Englewood Cliffs, N.J.: Prentice-Hall, 1967, 431 pp.

Zelany, Leslie D. *How to use sociodrama.* Washington, D.C.: National Council for the Social Studies, 1964, 8 pp. ("How-to-Do-It Series," No. 20).

Zelany, Leslie D. & Gross, Richard E. Dyadic role-playing of controversial issues. *Social Education,* December, 1960.

Role Playing: An Approach to Meaningful Social Learning

Fannie R. Shaftel

Last year, in a California college town an incident occurred which placed in sharp focus a critical aspect of American life.

In a student body of about 4000, forty students were Black. The Black students grouped together for support. One night, about eleven P.M., five Black students entered the single eatery open at that hour. All tables were occupied and the only seats available were six at the counter. At the hostess' invitation they seated themselves. Then a white man entered, and the sixth seat was offered him by the hostess. He protested, "I won't sit next to those niggers! You'll have to find me another seat!"

The hostess then turned on the five Black students, saying, "Why don't you get out! You're nothing but trouble!" Everyone in the restaurant heard this.

When the students tried to assert their rights, not one of their white classmates or the faculty members present came to their defense!

The next day some of these whites tried to apologize for not having the courage to speak up!

In a class on Sociodrama and Related Techniques for the Classroom Teacher, this writer used that incident with a group of teacher interns, their supervisors, and some experienced teachers. The objective was to help them explore their "hang-ups," many of them hidden, about their own interracial attitudes.

After describing the incident, a role-playing situation was established. The hostess was chosen and white students were selected to role play the five Black students. A group of people seated around a table were assigned the roles of faculty members, while the rest of the class were to play the other students in the eatery. The white man who objected was finally chosen.

From *Social Education*, May 1970, pp. 556-559. Reprinted with permission of the National Council for the Social Studies and Fannie R. Shaftel.

The enactment was started. When the white man began shouting, the hostess turned on the five students, venomously. The five Blacks protested angrily and refused to leave. In the midst of the controversy the faculty members got up and left!

A Black intern, "G," role-playing a white student, suddenly shouted, "Call the police!" Two men (exiting faculty) returned as policemen.

"What's happening here?"

"Those fellows (pointing to the students playing Blacks) started a fight here," said G.

The class began to protest, saying, "That's not what happened!"

"Yes, it is," said G quietly, now speaking as a Black. "That's the way it is. The Blacks get blamed, even when they're innocent."

There was a moment of silence. Then someone said, "I never quite realized it before," and the talk was on. The class stayed an hour past dismissal time, deeply absorbed in the experience of exploring why the whites did not respond, what each thought he might do in such a situation, and how it felt for whites to be Blacks in these circumstances.

The two Black interns plus one Brown (Mexican-American) intern suddenly became very articulate, and everyone was listening. If time had permitted, there could have been further enactments in which whites could have explored other ways of responding in this situation.

What had happened? The polite barrier where words are used as defenses against unpleasant realities had been broken; and, instead, ideas were being dealt with at a feeling level. The acting out of the situation encouraged spontaneous responses rather than guarded maneuvers. In this moment of truth, members of the class recognized that they had been so socialized in the process of growing up in American culture that they accepted forms of discrimination as realities of life, seldom aware that they themselves were participating in that discrimination.

In re-enacting the episode, some members had had their awarenesses enlarged by a confrontation with the real-life experiences of the Black and Brown members of the group.

THIS IS ROLE PLAYING

This is role playing, or sociodrama—a reality practice that permits groups to explore life-situations in a "safe" environment wherein feelings can be expressed, ideas of reality can be explored in action, and consequences can be delineated. Role playing is a powerful educative tool when used skillfully to deal with the many critical life situations in which we all are enmeshed.

THE CRUCIAL NEED

Today, more than ever before in man's history, skills are needed for social problem solving, along with a commitment to the human good. How do we help children and youth to develop into caring, aware human beings, committed to the solution of society's critical problems? What, for example, went into the life experience of Ron Ridenhour, the young soldier who precipitated the My Lai investigation, that he could not rest until he had done something about his knowledge of this human tragedy? It is this quality of concern of human beings for each other that will be needed to solve the problems of interracial strife, pollution, poverty, overpopulation which threaten our very survival.

Social studies teachers, if they are to be effective, must address themselves to creating such concern and must have the courage to unwrap the curriculum packages to develop a survival curriculum.

Role playing is a teaching procedure which by its very process provides experiences vital to the achievement of this goal. What is role playing or sociodrama? To the novice it looks like dramatic skits in which an event is acted out, then talked about. But role playing as an educative process is much more than that when used skillfully and sensitively.

A GROUP PROBLEM-SOLVING METHOD

Role playing is a group problem-solving method that enables children and young people to explore human problems in spontaneous enactments followed by guided discussions.

Usually, a role-playing session consists of an incident or problem situation, involving two or more people, in which some action must take place to solve a problem. Since it is an open-ended situation (no solution is offered to the group; the description stops at the dilemma point), there must be some analysis of what is happening, with some proposals being given for possible action that might solve the problem.

Typically in real life, when we find ourselves in such circumstances we feel, we act, and *then* we think (often wishing we had behaved differently). Young people should be taught to feel, to think (who is involved, how do they feel, what will happen if—), and *then act*. In role playing there is always another chance to try out new ideas; one can thus learn from his mistakes. Customarily, the sequence of activities in role playing involves: delineating a situation; proposing a course of action; conducting an enactment; and discussing. The group may decide that the portrayal was adequate (realistic), and explore in further enactments what could happen if that line of action is followed. Thus, the consequences of that alternative will be identified. Further discussions might generate additional alternatives, and each can be explored in action to its consequences.

Role playing typically involves the following steps:

1. 'Warming up" the group (problem confrontation);
2. Selecting the participants (problem confrontation);
3. Preparing the audience to participate as observers;
4. Setting the stage;
5. Role playing (an enactment);
6. Discussing the enactment;
7. Further enactment (replaying revised roles, suggested next steps, exploring alternative possibilities);
8. Further discussion (which may be followed by more enactments);
9. Sharing experiences (relating the role playing to one's life experiences) which may result in generalizing.

A TRANSACTIONAL PROCESS

A unique element in role playing which makes it more powerful than discussion alone is that when a person gets up to act out a proposed line of action, *with other role players* in the other roles, the situation is no longer entirely in his control. *It has become transactional.* His ideas are complicated by the unpredictable responses of others in the situation. How much like life itself! One has to act and respond to the action of others.

LEARNING TO USE ONESELF AS A RESOURCE

Many personal perceptions of the students are delineated in enactments; consequently, their life experiences become a resource for use. As each offers his idea of what is happening, the group becomes aware that different people see different things in a commonly-experienced event. The many perceptions offered should widen the awareness of each participant. In the college incident described above, the Black students experienced that event quite differently from the whites.

In a skillfully led role-playing session, beliefs are challenged and the variety of ways in which an incident is experienced enables each participant, no matter what his experiential background, to contribute to the situation. The result is that students learn to respect and value a variety of interpretations of social realities. The following classroom episode is illustrative:

Mary comments, "Well, if my father says 'No,' I ask my mother."

Rick says, "It's his own money; he has a right to spend it any way he wants to."

But J., another ten-year-old, says, "There's another way to handle this. You go to your father and tell him you need a microscope. He'll give you money for that. Then you pay your club and borrow a friend's microscope to show your dad!"

The teacher can then respond, "People have many different ways of trying to solve a problem like this one. I wonder what will happen if we *try* each way." Now the children can enact the behaviors they think will work for them. At the end of each proposal the class discussion offers a range of insights into the consequences of such solutions. Expediency, such as J.'s, may be explored and found wanting. Some child may say, "You may get away with that, but if it was me, I wouldn't feel so good inside!" The sensitive teacher may say, "Sometimes we're pressed to use solutions that aren't very easy to live with. . . ," and she opens the door to safe but honest discussion. New proposals may offer the children a range of resources that give them more productive ways to solve the problem. They have learned from the support and opposition of their age-mates. And the teacher has contributed by asking facilitating or clarifying questions such as "How will _____ feel if we do this?" or "What will happen now?"

ANOTHER CONCEPT OF INDIVIDUALIZATION

In a society and educational system where individualization has been interpreted as "doing your own thing," and going at your own pace in order to achieve more sooner, role playing can provide a much more profound concept of individuality. The teacher in role-playing groups works for a climate wherein it is safe to try out all ideas: socially acceptable; expedient; and even anti-social. Each is a reality to be actually tested in a public arena. The focus is not on right answers, but on open inquiry. Both teacher and group "listen" with full attention to each other. The teacher models this by probing with such questions as "If I understand you, you are saying that . . . " And a child can say, "Yes, that's what I mean" or "No, I mean. . . ." The observing class is asked to listen and watch carefully so as to be able to respond to a proposal in terms of: How are people feeling, who is affected, could this really happen, and what will happen now?

Instead of a competition where each student is attempting to display a better idea, the group is guided to give full support to the exploration of Debby's idea, for example, before going on to Bob's proposal. This cooperative process can build a cohesive group in which individuals learn to like one another, respect each other's thinking, and support variability. Such a group can become a "community" in which children develop the courage of their convictions and can both support group efforts and sometimes oppose them. It is in such groups that children learn who they are, what they believe, what they value.

Kenneth Benne has said so eloquently, "Self emerges originally in the process of interaction and interchange with others." He goes on to say, ". . . If . . . the standards of a group elicit and reward honest, individual self-expression and self-searching by its members and meaningful encounters and conflicts among members, its effect upon those to whom the group is important will be to support their quest for identity."[1]

The teacher who is unafraid to say, "You two seem to have opposing ideas of what has happened (or what will work); can we explore these differences and try to understand how each of you came to your opinions?," is guiding students to respect individuality.

CONTENT IS IMPORTANT AS WELL AS PROCESS

As children learn to consider consequences by taking roles and learning how it feels to be on the receiving end of an action, the *content of life* that they explore is as important as the process itself. Children make decisions every day that both shape and reflect their values. In these daily life encounters, they can learn to care about others, or to use others for their own selfish purposes. They may decide to go ahead with a crowd when a cruel prank is planned rather than risk ostracism. They may stand by, mute, while a friend is teased or rejected. Sometimes a child stands against the group and follows his convictions. But this is very difficult to do.

Children need help in confronting these dilemmas. They can be helped to learn from their own experiences, helped to seek socially-productive solutions that consider the welfare of others as well as themselves. Such early learning becomes a basis for the development of caring, concerned human individuals.

In the writer's opinion, it is futile to present the larger critical problems of society to children who have not yet learned to relate empathically to others. Significant social learning starts with children's own deeply-felt experiences. When they explore through a group process like role playing how it feels to be left out or to be discriminated against, what it means to be a friend, and whether it is worth the price to just go along with a crowd, they are gradually making explicit the values on which they have been basing their decisions. In this forge they can reconsider values in the light of the clarification that comes from the group controversy. When a child says, "I had to snitch something from the dime store to join a gang . . ."; and the teacher responds, "What happened?"; and the child answers, "Nothing, I only took an eraser but it bothered me . . .," the way has been opened to

---

[1]Kenneth D. Benne, *Education in the Quest for Identity and Community*. The College of Education, Ohio State University, 1962, pp. 39-40.

candid discussion of pressures, feelings, social consequences. Thus, children can conclude, after many enactments and discussion, that friends who have to be won by going along with vandalism may not be friends one wants after all.

For very young children, problem situations may center around such developmental problems as how to shift to the role of brother or sister when the new baby comes, how to defend your rights on the playground, or how to cope with property damage. They can learn gradually through role playing to accept their feelings, to begin to think in terms of consequences. A simple and effective way to present problems to children is through the use of problem pictures or through the narration of a brief problem story.[2] Many situations emerge naturally out of the daily living on the playground and in the classroom.[3]

Older elementary children today are increasingly exposed to pressures to try drugs, to participate in vandalism, and to show bravado in petty thievery. How can they be helped to resist the pressures of their environment? A role-playing curriculum can present life situations that range from the less threatening problems such as how do you reconcile loyalty to a new friend with the counter-demands of your group, to such anti-social ones as what do you do when the club says you have to demonstrate courage by stealing something from the supermarket.[4]

When children feel free to candidly explore such pressure situations in the role-playing "community," they can share their fears, admit their desire to please or be liked; they can accept their impulsive or expedient solutions as ideas to be explored in public and perhaps modified by the group discussion that role playing generates.

A teacher who has mastered the technique of being non-judgmental, of accepting all ideas as worthy of exploration, is in a position to help children to clarify values, and help them learn from experience. Pupils can be helped to realize that usually we cannot solve all of our problems. We often must make choices. We often must give up one "good" for another. As children

---

[2]Fannie Shaftel and George Shaftel, *Words and Action: Role-playing Photo-Problems for Young Children.* New York: Holt, Rinehart and Winston, 1968; *People and Action: Role-playing and Discussion Photographs for Elementary Social Studies.* New York: Holt, Rinehart and Winston, 1969. See also Hildred Nichols and Lois Williams, *Learning about Role Playing for Children and Teachers.* Washington, D.C.: Association for Childhood Education International, 1960.

[3]Marie Zimmerman Solt, "George Wanted In," *Childhood Education,* April 1962, pp. 374-76.

[4]R. Chessler and R. Fox, *Role Playing for the Classroom.* Science Research Associates, 1968. See also Fannie Shaftel and George Shaftel, *Values and Action: Role-playing Problem-Situations for Intermediate Grades* (film strips with dialogue). New York: Holt, Rinehart and Winston, 1970; *Role-playing for Social Values: Decision Making in the Social Studies.* Englewood Cliffs, N.J.: Prentice-Hall, 1967; *Building Intelligent Concern for Others.* New York: National Conference of Christians and Jews, 1968.

recognize this, and struggle to decide which "good" to give up, they steadily grow in their capacity to choose that good which does the least harm.

Underlying successful guidance of role playing is the belief that each individual has the ability to cope with his own life situations, and that when he is helped to be honestly in touch with his innermost feelings and can explore them in a supportive group he and the group grow in the direction of more humane and enduring solutions to human problems. When one works with children using role playing to explore the areas where children make their daily life decisions, this view is supported over and over again. Social life will be filled with controversy in the years ahead. The problems will be critical and complex. Elementary school children need to learn from early years to confront problems confidently and skillfully. They should be encouraged to welcome conflict as evidence of ideas passionately held, to explore divergent ideas with interest and compassion. In this process they will grow up to be rational, caring, human beings.

The Arts of Contributing: A Role Play

Alfred Alschuler

PURPOSE

The goal of this first session, in addition to general ice-breaking and helping people get acquainted, is to develop guidelines for individual behavior that will help the group reach its goals. This will be done through role plays of groups working on tasks. In the discussions after role plays, the group will draw conclusions about what helped and what hindered progress.

PROCEDURES

10 minutes	Leader for the session explains the purpose of the session and introduces the role-play activity. He allows time for people to read the introduction, which follows.
20 minutes	Members of the group role play a faculty committee gathered to work on a specific problem. Each person receives from the leader a slip of paper describing his role (another person than himself) in the group. The leader does any necessary briefing, allows people a moment or two to settle into the roles, then calls for the scene to begin. After the action has developed (about 5-10 minutes) the leader stops the role play at an appropriate time.
30 minutes	Discussion.
10 minutes	Instructions for second role play.

Reprinted from *Teaching Achievement Motivation: Theory & Practice in Psychological Education*, by Alfred Alschuler, Diane Tabor, and James McIntyre. Middletown, Conn.: Education Ventures, Inc., 1971. Used with permission.

20 minutes	This time members are to be themselves. The leader assigns the "faculty committee" a new problem, and everyone tries to be a perfect member and cooperates with the role-play leader to make progress on the task.
30 minutes	Discussion.
30 minutes	Evaluation of session and preparation for session 2.

FOLLOW-THROUGH READING

Miles, M. *Learning to Work in Groups.* New York: Teachers College Press, 1959.

INTRODUCTION

Recently a school administrator lamented that a new disease of epidemic proportions was running rampant through school systems across the country. He called the disease "committee-cocchus" and recommended that strong antidotes be developed. While it is true that most of us spend a great deal of time "in committee" and in working groups, there is no intrinsic reason why this has to be an unrewarding, fatiguing experience characterized by antsiness, impatience, daydreaming, and ever-so-polite infighting. We all can recall those relatively rare meetings that started on time, finished on time, and accomplished a sizable chunk of work in between. The problem is to figure out how to have more of these productive meetings.

The common philosophy of inevitability about group work is caught in such cliches as, "Well, it depends on the combination of personalities"; "What's needed is a really strong leader"; "He really cracked the whip—we hated him but we got the work done"; "Committees of more than three never accomplish anything"—and on and on. Groups are not ultimately doomed to be ineffective learning and working forces. Otherwise we wouldn't be proposing a "self-run" group as a way of learning about achievement motivation and Psychological Education. But groups need training in how to work together—something that is rarely done and may be the main cause of "committee-cocchus." This is especially true of a group without a recognized expert or elected leader. Members need to become aware of what particular behaviors and interactions make for good feelings rather than bad ones. Members need to identify processes which facilitate progress toward the goal and processes that bog things down or provide tinder for an explosion. Members seldom are fully aware of how they come across in groups, what kinds of helpful contributions they make, and what they do that irritates other members. Any group that works together over a period of time needs to develop "ground rules," a common "process vocabulary," and sympathetic awareness of others' needs and desires.

By these allusions to ground rules, process vocabulary and awareness, we mean that your group will need to develop a way of dealing with the second conversation that always goes on in groups. One conversation, the audible one, will center around the task of the day. The other conversation emerges through the group's style of communicating. It consists of the unspoken sentences hanging in silences and the messages implicit in the explicit remarks. For example, sometimes it happens that members of groups fall into certain patterns with each other. Whenever Mr. Krug makes a comment or proposal, Mr. Almenden disagrees. On the surface of it, perhaps the two hold incompatible sets of ideas, and can never agree about anything. But more likely there is a deeper conflict between them. In the group they fight each other, using slight differences of opinion as camouflage for the real struggle that is going on. These problems can seriously interfere with the group's progress. An awareness of these kinds of issues, along with ground rules about when and how to deal with them, plus a process vocabulary to use in working them through, will enable you to overcome difficulties experienced by the group and enhance the personal meaning of every workshop session.

One way to develop these group assets and your personal skills in contributing is to observe the group itself as it goes about its business. We have chosen a slight variation on this direct method. To create concrete behavior for the group to analyze, we suggest you role play, spontaneously improvising and acting out the way people behave in a faculty meeting. The session leader will assign you a role not typically your own. After the play is over you will have a chance to identify the various roles and their effects and how to deal with them constructively.

TO THE LEADER

Typically, people in a group back away from looking closely at their own behavior. In a role play, however, the characters can be held responsible for what happens, and even accused directly of botching up the meeting because they are playing a role, not being themselves. In a role play, people are pretending, reacting off the top, exaggerating. The projected characters will be realistic and familiar enough to talk about, but not accurate or personal enough to force group members into defensive postures. People can observe honestly, say freely what they think and practice appropriate ways to make candid remarks. In other words, this exercise sets a precedent for group members to give others feedback about their effect on the group. Part of your job as leader will be to help everyone decide on ground rules for giving feedback that will be helpful and productive when you are yourselves again and not these pretend characters.

The role definitions themselves suggest one feedback procedure, since the name of the character in most cases indicates his typical behavior. In a later meeting if one member says to another, "You're playing *conspirator*," everyone will quickly know what he means. In this way the role-names are the beginning of your process vocabulary.

The role play also teaches the possibility of change. Role plays are not little dramas that, once acted out, freeze into scripts. It is obvious that each rendering is one way people behave and one way it could have happened. There can be as many ways as people are willing to try. This is the feeling we hope to convey through the exercise—that a meeting, too, can be played or acted out in many ways. People can change their roles by behaving differently if they choose. In fact, you should state explicitly to group members that the whole workshop is a laboratory of human behavior, a place where they can try out new roles and new ways of reacting. This role play is the first opportunity to see the effects of various attitudes and behaviors and to practice new ways of acting to see how it feels.

Other resources that describe role playing are: *Handbook for Staff Development and Human Relations Training.* p. 226ff; *Learning to Work in Groups,* p. 191ff; and *Improvisations for the Theater.* The first two have bibliographies and appendices that contain several references to sources on role playing. *Learning to Work in Groups* (p. 121) describes an exercise related to the one presented here.

SPECIFIC INSTRUCTIONS

As leader, explain the role play situation to the group: "You are a faculty steering committee elected by the faculty as a whole to influence policy decisions and attend to schoolwide issues. You are now in one of the weekly after-school meetings that start at 3 p.m. and extend usually to 5 p.m. and sometimes beyond. You are meeting in the teachers' cafeteria, a small and stuffy room. The chairman has just introduced a new problem and invited discussion."

The problem can be any of the following, one of your own choosing, or a real school issue: revisions in the dress code, drugs in the school, choice of a gift to commemorate the head custodian's 50th year of service, black-white tensions, granting in-service credit for a group of teachers taking some strange self-run motivation course.

Now pass out the brief role descriptions listed at the end of these instructions. Explain that everyone has been assigned a role, that he is to tell no one else what his role is, but simply to act that part as the meeting proceeds. However, you should identify the person playing the chairman role. Give everyone two or three minutes of quiet to settle into the part. You can suggest that they warm up by saying a few sentences to themselves, or ask them to react to a remark by saying silently the first role response that comes into their heads. Don't overdo this preparation since it may cause nervousness and hamper people's impulse to act spontaneously.

In advance you will have typed out the role descriptions. Our list of roles includes 12 brief descriptions. Choose those that appeal to you (but be sure to include the "chairman" role). Add roles or make changes if you like, so long as you don't burden the player with an excess of cues. If the group has several more than six or eight players, have the extras form a second role-play group or be an audience. If only one or two people are extra, assign them the role of observers. The audience or observers also should be briefed about what to watch for. You might compose a list of suggestions from the questions in the discussion guide for this session.

We would urge two cautions in assigning roles. Introduced in the right spirit, the exercise will catch people's imagination and they will willingly participate. If someone is reluctant, encourage him, but don't press. The first commandment in group work of this kind is "No one has to do anything he doesn't want to do." If you know the people involved, you can take care to avoid assigning a role that is too close to the person's real character and therefore potentially uncomfortable. Give the brasher roles and those likely to warrant much comment, or perhaps controversy, to people who can handle both the role and the reaction to it.

Once the role play begins you should generally keep out of it. You should be generous about waiting for players to warm up and settle on an issue to develop. But if it's cold and nothing seems to get started or if it swings off in too bizarre and ham-like a direction, you can gently bring it back to the problem by saying, "Remember the focus" or "Take one minute more." The knowledge that the role play will end soon helps people get back on the track. Assuming all goes smoothly, 5-10 minutes should be enough time for behavior to appear that will give the group a basis for discussion. At that point, or at some moment of natural closure, step in and call "cut."

LIST OF ROLES

Chairman: You see yourself as a coordinator of the group. You frequently take leadership roles in groups, tend to be more directive than non-directive, and are comfortable taking this role.

Wallflower: Most of your participation in meetings goes on internally. That is, you follow the proceedings, have opinions and good ideas, but think them to yourself unless someone specifically invites your comments, or makes an effort to draw you out. Shyness prevents you from speaking aloud unless you have in advance the psychological safety of knowing people really want to hear you.

Napoleon: You have a vested interest in being leader. You are positive you could be doing a better, more efficient, livelier job than the assigned leader. Your tactics are all aimed at getting the leadership role.

Court Jester: You have lost hope of an interest in reaching a solution. Your usual behavior involves keeping things on the light side. Your entries are designed to get a laugh. Sometimes the humor has a cutting edge.

Harmonizer: You try to make sure that no one gets put down. Support other people's ideas—agree with others. Try to preclude or ameliorate discord.

Mad Hatter: You have other places to go and other things to do. Lately it seems your whole life has been spent in committee. You are on the verge of leaving—mentally, and maybe physically, too. You definitely and vocally want things to go along faster.

Conspirator: You may not be planning to overthrow the leader, but all of your conversation is low and directed to those near you in very confidential tones that make others wish they could hear what you are saying.

Logical Thinker: You believe that progress is made when the task is defined clearly. You want a concise statement of the problem. Personal issues don't concern you and you are impatient with those who let their emotions show in the discussion.

Butterfly: You really are interested in helping the group work on the problem at hand. But your interests are many and your mind skips along from dinner menus to Nationalist China. One thing makes you think of something else, and you are prone to lead the group off on a tangent.

Dashing Basher: You interrupt. You know what the other person has to say after half a sentence so there is no need to waste time on his sentence when you could be getting yours out. You make up your mind quickly and don't want to hear an excessive rationale about anything.

Host (Leader for the Second Role-Play): You are helpful, competent, warm, supportive, imaginative and all the other Boy Scout virtues—and still human. You are intent on getting the task accomplished, but not at the expense of group harmony. Thus you concentrate on encouraging everyone's best efforts and try to be more guiding than directive.

Observer: You are not one of the role players, but instead an audience member. Watch the role play with the intent of commenting later during the discussion.

THE DISCUSSION

The following questions suggest a focus and sequence from here-and-now concrete observations to "there-and-then" group strategizing about how to work together effectively.

1. What roles were people assuming? Have them describe the way they saw each other.

2. What effect did various members of the group have on each other?

3. How did that make you feel? What specific behaviors (remarks) caused the various feelings you describe?

4. How did the leader feel, and how did people feel about him?

5. How else might the situation have been handled?

6. Have you seen these roles played before in real groups?

7. How realistic is all of this? What are some of the typical problems groups encounter when working together?

8. What agreements, behaviors, or strategies would help to avoid some of those difficulties?

9. List the kinds of contributions that help progress on the task and the feeling that the group is working together. Draw up a similar list of behaviors that hinder group progress.

10. As a group, establish at least five ground rules that will help you work together productively and enjoyably.

To start the discussion it is useful to ask the group to guess each person's role and the specific behaviors that define that role—*e.g.*, typical remarks, posture, gestures, tone of voice. When a role is identified, give the actor a large name card with his role title on it. This will serve two purposes, getting group members to use the role names as part of their vocabulary, and keeping individuals from being identified with their roles. Once the roles are clearly specified it will be easier to move to the more general issues suggested in the discussion questions listed above.

The criteria of success for this session are long-range and behavioral: more aware, productive group behavior. However, it helps to have a concrete product at the end of this group meeting: a list of behaviors which helps group work and a list of behaviors that hinder it. For example, going off on tangents, late arrivals, failure to confront conflict, and needless leadership competition are all obstructive behaviors. The group should suggest ways of dealing with these obstacles. In contrast, stopping for clarification, repeating what someone has said to make sure you understood, checking for group consensus when there is a sticky controversial issue, are all examples of constructive group behavior. Whatever discussion tack you follow, we would strongly recommend that the group draw up a list of blocking and facilitating behaviors.

Another kind of list that would prove helpful is a set of ground rules that the group agrees to accept and abide by. For example, the group might decide that it is legitimate and helpful to give people feedback when their behavior affects progress on the task. The group could define ways of giving feedback candidly, yet non-evaluatively. For example, people in the group should speak personally, and *only for themselves:* not "You got us off the track!" but, "When you kept joking I lost interest in the task because I thought you were interested in something else. Did anyone else feel that way?" Feedback should be directed toward specific behaviors, not the total person. "I don't like the method you are proposing" doesn't mean that "I don't like you."

The issue of giving personal feedback is such an important one that, if it does not come up in the conversation naturally, you should make a point of introducing it for discussion. However, this is only one of the many guidelines that may concern your particular group.

The second role play follows this discussion. If discussion has been extensive and members do agree upon basic procedures, then this second role play provides the opportunity to practice the behaviors discussed, and to expand on the list of facilitating behaviors. Members can try meeting the standards they have set for themselves, and ask the group for feedback on how well they do. The procedure is the same as for the first role play, except that the leader introduces a new problem and instructs the members to be themselves and to be "perfect members." If they are hesitant or reluctant, then use this variation exercise: ask each of them to choose one of the roles in the first role play that they want to try out, but to keep in mind that they are to cooperate with the leader. Discussion after the second role play should emphasize giving feedback in ways the group defined after the first role play. The emphasis should be on discovering new ways to participate constructively on the task and support each other at the same time.

Some Gestalt Role Plays

Dale L. Brubaker and John A. Zahorik

LANDLORD-TENANT CONFRONTATION (INTERGROUP RELATIONS)

Objectives

As a result of this lesson, students may conclude that:
1. A given action or event has many causes.
2. People concerned with an event interpret what occurs according to their priority of values (belief systems).
3. People who wish to influence the outcome of an event behave on the basis of their own priority of values.
4. Landlords commonly have different priority of values than do tenants.

Methods and Materials

1. Announce to the class that a landlord has just asked his financially poor tenant's family to leave their apartment. The class's task is to identify reasons that this confrontation has occurred. Tell them that two students can act out the meeting between the landlord and tenant, and by viewing this scene the class may be able to estimate why this event happened.
2. Select one volunteer to play the role of landlord. Hand him a card labeled *Landlord* citing some reasons for why he is evicting the tenants. Tell him that he should add other reasons as well.

Reprinted from *Toward More Humanistic Instruction*, by John A. Zahorik and Dale L. Brubaker. Wm. C. Brown Co., 1972. Used with permission.

3. Select another volunteer to play the role of tenant. Hand him a card labeled *Tenant* citing some reasons he has not paid the rent. He can also think of other reasons.

4. Before the role playing begins, suggest that each student mentally or actually divide a sheet of paper into two columns, one titled *Landlord* and the other *Tenant*. As the scene is acted out, they are to record the reasons for the actions of the two characters.

5. Have the two actors come before the class and describe the setting somewhat in this fashion: "We'll imagine that the landlord has just knocked on the door of the tenant's apartment. When the tenant opens it, the landlord steps in and says that the family will have to move. When the tenant asks why, the landlord starts to give his reasons. Then the tenant answers back. Now, let's begin with the landlord knocking on the door."

6. When the sociodrama has gone far enough to elicit a variety of reasons or arguments on both sides, ask the two characters to switch roles and play the scene again.

7. After the second playing of the scene, conduct a discussion of the event focusing on individual viewpoints, values, and feelings in regard to the event, its causes, and its solutions.

Evaluation

Observe student responses in the role playing and discussion. Using a controversial event from the newspaper, hold another discussion on why the event may have occurred. More than one cause should be proposed.

In the preceding lesson, the roles of the landlord and tenant were apparent to the class from the beginning. In the following lesson plan, the class is asked to identify what the participants are doing—their roles. Only the participants or actors are informed by the teacher as to their roles. In this way the role-playing method invites the class to evaluate how well the participants are playing their roles.

COMPARING CULTURES (INTERGROUP RELATIONS)

Objectives

As a result of this lesson, the students should be able to:

1. Identify some basic tasks common to all people.

2. Describe what is meant by the *culture* of a particular society.

3. Compare and contrast briefly the culture of a given society with their own culture.

Methods and Materials

1. Choose three volunteers to go to the front of the room. Tell the three students that they are to pretend they are eating. Give one student chopsticks, the second silverware, and the third nothing. Instruct the student with the chopsticks to pretend he is eating rice and seaweed, the student with the silverware to pretend he is eating roast beef, and the third student with no utensils to pretend he is eating whale blubber.

2. Ask the class a series of questions concerning what the three students are doing. Once they have identified the common task—eating— ask more specific questions as to what cultures or societies use such implements. Help the students discover the conclusion that although all of the students are performing the same task, the way in which this task is performed varies from society to society and culture to culture.

3. Choose three different volunteers to role play. Instruct the three students that they are going to use different methods to seek food. Give one student a fishing net, the second a makeshift spear, and the third a shopping list.

4. Ask questions similar to the ones asked previously. Have the students discover the conclusion that although all people seek food, they fulfill this need in different ways from society to society and culture to culture.

5. Show the class a picture of an Eskimo family outside of their house and have the students compare their own housing conditions with those of the Eskimos. Have the students discover that all men have a basic need for shelter although they meet this need in different ways in different societies and cultures.

6. Discuss what is meant by the term *culture*.

7. An alternative procedure to using a role play-discuss-role play- discuss sequence is to do all of the role playing first and then have one lengthy discussion.

Evaluation

Have the students list four basic tasks common to all people. Then read an account of the kind of education an Eskimo child acquires. Ask the students for a verbal comparison of this education to their own. Ask the students to compare other aspects of Eskimo culture to their own.

In the first two examples of the role-playing method, the students directly involved in playing roles were given very specific information as to the subject-matter content of the role. If the actors had had no experience in playing the roles, they still could have played the roles because of prescribed content. In the following lesson, students are asked to draw on their own experience—affective and cognitive—in order to play the roles.

CONFRONTATION WITH SOMEONE YOU DISLIKE (INTERGROUP RELATIONS)

Objectives

The following experiences should enable students to:
1. Identify a national figure they dislike.
2. Relate the emotional feelings they have toward this person as well as the reasons for such feelings.
3. Play the role of this national figure in order to empathize with him.
4. Draw the conclusion that feelings of dislike as identified in relation to national figures may be similar to feelings of dislike for those in their more immediate environment, and feeling empathy for such people usually reduces the amount of conflict between hostile parties.

Methods and Materials

1. Have students form several small groups—5 students per group—with each group sitting in a circle. Place an empty chair in the middle of each circle.
2. Ask the students to begin discussing some national figure they have seen on television, heard on the radio, read about, or heard of through conversations with other people. (This national figure may be a recording artist, artist, politician, or member of any other profession. It should be *anyone* who has caught their attention.)
3. Ask the students to limit their discussion to those national figures who make them angry—someone they dislike.
4. Ask a student from each circle who seems to be quite emotionally involved to pretend that the empty chair in the center of the circle is the person they have identified. Have any students in the circle who share feelings of dislike openly confront the "target" with their views.
5. After they have vented their feelings, have "hostile" students play the role of the "target" and respond to their previously-made criticisms.
6. Ask other students in the circle to stand behind the "hostile" chair or "target" chair and enter into the confrontation.
7. Have each student in the room face an empty chair and replay a situation in which they recently confronted someone toward whom they were angry. Then have each student sit in the empty chair and respond to their criticism.
8. Discuss the role-playing incidents and the empathy the students felt.

Evaluation

Have each student write a few sentences in which he describes how he felt in the role of someone he had previously criticized. Write the conclusion stated in objective 4 on the board and determine whether students agree or disagree with the statement. Discuss reasons for students' views.

An even more open-ended role-playing situation would be the following: Haved students write and present a brief skit on the subject WHAT POLLUTION MEANS TO ME.

In summary, role playing or sociodrama is the primary *method* used in Gestalt game approaches. Role definition may be viewed on a continuum from tightly prescribed to open-ended. This method facilitates humanism because the content of the games is humanistic content and the behavior of the teacher and the students during and following the game that results from this approach often meets the criteria of humanistic classroom behavior.

Two Role Plays

Ray Eiben

MAGIC GLASSES ROLE PLAY

Objectives

1. To point out that there are a number of ways in which a situation may be viewed.

2. To communicate to students that one's feelings influence one's views.

3. To develop an awareness that an individual responds to others based on his own views.

4. To demonstrate the consequences of how one behaves, e.g., if a person acts with others in a cheerless manner, he is likely to elicit a cheerless response from them.

Procedure

The facilitator may distribute a pair of inexpensive eyeglasses to each student who will be playing one of the roles listed below. If glasses are not available, the roles may be written on cards, with the instruction that the participant is to imagine that he is wearing a pair of glasses that cause him to respond in a particular way.

Examples

One type of glasses may be "suspicious" glasses. The person who wears them is instructed to regard whatever he sees or hears with suspicion. A second type of glasses the student may wear is "rose-colored." Whoever

Adapted from G. Weinstein and Mario Fantini, *Toward Humanistic Education: A Curriculum of Affect*. New York: Praeger Publishers, 1970.

wears them is to see and hear with the feeling "No matter what anyone says to me, I know he really likes me."

Other types of glasses that participants may be asked to wear are:

cheerful	gloomy, angry
confident	unloved
humorous	serious, studious
bossy, stubborn	diffident, acquiescent
tough, proud, conceited, show-offish	frightened, timid, bashful
helpful, loving, open	prejudiced, judgmental, hateful
mature, independent	childish, confused
investigative, curious, flirtatious	bored, reclusive

A topic or problem can be introduced by the group leader, or someone in the group might be asked to initiate the discussion. In a group of teachers, the topic might deal with the reason why members chose teaching as a profession. The person wearing "curious" glasses might ask, "Why did you choose to become a teacher?" The person wearing "gloomy" glasses might enumerate all the problems facing teachers today—lack of jobs, lower enrollments, apathetic students, etc. The person wearing "bored" glasses might say that he is unable to become interested in the topic and that the group could be talking about something more worthwhile. The individual wearing "conceited" glasses might boast about his skill as a teacher.

A student group might role play a situation wherein a student has been caught smoking marijuana or stealing. Group members might wear glasses that "see" the various ways that a student having a problem might be dealt with.

Some questions for processing:

1. What happens in a meeting when each person "sees through" different glasses?
2. Have you found that this happens in real situations?
3. Are some of the views contradictory?
4. Do people usually see things the same way?
5. How did I react to each person in this activity?

ROLE PLAYS FOR CAREER EDUCATION

Procedure

1. Divide the participants into two groups. The first group selects one of its members to role play an employee (or job applicant). The second group selects a member to role play the employer. If a role player gets into a difficult situation, he may recaucus with his group to receive suggestions and comments.

2. The total group provides process comments following the role play. Some topics for discussion are: Did the (prospective) employee seem confident and relaxed during the role play? Were the questions asked by the participants relevant and helpful? What would be the chances of the (prospective) employee keeping (getting) the job after an interview similar to the role play? Would you want to work for a company such as the one represented by the employer during the role play?

Variations

1. Develop a role play involving a student and his parents. Suggest that the situation is one in which both parents feel strongly that the high school student should attend a four-year college or university. The student wants to get a technical job after high school graduation. The intention of the group discussion will be to focus on differences between parental and youthful values, the arguments for and against a college education, and the decision to attend a technical school or obtain a job immediately following high school graduation.

2. Develop a role play in which a female high school senior seeks information from a male employer who feels very strongly that women should pursue only typically female occupations. The group discusses the issues involved in this kind of situation and provides feedback to the participants as to how they appeared during the role play.

Six-Part Valuing Process: A Framework for Post-Role-Play Discussion, and Two Role Plays

Robert C. Hawley

A useful framework for organizing a post-role-play discussion is the six-part valuing process.[1] The first four parts deal with choosing a value, the last two deal with acting on the value.

Choosing

1. Identification of preferences: What do I really like, what do I want? What can make me happy?

2. Identification of influences: What influences have led me to these preferences? How much is my choice determined by my parents, my peers, by the subtle pressures of the media? How freely have I chosen?

3. Identifying alternatives: What are the possible alternatives to this choice? Have I given sufficient consideration to these alternatives?

4. Identification of consequences: What are the probable and possible consequences for each alternative? Am I willing to risk the consequences? Are the consequences socially beneficial or socially harmful?

Acting

5. Acting: Am I able to act on the choice I have made? How do my actions reflect my choice?

From *Value Exploration through Role-Playing*, by Robert C. Hawley, Ed.D. (Amherst, Mass.: Education Research Associates, 1973). Used with permission.

[1]This is an adaptation by Robert C. Hawley and David D. Britton of the seven valuing criteria presented in Louis Raths, et al., *Values and Teaching*, Charles E. Merrill, 1966.

6. Patterning: Does this choice reflect a continuing commitment through action? How can I change the patterns of my life so that this choice is continually reflected in my actions?

As the teacher listens to the role-play, he may become aware of the expression of preferences, the identification of influences, the search for alternatives, and the eliciting of probable and possible consequences. He may also hear some planning for action and identification of possible ways of patterning. When the teacher hears some of these areas being touched upon in the role-play, he might jot down notes to use for later reference in the post-role-play discussion.

The list of clarifying questions for post-role-play discussion which follows contains several questions that are based directly on this six-part valuing scheme.

CLARIFYING QUESTIONS FOR USE IN POST-ROLE-PLAY DISCUSSION

1. What alternatives did the players consider?
2. Can you think of some alternatives that were not considered?
3. What would be the probable consequences from the line of action that was being taken?
4. What risks were involved?
5. What is the probability for a satisfactory outcome at this point?
6. What would you consider a satisfactory outcome at this point?
7. Would both parties consider this a satisfactory outcome?
8. What kind of relationship did you hear being portrayed?
9. How well did they define the problem?
10. Did you hear some hidden messages being passed?
11. How would you characterize the communication that took place?
12. Did the discussion shift to the personalities of the individuals, or did they concentrate on the problem?
13. Were there some assumptions made by either of the individuals about the other that might not be justified?
14. What are some of the influences that have led these people to act in the way that they have?
15. How clear are their objectives? Do you think that they have some objectives that even they don't understand very well? What are they?

CAUTIONS

1. I've found it best to proceed on the assumption that there are "no wrong answers." That is, that any response within the role-play or after it may be valuable for study. The more the teacher can take the "no wrong

answers" approach, the more likely he will be to convince his students that he has no hidden agenda or secret purpose.

2. Avoid as much as possible even the appearance of a hidden agenda. If the students sense that you're out to teach them that "honesty is the best policy," then they will make nice noises to please the teacher on that point (or perversely, they will bring up all the special cases where honesty doesn't pay so as to cloud the whole issue).

3. Avoid commenting on the authenticity of a role-play or on the appropriateness of any response. Consider all the material elicited as useful for analysis, even that which seems "phony." —Why was it phony? is a good point for discussion. Have faith in the class as a self-correcting device. Students will be sure to police one another on the point of realism or of logic. (But don't let them interrupt the role-play in progress to make negative criticisms.)

4. Avoid over-directing. Let the role-players move in their own direction, even if it seems to be away from what you had planned as the objectives for the lesson. (Remember, the role-play need last only three to five minutes.)

5. Remember that role-playing is not a theater situation—there should be no criticism of expression, acting ability, etc.

6. Review the "right to pass" often. Every student should have the unalienable right to pass, to decline to take part or share his views, at any time, including all the time.

7. Avoid confronting an individual with a level of risk which is too high for him. One of the strengths of the open-chair technique is that it lowers the risk-level to participants. I strongly believe that no one should be appointed or "volunteered" or urged to take a role by himself. The individual knows best what's best for him.

8. Avoid putting an individual on the spot for his views. "Do you *really* feel that way?" or "How can you defend that position?" or "You can't really be serious about that?" can all be very damaging to a weak ego. Appropriate ways to probe further would be, "Can you tell us more about that?" or "Would you like to go into that?" or "Do you want to add anything to that?"

9. Be careful not to focus too narrowly on predetermined objectives. It is important to have learning objectives in mind for role-playing, but the medium is so powerful that often a more important or more meaningful path to discovery will be opened. Students are very good judges of this. If they find an area to explore that is outside the objectives that you have set down, then the new area is probably worth spending some time with.

10. And finally, don't beat a dead horse. Much of the learning that takes place in role-playing is private and individual. The fact that an individual doesn't respond in a given way to a teacher's question is no indication that he hasn't learned anything.

THE TIBETAN MONK

In a broken-down monastery high in the mountains of far-off Tibet there sits an ancient monk in a narrow cell. You have it within your power to press a single button on your desk and thereby destroy the monk. This act will release the entire world from its misery of human suffering, from wars and famine and pestilence. Will you press the button?

Role-play two individuals seated with the button between them. One wants to press the button. The other wants to talk him out of it.

THE HEINZ DILEMMA

In a certain town in Europe a woman was dying from a special form of cancer. The doctors had little hope for her except for the possibility of one drug which had recently been developed by a druggist in that town. The drug cost the druggist $200 to make, but he was charging $2,000, 10 times the amount that it cost him to produce it. Heinz, the sick woman's husband, could not afford the drug. He tried to borrow money from everyone he could think of, but he could raise only $1,000. He asked the druggist to let him have the drug for less money or to let him pay for it later, but the druggist refused. Heinz considered breaking into the druggist's store to steal the drug.

Role-play the two halves of Heinz—one wanting to steal the drug, the other not wanting to. Or role-play Heinz and the druggist, Heinz trying to persuade the druggist to take a cheaper price. Add Heinz's wife.

Extensions

1. Heinz stole the drug and was caught. Role-play Heinz and the judge whose court has just found Heinz guilty of stealing.

2. The drug didn't work; in agony, Heinz's wife asks the doctor to kill her and end her misery. The doctor does, but he is caught. Role-play the doctor and the judge.

3. Heinz is sent to jail. He escapes, settles in another town, and lives there as a model citizen, devoting his spare time and energies to local charity work. One day, five years later, the judge visits the town. He sees Heinz and recognizes him as the escaped convict. He makes inquiries and discovers that Heinz has led an exemplary life. Role-play the two halves of the judge, one wanting to bring Heinz back to jail, the other wanting to let him go. Or role-play Heinz and the judge.

Part Three
Change Strategies

Typically, schools invest a great deal of time and money in workshops and training programs focusing on educational innovations. The impact of many of these programs is minimal because they are discrete entities and do not fit meaningfully into the total program of the school. Teachers make the same mistake when they use exercises and activities having a humanistic focus but having no identifiable relationship to the students' educational program and which do not help to develop the students' awareness of what the activities are going to do for them. It is suggested here that planned change become a part of every teacher's philosophy and that the exercises and programs included in this book be used only as they fit into a total plan for change for the individual teacher and the school in which she teaches.

Within the humanistic context, normative goals of change agents include improving interpersonal competence of teachers and administrators and effecting a change in values so that human factors and feelings come to be considered legitimate. Additional goals are to increase understanding among and within working groups in the school community, to reduce tensions, to develop better methods of conflict resolution, and to view the organization as a system of relationships marked by mutual trust, interdependence, multigroup membership, and shared responsibility—all to be accomplished through systematic training or problem solving.

Change or growth in education without goals and planning is no longer justified. From the superintendent of schools to the teacher, the concept of change and how it ultimately affects the learner is of paramount concern. We can no longer merely ask the question "Is change appropriate for education?" There is unanimity that the answer is yes; the major task of educators is to find strategies that make the process effective and meaningful to learners in terms of goals and values that have a high priority for them. We cannot afford to push aimlessly forward, gambling that the suggested changes might have some relevance to the learner. If new and better techniques are to be developed in response to the many crises and conflicts in our educational system, educators will need to have a knowledge of the process of change, of techniques that can be used at various steps in the process, and of procedures for obtaining feedback on the effect of the innovation once it has become an integral part of the system.

In this section, the major focus is on planning changes that affect what goes on in the classroom, especially as those changes are related to humanistic education. Even though it is probably not within the province of every teacher to be an expert on change, each teacher should have the ability to determine the desired future goals for her classroom and systematically develop strategies for achieving them. Truly, each member of the school community must be involved in change. Administrator involvement is in the form of providing financial and emotional support to teachers who wish to engage in planning for change. The teacher, who has the most contact with students, is in a position to perform a linking function—she feels the pulse of students in respect to their needs and is sensitive to the administrative and community pressures related to new developments. The kinds of strategies and plans suggested here are helpful only if there is a meaningful interchange between students, teachers, and administrators.

As envisioned in this book, planned change affecting the educational community involves:

1. Improving the interpersonal competencies of teachers, administrative staff, and students;

2. Effecting a change in the educators' priorities so that humanistic concerns have a higher value;

3. Enhancing understanding among all members of the school community with the end result of decreased tension and lessened anxiety;

4. Developing programs that have as their goal more effective team approaches to curriculum planning and problem solving;

5. Providing assistance to the educational community in the resolution of conflicts and the improvement of communication;

6. Assisting educators to view the school organization as an entity wherein mutual trust, shared responsibility, and creative risk taking become operational norms;

7. Selling the process of change to all members of the school and community organization to the point where all have a commitment to invest time and energy in planned change.

The materials included in this section should be appropriate for: (1) teachers who are interested in adding a new dimension to their planning of classroom programs; (2) school administrators who want to acquire a basic understanding of change as it affects education and who want to acquire a knowledge of skills and activities they might use in educational planning; (3) planning experts who want to acquire a repertoire of specific change-agent skills related to education; and (4) individuals in other settings —hospitals, churches, or other organizations—who see a relationship between educational change strategies and planned change in their own work environment.

Organizationally, the following selections begin with an article that is intended to give a theoretical overview of humanistic change processes. This is followed by a number of goal-setting, problem-solving, and other data-gathering instruments and exercises. So that the reader can gain an understanding of how individual activities fit into a total plan for change, a number of synthesizing, total programs of planned change are included. The reader is reminded that these materials may have to be adapted as organizations discover needs for specific kinds of change programs.

GOAL-SETTING APPROACHES

Whatever it is called, the establishment of current and future priorities for action is essential. The selections on goal-setting approaches include descriptions of exercises that can be used for the purpose of helping individuals and groups to focus on what they perceive to be their current situation or on where they wish to go at some subsequent time.

Most of the exercises can be adapted to either individual or system use and are appropriate for most kinds of organizations. The use of goal-setting and aim-setting activities serves a twofold purpose: they generate data about the individual or organization for future reference and they serve as a foundation for the use of the "here-and-now" group for processing purposes.

Toward a Strategy for Humanizing the Change Process in Schools

Robert L. Heichberger

Make no mistake about it, change appears to be a fact of life. If there is one thing we can be certain of in the passage of time, it is change. Oh yes, we may be shocked at its speed and it may strike us from an unexpected quarter but, as they say about death and taxes, it's coming!! But, if we sharpen our skills of prediction, we can reduce much of the uncertainty.

Most change is good and can be anticipated, studied, and planned for. If we train ourselves to accurately predict changes that may well affect our schools, we can better prepare ourselves, the faculty and students, as well as the community, to meet these changes in a positive way; there should be a few great surprises or blind spots. The futurists are giving us ample warning of things to come. It is up to us to be prepared to guide the direction of change and to build in measures which tend to humanize the shock.

Too often change catches one by surprise. Indeed, change may have the tendency to frighten the individual causing him to fortify his natural defenses. When one experiences a feeling of an unusual degree of stress or he is fearful for his own security, he may have little time or concern for the problems of others. One may react instinctively and not always in a very humane way. At the present time, to be sure, there is a real need to humanize our schools. Our schools will become more humane when those individuals connected with the schools learn to anticipate and plan for change.

Clearly, it would seem, whenever we increase the pace of change, we need to seriously take into consideration the effect this change has on the human ability to cope with it. We may need to develop "shock absorbers" into the very fabric of society itself.

It is the purpose of this paper to:

1. Review selected literature related to behavior change processes;

Reprinted from the *Journal of Research and Development in Education*, Vol. 7, No. 1, Fall 1973. By permission of the author and publisher.

2. Offer a "future-shock absorber," a systematized approach toward *humanizing the process of change* in the schools, and, thus, reduce the gap which appears to exist in the preservice and inservice preparation of teachers and educational administrators.

PLANNING OF CHANGE

Because it is often possible to predict change, it is also possible to plan for change. Change can occur systematically and with plenty of warning if schools of education, boards of education, teacher organizations, and educational administrators are alert. A systems approach to organizational change includes both long and short range planning.

When the "early warning systems" alert educators to change, the process of change can be well planned, unhurried and humane. When change comes unexpectedly and there is little time for preparation, the effect on humans, both young and old, is often disastrous. Change can come by decree from on high, or it can come as the result of expressed needs, and team decision making. It can be manipulated and secretive or it can be open and honest.

The process of change will be more humane if the stimulators for change realize that feelings and emotions are of primary importance. These prime movers must realize that the individuals they are asking to change are, first of all, human; they have deep underlying feelings, wishes, defenses, and fears that must be considered. Those involved in change must be allowed to be authentic persons, living, breathing, human beings. They must be allowed to think for themselves, to initiate, to imagine, to work without constant "over-the-shoulder" supervision; they must learn to be empathetic; they must be willing to show concern and compassion. And, they must be supported and trusted as they risk themselves in openness.

Obviously there is no one successful way to bring about change. All of the various strategies, however, may be grouped under two headings: Theory X and Theory Y, as articulated by McGregor (1958). Theory X strategies usually come by decree and are imposed by the administration with little or no faculty involvement in the decision making process. In most cases this is not a very humane way to bring about change. It usually leads to bitterness, resistance, and impedance. It is suggested here that little is positive or long-lasting that comes from the Theory X strategies.

Theory Y, as presented by McGregor, places the emphasis on man as a proactive, growth-seeking, inquiring, confronting person. It involves open and trusting communication, confronting conflict and managing it through rational means, true collaboration, relying on here-and-now, and publicly sharing experiences. It is suggested that Theory Y is a much more "humane" strategy for bringing about change and, therefore, will be the basis for ideas presented in this paper.

THE SCOPE

There is much in the literature concerning the need to humanize the schools, at both the teaching and the administrative level. Educators have recently called for a renewed atmosphere of trust and openness in the classroom. Little has been written to help teachers achieve this open classroom climate; and, even less has been written to assist administrators to bring about this atmosphere within their school systems. In short, little has been written specifically on how to humanize the process of change.

The Hawthorne studies (1933) showed that people will be happier and more productive if they are treated humanely—namely, involved in the decisions that affect their professional lives. Chris Argyris (1965) and Rensis Likert (1967) showed through their studies that it is important to involve the people who are going to be affected by a change. These authors stress the importance of collaborative role arrangements which tend to lead to productive and successful strategies for change. Teacher preparatory programs have placed painfully little emphasis on the development of teacher collaborative skills. This is a serious omission and a great deterrent to improvement and change.

In the last decade we have begun to listen to the behavioral scientists who are beginning to amass a considerable amount of information from their laboratory experiments. Not all of it applies specifically to schools; industry and hospitals have also recognized the importance of understanding and using the human approach. But, we can gain from their work with "change agents," "motivation research," "T-groups," "social systems theory," leadership theory, evaluation and feedback techniques. In order to limit the scope of this paper, we will use as a base the Lewin Equilibrium Theory (1952) and the Theory Y formulation of McGregor. We recognize that there are many theories from which to choose; our choice is to draw extensively from the work of Lewin and McGregor. Certainly there is no one right way to bring about change humanely, especially within a bureaucracy.

CHANGE ACCORDING TO LEWIN

Part of anticipating change is the need to understand the elements of change. According to Lewin there are many forces, not one or two, counterpoised in "dynamic tension." Change takes place when an imbalance occurs between the sum of the restraining forces and the sum of the driving forces. By identifying the individual forces at work, decisions may be made concerning where to concentrate the efforts. Care must be taken, however, so that a change in one part of the system is supported by necessary changes in other parts of the system. Too much pressure for change can result in tension, unstable and unpredictable conditions. Lewin suggests that the place to begin change is at those points in the system where some stress and strain exist. Stress may give rise to dissatisfaction with the status quo and thus become a motivating factor for change in the system.

ADMINISTRATOR HAS IMPORTANT ROLE IN CHANGE

The administrator has several important roles to play:

1. He must be well read and alert to changes on the local, state and federal levels;

2. He must educate his board and the staff to these possible changes and assess their impact on his school;

3. He must predict where along the equilibrium the greatest stress will occur;

4. He must judge at what point counteracting pressure must be applied;

5. He must consider who will act as the change agent or agents to begin involving the entire staff in the change process;

6. He is responsible for establishing the proper atmosphere and communication channels;

7. If balloons are to be sent up to test the air, then he must also be ready to evaluate the feedback.

He needs to recognize that most teachers will be more interested in the "how" rather than the "why" of the new program; he will need to make a judgment as to where his responsibility should phase out and where the teachers should take charge.

Carl Rogers (1960) suggests that once the administrator has called attention to a change or has given his consent to a change proposed by the staff, he is responsible for "organizing the resources of the institution . . . in such a way that all of the persons involved can work together toward defining and achieving their own goals" (p. 207). It is up to the principal to do his best to remove obstacles and to create a situation where students, teachers and administrators can and will be creative. As people are risking, he must be trusting; when people falter, he must give support. According to Rogers, the leader must help each person in the process "believe that his potential is valued, his capacity for responsibility is trusted, his creative abilities prized" (p. 208).

A long time before we had ever heard of "individualized instruction," "self-actualization" or "do your own thing," Thoreau wrote, "If a man does not keep pace with his companions, perhaps it is because he hears a different drummer. Let him step to the music which he hears, however measured or far away."

Because so many things around us are changing and changing at an ever increasing rate of speed, there is a normal feeling among many, including teachers, to resist change wherever possible. Brown (1971) says that one way some people attempt to avoid change "is by creating in their minds imaginary catastrophies that might happen if they . . . move into the unknown of new experience" (p. 12). People build up defenses. Clearly, there is no use in trying to destroy the defenses; this will not serve learning. Instead, it increases the anxiety of the person that he will lose the more or less effective conceptual systems he has with which to understand and relate to the world; and, thus, he may drop back to an even more desperate and perhaps unrealistic defense than the one destroyed. Though it may seem paradoxical, we cannot increase learning by destroying the defenses which block it; people need their defenses most when they are under threat and pressure.

Teachers must be convinced that the change is worth the risk and that by becoming involved in the change process, the outcome can be controlled and the threat of the unknown diminished. It is important to include the individual in the process. It means that administrators must take the teachers into partnership and respect and encourage them all the way. Without a doubt, teachers will find cause for despair; but, if they feel supported and are helped to conceptualize the problem to be solved, one can build up their tolerance of ambiguity. In short, future shock—that is to say too rapid a change—brings on feelings of isolation, alienation, frustration, and impotence, along with the loss of identity and purpose. It is significant to note that programs designed to prepare teachers and administrators are not well geared to provide their clients with tools for coping with future shock.

WAYS OF OVERCOMING RESISTANCE

It is up to the change agent and other staff members to help threatened colleagues maintain positive images of themselves and to understand that change involves a certain amount of discomfort for everyone. Teachers need to have an opportunity to think about the various alternatives open to them. It is important that alternatives exist so that no one feels compelled to move in lock-step fashion, ready or not. Change is an individual matter. The way something is learned is determined primarily by the internal structure of needs, perceptions, readiness, and motivations of the individual; it is usually not determined by the external conditions of an outside person desiring change. Adjustment comes at different speeds for different people. During this time of threat and uncertainty, school administrators should keep other threats to a minimum.

Time is the one element that most teachers and students of teaching need in order to help in the adjustment to change. They need time to take stock of themselves and set new goals. They need time to participate in formal and informal discussions with other teachers and this experience is almost totally devoid in teacher education programs. They need time to seek out and participate in such personal growth experiences as motivation workshops and other inservice education opportunities.

GROUP CHANGE

If it seems difficult to bring change humanely in individuals, it becomes almost an overwhelming task to change group behavior. But there is hope!

Each group is unique, but all groups have certain characteristics in common. Each has its own social system, leadership, norms, and boundaries. Kimbough (1968) points out that most social systems tend to stay near a state of equilibrium and new ideas are usually seen as a threat to the system (p. 13). Social systems have a great capacity to resist forces that challenge them. The norms of a faculty will not vanish easily. The system will react in ways yet to be invented to resist what it believes to be the crackpot idea of a new principal. Each social system is more or less open or closed. Each has its extreme toleration point beyond which it will reject further attempts at input. In fact, such as a new instructional innovation [sic] may temporarily throw the system into disequilibrium. However, the trained and sensitive administrator can successfully work within these limits.

Again the key factor to success is time. It takes time for a principal to learn the ins and outs of the social system and subsystems in his school. Homans (1950) suggests that the one avenue to success is for the principal to accept and support the norms of the faculty social system. But here the principal may face a dilemma, for he may be unable, because of his own value system, or his role, to accept the group's values. How does he then bring about changes in undesirable norms?

It is suggested that there may be an advantage for the administrator to be one step removed from the social system he is trying to change. If you look at a system from its own values, you are not going to come up with anything very startling and different for it to do. You must be able to step out of it and say, "What really would make sense here?"

THE PLANNING OF CHANGE

Confrontation has been the missing element in behavioral science practice. One must be open, direct, and explicit. Administrators and teachers of teachers must establish a "systems approach" to planning: establish a philosophy, state long and short range goals, set priorities, work out strategies, implement and then evaluate.

Rogers would make use of outside consultants who may or may not be acting as change agents. He would directly confront the faculty with proposals and establish various techniques for feedback. He would be empathic and would be willing to adjust the process of change for individuals.

Rogers would build, during the process, a structure within the faculty to deal with change on an on-going basis. He would couple action with critique, one eye on content, one eye on process, encouraging the staff to analyze as they act. And, he would encourage the testing of choices, encourage the trying of new ideas, evaluate and try again. Most faculty want the principal to be a leader and they are disappointed when he is not. He does not have to win his position; leadership is his role.

THE MODEL

Fundamental to humanizing the change process is the ability to anticipate and plan for the impact of change on the school. Accurate prediction gives us better control. There are several good ways that a school system can plan for change. A school, beginning with the Board of Education, must begin to use a systems approach to planning. The school must develop its philosophy of education. It must set long and short range goals and arrange these goals according to priorities. It must assess the resources of the district and look at the objectives in the light of present resources and ability to acquire the necessary resources. The school must plan long and short range strategies to reach its goals. It must implement strategies and at the same time develop tools with which it may evaluate strategy outcomes. Once the cycle is completed, it must begin the process again.

Each subsystem (high school, middle school, elementary school, department, grade level, classroom teachers) within the school system must work with the established philosophy and objectives as its guide. At each level of operation, from Board to the teacher in the classroom, the desired behavioral outcomes must be stated. Using this approach, open communication clearly becomes a necessity.

A curriculum council should be established at each administrative level throughout the district. All elements of the school staff should be directly represented including: administrators, teachers, secretarial, food, custodial and transportation people. Communication must be articulated among the various councils. Within each council, efforts should be made to keep up on "what's happening out there." Other efforts can be directed toward diagnosing and evaluating what is going on within the system; still other time should be spent prescribing for the needs of the system. Needs will include those of students and adults, individually and collectively, at each level. It is suggested that various tools be used frequently to determine the organizational climate; other tools to monitor the tension along the equilibrium should be devised and used.

Preservice and inservice education experiences should grow out of the expressed needs of the subsystem(s); schools of education can make a significant contribution in this critical area. Information should be made available through a professional library of books, tapes and films. Resource people should be utilized. Motivation and sensitivity workshops should be offered. Intra and inter school visitations should be arranged. Individuals and groups should be trained to predict, identify and deal openly and honestly with areas of stress within the system and subsystems.

Changes may be suggested from any quarter, members of the PTA, the faculty and staff, students, the Board of Education, parents, and other citizens. Everyone in the district should have a channel through which he may make suggestions and those suggestions should be acted upon and the outcome, pro or con, should be communicated back to the person making the suggestion.

STRATEGIES OF IMPLEMENTATION

Change takes place when an imbalance occurs between the sum of the restraining forces and the sum of the driving forces. The monitoring devices such as Decision Point Analysis, curriculum councils, and teachers' room banter should signal that there are forces driving toward an imbalance in the equilibrium; relationships should be identified between these forces and the various "target areas."

In order to guide the action of a change agent, answers should be sought to several key questions; they are:

1. Who is involved in the target area or who is the "client?"
2. Where is the point of entry or at what level of the system are we aiming?
3. What subsystems are involved?
4. Are the changes consistent with the philosophy and goals of the system?
5. Are the key people involved?
6. To what extent can the change agent involve the target system in planning and executing the change?
7. Are there any value conflicts?
8. Is the target system open to change?
9. How does the faculty perceive the proposed change? Is it a threat; does it violate their norms? Will it take time? Will they be paid?
10. What assumption has the target system already made about the proposed change?

The change agent must gain answers to most of these questions in order to accurately diagnose the climate for change, the degree of resistance to change and the strength of the forces pushing for change. The next step is prescribing strategies for countering forces along the line. These might include:

1. Making a timetable and setting deadlines for things to be done. He should allow plenty of time.

2. Recruiting teacher involvement.

3. Developing alternatives (choices).

4. Testing the staff concerning assumptions, styles, norms, expectations and role perceptions.

5. Clarifying roles of change agents, administrators and staff.

6. Planning preservice and inservice education experiences with area schools of education: reading, discussion, resource people, field trips, motivation workshops, T-groups, and intra and inter system meetings to articulate the change program.

7. Anticipate the effects of the change on other parts of the system and make the necessary provisions.

8. Monitor feelings and suggestions of all concerned.

9. Devise methods of educating the public concerning the change.

10. Write behavioral outcomes desired from the change.

11. Create tools to evaluate the report outcomes.

12. Outline the "Plan of Work" to achieve the change.

The process and tempo of change are most important. Teacher involvement, where desired, is a must; and, teachers must be adequately prepared to be effectively involved. Research indicates that morale is directly related to participation. It takes time to be humane. Change cannot come suddenly and without warning. It must grow logically out of the expressed needs of the people in the system and it cannot be forced. Manipulation is possible but must be handled openly and honestly. Change agents need to constantly encourage and reinforce their clients and gain their support and trust by removing as much of the risk as possible.

The pace of change needs to be one of ebb and flow, surge and slack off, venture forth and regroup. Change requires adjustment and people have a tolerance beyond which change brings on the symptoms of "future shock," and shock is less than humanizing.

REFERENCES

Argyris, Chris. The individual and organization: Some problems of mutual adjustment. In W. G. Hack (Ed.), *Educational administration: Selected readings.* Boston: Allyn and Bacon, 1965, p. 178.

Brown, George. *Human teaching for human learning: An introduction to confluent education.* New York: Viking, 1971.

Kimbough, Ralph B. *Administering elementary schools.* New York: Macmillan, 1968.

Lewin, Kurt. *Field theory in social science.* (Dorwin Cartwright, Ed.). New York: Harper & Row, 1951.

Likert, Rensis. *The human organization.* New York: McGraw-Hill, 1967.

McGregor, Douglas. *The human side of enterprise.* New York: McGraw-Hill, 1958.

Rogers, Carl R. *Freedom to learn.* Columbus, Ohio: Charles E. Merrill, 1969.

Force-Field Analysis: A Tool for Change

Ray Eiben

"Force-field analysis" is a commonly used strategy for analyzing change situations. As defined by Lewin (1951), force-field analysis is applicable to individual, group, and organizational change. By definition, "force field" is the total of all forces, positive and negative, that affect a particular situation. The lines surrounding the diagram represent the limits of the force field; the arrows represent the particular forces that act upon the situation, either facilitating movement in the direction of change or impeding such movement.

Jenkins (1949) identified four steps that must be taken before desired changes can be effected: (1) analyze the present situation; (2) determine the changes that are required; (3) make the changes indicated by the analysis; and (4) stabilize the new situation so that it can be maintained. In addition to completing these four steps, it is important that the change agent determine the limits of the force field to make sure that the forces being discussed are really pertinent to the change situation. For example, it often happens that a great deal of time is spent talking about the strength of a particular restraining force, and only later is it discovered that the individual or group that has been perceived as an impediment to change is, in reality, a supportive and driving force.

In educational systems, particularly within the boundaries of a local school district, many forces exist. These proximate forces include teachers, administrators, parents, influential citizens, student representatives, and business leaders. The change agent must identify these individuals and determine the amount of support or resistance they generate before he can utilize appropriate strategies for changing behavior or before he can secure the assistance of others who might help minimize resistances.

It is often necessary to look beyond the proximate field to discover other positive and negative forces that influence a situation. These forces are representative of the extended force field and might include such people as state educational leaders, representatives from accrediting agencies, university experts, and state and Federal officials. The following analysis, which involves a school district dealing with Title IX (sexual discrimination), identifies both proximate and extended forces.

Question: Should this school district have an athletic program for girls?

Possible Analysis: Human Forces.

Proximate Positive Forces
1. Girls interested in sports
2. Parents of girl athletes
3. Physical education teachers
4. Members of American Civil Liberties Union

Proximate Negative Forces
1. Coaches of boys' sports
2. Parents of boy athletes
3. Intramural directors
4. Members of board of education
5. Athletic director
6. Representatives of local conservative groups

Extended Positive Forces
1. State superintendent of public instruction
2. Federal officials
3. Representatives of amateur athletic union
4. Outstanding female athletes
5. Attorneys for the state

Extended Negative Forces
1. State and national medical association officials
2. College coaches for male athletics
3. Male professional athletes

It can be surmised that the forces outside the proximate force field will strongly influence the implementation of the program. A Federal law or court ruling, for instance, can produce a force powerful enough to counteract a long list of local negative forces. Although the cost of change may be a significant factor in the local board of education's opposition to the program, an interpretation by the courts can force a reevaluation of the board's position.

Stabilizing the change, or determining its degree of equilibrium, is of primary importance in force-field analysis. The desired effect is to achieve some degree of comfort with the change but not a situation that is devoid of all reactions and feelings. A philosophy of dynamic change must be accepted by members of the organization. Thus, the goal of change agents is to make force-field analysis a present-oriented process of cataloging data whereby the situation is subject to further change as soon as it becomes stagnant.

After identifying the forces and assessing their strength, the next step is to determine which strategies will be used to facilitate movement. According to Golembiewski and Blumberg (1970), the available strategies include: (1) increasing old driving forces; (2) adding new driving forces; (3) reducing the number and strength of old restraining forces; (4) converting previous restraining forces into driving forces; and (5) employing various combinations of the first four strategies. Whether the change agent will be able to maximize the impact of the above strategies will depend on his effective use of such interventions as group methods, interviewing, teleometrics, and conflict resolution with individuals who are part of the force field. Force-field analysis, like any other technique in organization development, is a component of a total plan; it is not the total program for change.

Force-field analysis and field theory have broad implications for the field of education. In counseling, for example, the client would define the problem and, with the assistance of the counselor, compile a list of all driving and restraining forces. Another application would be to help a student define his psychological field and determine the effect that various personal and environmental forces have on the learning process. Mey (1972), in viewing field theory from the standpoint of total educational change, states, "Educational change cannot take place without the force field of society undergoing a change in the same respect." It may be concluded, then, that force-field analysis and field theory are an integral part of individual and group learning as well as a change in the total system.

The exercise that follows is based on theories and procedures that have been discussed as relevant for force-field analysis. It can be adapted for particular work settings and is suitable for a variety of groups.

EXERCISE: ANALYSIS OF FORCES

Introduction

Once a problem has been identified, it may be viewed in terms of the forces that provide both positive and negative impetus to its solution. This analysis of forces is appropriate for any problem that has been identified within an organization.

Individual Worksheet

Identify as many problems or areas of concern that you can think of that pertain to the organization to which you belong. For each of the problems, identify the forces that might assist in the solution of the problem and the forces that might hinder the problem-solving process.

Problems or Areas of Concern	Forces Related to This Problem or Concern	
1.	Helping Forces	Hindering Forces
	1.	1.
	2.	2.
	3.	3.
	4.	4.
	5.	5.
2.	1.	1.
	2.	2.
	3.	3.
	4.	4.
	5.	5.

Group Worksheet

Form groups consisting of four to eight members each and make a composite list of all the problems or areas of concern that have been listed on the individual worksheets. Identify the four or five most frequently mentioned problems as well as those that seem to be the most important. For each of the major problem areas, identify the helping forces and the hindering forces. These forces should be ranked in order from the most important to the least important.

Problem or
Concern One

Forces giving impetus to solving the problem:

1.
2.
3.
4.
5.

Forces restraining or hindering the solution of the problem:

1.
2.
3.
4.
5.

Problem or
Concern Two _____

Forces giving impetus to solving
the problem:

1.
2.
3.
4.
5.

Forces restraining or hindering the
solution of the problem:

1.
2.
3.
4.
5.

EXERCISE: DEVELOPING A PROGRAM OF PLANNED CHANGE

In an educational system, change is frequently haphazard and inconsistent.
In the section that follows, a structure is provided that can be used to effect
change in a particular area. A total change plan relating to a particular goal
is included in the structure. (Many planned-change activities can be used
with equal effectiveness in church groups, business organizations, and
schools.)

   I. Write a goal statement. A goal is a written description of desired results that do not now exist but that can exist at a specified time in the
future. Example: To have employed elementary counselors in four
district elementary schools by the fall of 19___.

  II. Use a force-field analysis to determine those forces promoting change
and those forces resisting change. Example:

Promoting Change	*Resisting Change*
1. High school counselors	1. Conservative teachers
2. Progressive teachers	2. Superintendent of schools
3. School principals	3. School board
4. Parent groups	4. Conservative community groups

III. Identify as many resources as you can that relate to the achievement
of your goal. These are to be broken down into human and material
resources. Examples:

Human Resources	*Material Resources*
1. Out-of-district elementary counselors	1. Elementary guidance journal

2. State department of education consultants	2. Samples of other guidance programs
3. University personnel	3. Current textbooks in elementary guidance
4. Child-development experts	4. State department of education guidelines

IV. Strategies. A strategy is an intervention that is used by the agent of change to cause movement toward the goal. The best way to list strategies is by means of a brainstorming session in which each strategy is identified separately and no strategies are combined. A list of forty or fifty strategies could result from this process.

Sample strategies for the above goal:

1. Meet with teachers who support elementary guidance;
2. Gather statistics supporting the need for the program;
3. Establish objectives for the program;
4. Bring in speakers to talk to parent groups;
5. Have articles on the need for elementary guidance published in local newspapers;
6. Develop guidelines for specific areas of concentration.

V. Make a total plan for the first three or four months of the project. Use the grid outlined below.

Time (Months)	Event	Person Responsible	Materials Needed
0-2			
1-2			
1-3			
2-3			
2-3			
3-4			
3-4			

VI. First Meeting

1. Introduce members present; identify particular resources that each member brings to the change effort.
2. Check the expectations that group members have concerning the nature of their tasks—what is their charter?
3. Spend time discussing the existing situation and then have the group decide in what areas individual members might best expend their energy.
4. Test individual commitment in terms of work and availability.
5. Have the members agree on some realistic level at which to begin the planned change effort.

6. Assign specific tasks for group members to complete before the next meeting.
7. Have group members briefly critique the meeting—how well did they work together?

VII. Develop an action plan.

Step	Strategies by Number	Stage
1.		
2.		
3.		
4.		
5.		
6.		

Stages include: preparation, first move, point of contract (either proceed or drop plans), implementation, stabilization, and termination. If the answer to the question "Should we proceed?" is "yes," then the last three stages follow. If the contract is not made, then it is necessary to recycle back to the first step.

REFERENCES AND READINGS

Force-field analysis: Individual problem-solving. In J. William Pfeiffer and John E. Jones (Eds.), *A handbook of structured experiences for human relations training* (Volume 2), La Jolla, Calif.: University Associates, 1970, 1974, pp. 79–84.

Golembiewski, Robert T. and Blumberg, Arthur. *Sensitivity training and the laboratory approach: Readings about concepts and applications.* Itasca, Illinois: F. E. Peacock, 1970.

Jenkins, David H. Social engineering in educational change: An outline of method, *Progressive Education*, May 1949, 26(7), 193–197.

Lewin, Kurt. *Field theory in social science* (Dorwin Cartwright, Ed.) New York: Harper and Row, 1951.

Mey, Harald. *Field theory: A study of its application in the social sciences.* New York: St. Martin's Press, 1972.

Spier, Morris S. Kurt Lewin's "force field analysis." In J. E. Jones & J. William Pfeiffer (Eds.), *The 1973 annual handbook for group facilitators.* La Jolla, Calif.: University Associates, 1973, pp. 111–113.

The Ideal School

Ray Eiben

A major goal of any change program is getting the participants to generate data. "The Ideal School" is an instrument that can be used to help change agents determine if any difference exists between the way in which they perceive a school is operating and the way in which they believe it should operate.

The consultant may also use responses from the instrument to determine whether the operational climate of the school can be identified as "humanistic." For this adaptation, the participants would first be asked to rank items describing actions taken in a "humanistic" setting and then to rank the items on the basis of how their own school currently operates.

Administering the instrument and achieving consensus take a considerable amount of time: two or three hours should be allowed if the entire instrument is to be used. In some instances, it may be necessary to use only two or three sections.

HOW TO USE THE INSTRUMENT

1. Following individual identification of the ideal (or humanistic) school through the use of this checklist, participants can share their answers and attempt to arrive at a group consensus concerning the order of preference.

2. Following individual use of the checklist, group members can share opinions about the actual conditions in one school, and attempt to arrive at a team decision in each category.

Adapted from an instrument used as part of the Parish Life Development Project, Lutheran Church in America, Philadelphia, Pennsylvania.

3. In any category, it may appear to the group that no single statement represents the ideal for a specific school. The participants can then determine what is ideal for that school and write their own statement.

4. Individuals can also use this instrument to identify conditions existing in their schools.

5. The difference between the ideal and actual situations represents the "gap." When gaps have been identified, commitments and plans can be made to close those gaps and begin the process of school development.

SEARCHING FOR THE IDEAL SCHOOL

Consider the five alternatives under each item. In the left-hand column, place a "1" by the alternative that represents the ideal way for a school to operate. Place a "2" beside that alternative which you consider the next best, should it be impossible to operate in the ideal way. Place a "3" by the third most preferable, a "4" by the fourth most preferable, and a "5" by the least acceptable way in which to operate a school. In the right-hand column, rank the items on the basis of how your school actually operates at the present time.

Ideal   *Actual*

1. *Managing Conflict*

____A.   Disagreement is low because people avoid expres-   _____
            sions that would create controversy.

____B.   People step in to soothe feelings and maintain har-   _____
            mony among conflicting parties.

____C.   Negotiations take place toward positions that can   _____
            be accepted by as many people as possible; people
            do not push their own positions too far.

____D.   Conflict is brought into the open; attempts are   _____
            made to examine and to resolve underlying causes.

____E.   The administrator and staff try to be aware of all   _____
            conflict issues and regularly decide between con-
            flicting viewpoints. However, many issues remain
            unresolved in informal discussion and debate.

2. *Communication*

____A.   Two-way communication is achieved through (1)   _____
            a variety of means of informing staff and (2) pro-
            vision of ample opportunity for in-depth discussion
            of current school issues. Maximum flow of infor-
            mation undergirds school decision making and
            leader-member commitments.

____B.   Communication efforts are primarily designed to develop staff/student understanding and support of school programs. Staff/student viewpoints are utilized to improve current efforts.

____C.   Informative discussions of school concerns are encouraged among members of the school community. When there is resistance to program efforts, staff/student viewpoints are sought before further action is taken.

____D.   It is assumed that staff/students will read published bulletins and newsletters. There is little need for additional efforts toward communication.

____E.   Communication is chiefly informative, apprising members of the school community of key issues and decisions and of programs developed by the leaders.

3. *Readiness for Change*

____A.   Changes are attempted only when they are acceptable to the majority of the school community.

____B.   New ideas that find acceptance are basically improvements of existing policies and procedures.

____C.   There is sound experimentation throughout the daily routine of the school. Creativity and innovation are encouraged when they are within the framework of the school's aims and purposes.

____D.   When changes from present practices are suggested by members of the school community, they are vigorously analyzed by school leaders to determine cost, potential results, and side effects on the school's existence. Strong determination is usually required for proposed changes to pass these tests.

____E.   New approaches are usually not tried.

4. *Planning*

____A.   Planning is based on a clear-cut concept of the school's purpose and on an analysis of facts. Goals and flexible schedules are developed in such a way that those affected can clearly identify their contributions and make commitments.

____B.   Long-range planning is not considered necessary. Actions of the total school community are based on problems as they arise.

_____C.   Planning is based on past practices, school traditions, and immediate needs. Difficult issues are decided through meetings wherein the majority vote prevails.   _____

_____D.   Acceptance is seen as the key issue in planning. Acceptance by persons at every level of the school hierarchy is essential before plans are implemented. When friction develops, plans are delayed until solutions are found.   _____

_____E.   Planning is seen primarily as the responsibility of the leaders. Well-defined procedures are followed. Alterations suggested by individuals or committees must be approved by the leaders. Most plans are carefully steered to successful vote and implementation.   _____

5. *Evaluation*

_____A.   Most evaluations are made by concerned individuals who are encouraged to bring to the attention of the leaders those areas in which school development is needed.   _____

_____B.   Periodic evaluations are conducted to identify current program efforts that need improvement and to examine staff/student morale.   _____

_____C.   Evaluation efforts are primarily aimed at discovering those member attitudes or group processes that affect the quality of personal relationships within the school.   _____

_____D.   Evaluations are regularly made of the purposes, procedures, and results of the school's programs in order to identify strengths and barriers to effectiveness and to provide guidelines for development.   _____

_____E.   Results of school activities are carefully evaluated by leaders to determine cost and effectiveness. Follow-up responsibilities are assigned in cases of failure or inadequate results.   _____

6. *Overall Purpose of the School*

_____A.   The purposes of the school are considered adequately fulfilled when the objectives of the school are being met and provisions of the school's charter are being implemented.   _____

_____B.   The purposes of the school are considered fulfilled when needs of the students/faculty are being served   _____ through activities that build relationships, increase program offerings, provide administrative direction, and increase individual commitments to the school.

_____C.   The purposes of the school are considered fulfilled when members of the school community are helped by the school to function more effectively as human beings, either personally or within the institutional setting. Specific areas of human commitment are determined by the school in response to community and world needs and the willingness of individuals to participate.

_____D.   Since the state is responsible for education, it is felt that only the state can determine if the purposes of the school are being met. Members of the school community attempt to determine directions for school activity only in times of crisis.

_____E.   The purposes of the school are considered fulfilled when the school engages in service activities, responding to the demands of the community, both in terms of curriculum and human needs. Needs of individuals in the school community are important primarily in relation to corporate actions.

7. *Group Work*

_____A.   Strong efforts are made to have the traditional programs of the school carried out by groups. Participation by individuals is encouraged, but usually within the group framework.

_____B.   Belonging to groups is seen as a matter of individual choice. Existing groups are not disrupted as long as they function peacefully.

_____C.   A variety of interrelated instructional, study, and developmental groups function with the encouragement of the school administration. Quality of team action is stressed, so that through these groups, individuals find mutual support, and school and individual goals are implemented.

_____D.   Since the main function of groups is to produce results, every effort is made to avoid wasting the time of individuals in needless group and interpersonal process activities. Groups are evaluated frequently. If they are not producing tangible results, they are disbanded and their work is assigned to individuals.

_____E. Groups are formed for the purpose of fulfilling the needs of members for mutual support and understanding. Efforts are made regularly to discover the needs and interests of group members and to develop groupings that attend to members' concerns. _____

8. *Concern for Results*

_____A. There is a constant emphasis on the need to measure increases in student achievement and staff output. The assumption is that such evidence indicates increased response and commitment to the educational process. _____

_____B. There is an ongoing concern that total school development be consistent with stated objectives. The commitment of all who are part of the school community is seen as a key factor in development. _____

_____C. The primary concern is for development of staff/student morale, based on individual approval and group discussion of school actions and their results. The assumption is that without high morale, there will be few positive results. _____

_____D. The maintenance of steady progress with a minimum exertion of pressure is considered satisfactory. Stronger measures are taken only when a crisis develops. _____

_____E. It is felt that school actions should be in accordance with state, accrediting agency, and local guidelines. In order to insure proper results, only tested and approved procedures are used. _____

9. *Leadership Resources*

_____A. Programs to develop student and staff leadership are not considered necessary. It is assumed that individuals will show initiative and work to their best ability for the organization. _____

_____B. Leadership needs are identified on the basis of school priorities. An ongoing recruitment and training program results in an adequate number of trained leaders who are available to carry out necessary tasks.

_____C. The principal/administrator is the key leader in the school because of his contacts with members of the school community and his background and training. The recruitment and training of other leaders, although acknowledged to be his responsibilities, would require an adjustment of his present schedule and priorities. _____

_____D. Since quality of leadership is considered essential, high standards are set. Only persons thought to be qualified are placed in leadership positions. If there are not enough qualified persons available, programs are reduced in an effort to avoid overworking present leaders. _____

_____E. The school leaders recognize that many persons can serve adequately, even though their qualifications may not be ideal, as long as they feel enthusiasm for the school's work. Emphasis is placed on encouraging persons who are willing to serve as leaders. _____

Educational Goal Setting: Components of Change

Ray Eiben

An essential attribute of an effective change agent is the ability to assist members of an organization in defining appropriate goals. Establishing goals is crucial if an organization is to avoid creating the aimless, frustrating, and anxiety-provoking atmosphere associated with organizational indecision and lack of planning. Individuals cannot accurately determine what their role is to be if the institution has not articulated where it wants to be at various times in the future. In turn, it is difficult for the organization to reach its potential unless its members have a clear indication of what plan the organization has for its future.

Temporal Aspects

The *temporal dimension* is an important aspect of goal establishment, particularly in the field of education. Goals can be defined as: (1) short range, (2) medium range, and (3) long range. Within the school environment, short-range goals are those that relate to the fiscal year (or a similar time unit), which is used by the school for scheduling or budgetary purposes. For example, if a group of teachers meets in late August to work on instructional goals for the coming school year, the decisions they reach would be defined as short-range goals.

Medium-range goals are those that extend beyond the current academic or budgetary year but not beyond the length of time a group of students are present in a particular academic unit. For example, on the college level, medium-range goals might extend until the present freshmen class graduates from the institution. For the typical educational establishment, medium-range goals would ordinarily extend no more than three or four years into the future.

Long-range goals may extend into the future for as long as they will still be viable. In the typical school organization long-range goals usually extend five, ten, and fifteen years into the future. Population changes, reduction in revenues, and legislation are three forces that may necessitate long-range planning within an educational institution.

Operational Aspects

Goal establishment can also be related to the various *operational aspects* of the educational institution. In this sense, planning might cover such areas as (1) curriculum, (2) personnel, (3) buildings and grounds, and (4) budget and finances. Even though the focus of goal-setting activities might be quite different, a similar methodology is used. It is important to identify the specific area for which goal setting is desired and then to make certain that the goals being defined are consistent with that identification.

Organizational goals are frequently clouded by narrow vision on the part of educational leaders and by their confusion about the purpose of the organization. In some cases, the difficulty of planning for the future is compounded by the fact that tremendous energy must be expended merely to keep the institution functioning at its current level. For instance, if the present reality includes having to deal with riots and physical attacks on members of the school community, school personnel may find it difficult to think about the future, or to realize how defining future goals can have an impact on present operations. But if one takes an optimistic look at goal setting, it might be seen that careful attention to future goals could forestall problems similar to those that are currently creating confusion or anarchy. In addition, it is easier to assess the contemporary level of functioning when there is an awareness of future directions and potential outcomes.

EXERCISE ONE: GOAL SETTING

In the first exercise that follows, attention is given to specific activities that must be undertaken at crucial times if the goals are to be accomplished. A sample goal is defined and examples are given to show how the completion of certain tasks at key times can help assure that final goals will be met.

Definition of a Goal

A goal is a written statement that describes results to be achieved at a specific time in the future. The goal statement includes: date at which the goal will be reached, criteria used to determine achievement, and changes that will indicate progress.

Questions to Test the Stated Goal

1. Can it be measured?
2. Can it be obtained?
3. Does it show direction?
4. Is it desired?

Example

(Incorrect)   I want to gain strength.
(Correct)   By sixty days from now I will increase the weight I will be
              able to lift from 150 to 175 pounds.

Procedure

1. Select one area in which you wish to see improvement in your school
   by six months from now (other time limits are acceptable).
   a. Write out a specific goal using the guidelines mentioned above.
   b. Test the goal statement. If it is the consensus of the group that the
      statement does not meet the criteria, rewrite it.
      1) Can it be measured? How? List ways.
      2) Can it be obtained? Is it realistic?
      3) Does it point out direction? Identify the direction.
      4) Is it desired? In what way?
2. By means of a brainstorming session, generate a list of people or groups
   that could help the school reach this goal.

   Helpers   *Help to be given*

3. What situations could help or hinder the personnel of the school in
   reaching the goal? List these.

   Help   *Hinder*

4. List any additional resources needed to reach the goal.

   Resources   *Source*

5. As you work on your plan for goal accomplishment, include ways to
   overcome any obstacles noted; involve those who can help; and list ways
   to obtain the additional resources listed. Use the following guide.
   a. What must you be doing five months from today to attain your goal?
      Six months?
   b. What must you be doing four months from now to attain your five-
      month objectives?

    c. What must be done three months from now to attain your four-month objectives?

    d. What must be done two months from now to reach your three-month objectives?

    e. What must you be doing one month from now to attain your two-month objectives?

    f. What must you be doing one week from now to attain your one-month objectives?

Example: Goal Setting and Planning

Aim

To develop greater participation among faculty members in determining the objectives and programs of their school.

Goal

To have 50 percent of the school faculty involved in the preparation of recommendations for the board of education meeting of January 15, 19___.

Plan

By January 10, 19___, to have the recommendations for action in the hands of each board member and each faculty member.

By December 15 of the preceding year, to have edited and categorized the recommendations prepared by 50 percent of the school faculty in preparation for final editing and printing.

By December 1 to have conducted six faculty meetings focusing on the future of the school, examining present programs, identifying existing needs, and listing recommendations.

By October 15: (1) to have all committees and school groups examine what they are doing (in light of the objectives for the school established by the board and selected leadership at a program-development retreat) and list their actions; (2) to have selected and trained leaders for the six faculty meetings; (3) to have determined the locations for the faculty meetings.

By September 15 to have conducted a program-development retreat for members of the school board and selected leaders.

By September 1 to have established, written out, and given to each participant in the retreat a design for the total retreat program.

By August 1 to have established an awareness of the need to improve the district educational program and to have gained approval from the school board and citizens' advisory council.

EXERCISE TWO: HUMANISTIC AIM SETTING

A key element of planned change processes is their humanistic emphasis. To accomplish humanistic ends, the communication system within an organization must be two way. When those involved with change desire information about the future of the organization, they need to solicit data from as many organizational members as they possibly can. It also means that when data is collected and processed it is shared with people within the organization so that feedback and reactions are solicited. In the exercise that follows, the emphasis is on identifying the needs that exist for people within the organization. Once the expressions of individuals are catalogued and some consensus is reached, participants can take a look at the organization and seek to determine how changes might be made to make the organization more responsive to the personal needs of individuals within the work community.

Definition of an Aim

An aim is a qualitative state or set of conditions that one desires to achieve at some future time. This is not the same as a goal, which is a specific activity that is measurable and definable and which will enable one to achieve an aim or some aspect of an aim.

Step One

List aspirations and concerns of members of the school system, as in the following examples.

System:

1. State (list) your *aspirations* (hopes, desires) for this school in terms of the way it might fill the needs of its faculty, students, and community.

2. State (list) your *concerns* about this school in terms of the way it presently fills the needs of its faculty, students, community, and others.

Individual:

1. State your *aspirations* (hopes, desires) for yourself as a teacher in this community.

2. State your *concerns* about yourself as a teacher within this school.

Step Two

1. Collect, categorize, and summarize the lists of aspirations and concerns from all individuals and groups.

2. Share this information with the total organization. If any individual or group finds that his or its ideas are not included, review the collected lists, resummarize, and submit the results to the members again.

Step Three

1. Examine the aspirations and concerns that have been stated and list the possible aims that might arise from them.

2. Summarize and categorize the list of aims.

3. Examine the returned summary and categorization to see if the listed aims reflect the aspirations and concerns of all parties.

4. Add to or modify the list so that it reflects the aims of all members.

5. Discuss, in groups, whether these aims are consistent with the participants' understanding of humanistic education and what individual members should do to foster development of the humaneness they have committed themselves to achieve.

6. Adapt the aims of the school within the context of the developing humanistic model.

7. Establish priorities.

Step Four

1. Discuss the need to mobilize other persons to help achieve the stated aims.

2. List and discuss alternative ways to achieve these aims.

3. Define and list measurable goals that can help further the aims.

4. Identify specific procedures that might be used in reaching the aims.

Step Five

1. Discuss the form (structure) of the school as it exists presently in terms of whether it will help in achieving the aims.

2. If it is established in the preceding discussion that a new structure is needed, conduct a brainstorming session to discover the forms that may be available and list the advantages and disadvantages of each.

3. Participants reach a decision on which form is best.

Step Six

Write a statement of the times for assessment of aims and for evaluation of the organization.

EXERCISE THREE: HOW DO I FEEL ABOUT THIS SCHOOL

In a program of planned change, it is important to learn how individuals feel about being part of the organization. Through an objective measurement of the climate within the institution, individuals working with planned change can assess the levels of satisfaction or dissatisfaction experienced by those working in the system and pinpoint particular areas of stress. The instrument that follows can be used by consultants to gather objective data to be incorporated into subsequent activities within the planned-change model, or it can be used as a stimulus for small-group sessions following its completion.

Questionnaire

We are interested in understanding the feelings and atmosphere present in this school. Put a check in the spaces below that best represent your feelings of agreement/disagreement and satisfaction/dissatisfaction. A space for "comments" after each item allows you the opportunity to provide the rationale behind your responses. Work quickly but try to give your real feelings about this school.

1. The school regularly reviews and evaluates its purposes, aims, and goals.

5	4	3	2	1
Strongly Agree	Agree	Uncertain	Disagree	Strongly Disagree

5	4	3	2	1
Highly Satisfactory	Satisfactory	Uncertain	Unsatisfactory	Highly Unsatisfactory

Comments:

2. There are effective programs for recruitment and in-service training of staff.

5	4	3	2	1
Strongly Agree	Agree	Uncertain	Disagree	Strongly Disagree

5	4	3	2	1
Highly Satisfactory	Satisfactory	Uncertain	Unsatisfactory	Highly Unsatisfactory

Comments:

3. Individuality and creativity are encouraged.

5	4	3	2	1
Strongly Agree	Agree	Uncertain	Disagree	Strongly Disagree

5	4	3	2	1
Highly Satisfactory	Satisfactory	Uncertain	Unsatisfactory	Highly Unsatisfactory

Comments:

4. There is a high level of motivation among teachers and administrators.

5	4	3	2	1
Strongly Agree	Agree	Uncertain	Disagree	Strongly Disagree

5	4	3	2	1
Highly Satisfactory	Satisfactory	Uncertain	Unsatisfactory	Highly Unsatisfactory

Comments:

5. Channels of communication are open and working.

5	4	3	2	1
Strongly Agree	Agree	Uncertain	Disagree	Strongly Disagree

5	4	3	2	1
Highly Satisfactory	Satisfactory	Uncertain	Unsatisfactory	Highly Unsatisfactory

Comments:

6. The structure of the organization is flexible and adaptable.

5	4	3	2	1
Strongly Agree	Agree	Uncertain	Disagree	Strongly Disagree

5	4	3	2	1
Highly Satisfactory	Satisfactory	Uncertain	Unsatisfactory	Highly Unsatisfactory

Comments:

7. The school's leadership includes individuals of varying experience, backgrounds, interests.

5	4	3	2	1
Strongly Agree	Agree	Uncertain	Disagree	Strongly Disagree

5	4	3	2	1
Highly Satisfactory	Satisfactory	Uncertain	Unsatisfactory	Highly Unsatisfactory

Comments:

8. Disagreements and conflict are dealt with adequately.

5	4	3	2	1
Strongly Agree	Agree	Uncertain	Disagree	Strongly Disagree

5	4	3	2	1
Highly Satisfactory	Satisfactory	Uncertain	Unsatisfactory	Highly Unsatisfactory

Comments:

9. The school's accomplishments and shortcomings are evaluated regularly.

5	4	3	2	1
Strongly Agree	Agree	Uncertain	Disagree	Strongly Disagree

5	4	3	2	1
Highly Satisfactory	Satisfactory	Uncertain	Unsatisfactory	Highly Unsatisfactory

Comments:

10. Members of the school community—parents, teachers, students—help shape decisions in person-to-person groups.

5	4	3	2	1
Strongly Agree	Agree	Uncertain	Disagree	Strongly Disagree

5	4	3	2	1
Highly Satisfactory	Satisfactory	Uncertain	Unsatisfactory	Highly Unsatisfactory

Comments:

11. The school is able to cope with change.

5	4	3	2	1
Strongly Agree	Agree	Uncertain	Disagree	Strongly Disagree

5	4	3	2	1
Highly Satisfactory	Satisfactory	Uncertain	Unsatisfactory	Highly Unsatisfactory

Comments:

12. The school administration supports and encourages its staff.

5	4	3	2	1
Strongly Agree	Agree	Uncertain	Disagree	Strongly Disagree

5	4	3	2	1
Highly Satisfactory	Satisfactory	Uncertain	Unsatisfactory	Highly Unsatisfactory

Comments:

EXERCISE FOUR: STRENGTHS AND WEAKNESSES

The assessment of organizational strengths and weaknesses may be of value to change agents as they work on determining the feasibility of certain goals. In this type of exercise, it is important that the lists of strengths and weaknesses be approximately comparable in length. Listing only weaknessess may create an atmosphere of negativism that will interfere with constructive progress. Accordingly, listing only strengths may create a sense of complaisance with the present—an atmosphere that will make it difficult for members of the organization to see a need for change.

Purpose

The intent of this activity is to provide a means by which members of an organization can systematically view the organization's strengths and weaknesses.

Instructions

1. Participants are directed to take fifteen minutes to think about the strengths and weaknesses of this organization and to list a minimum of five of each on the paper provided.

2. When members have completed their lists, the facilitator combines the entries and presents a master list to the entire group.

3. Individual group members are asked to rank the master list of strengths and weaknesses in order of importance.

4. Small groups are formed, and members are instructed to devise a priority ranking that represents the consensus of the small group.

5. The large group reconvenes, and either through fishbowling (see "Inner-Outer Group Technique") or by voting, one list is prepared that represents the consensus of the entire group.

Goal Setting

GUIDELINES FOR GOAL SETTING[1]

Once a person has decided where he is, who he is, and where he wants to go, he has identified what success means to him. Now he needs to learn how to establish goals to carry him along the road to success.

One of the valid criticisms of psychological and educational behavior-modification theories has been that the professionals have used them to try to manipulate people. They decide what others should do and then devise ways for them to get into action. The purpose of our Motivation Advance Program is to help people *decide for themselves* what they want to do and then devise *their own* systematic procedures for achievement.

Thus, learning how to establish goals is at the root of our system of motivation. It is important that one observe the following guidelines. A goal must be:

Conceivable

You must be able to conceptualize the goal so that it is understandable and then be able to identify clearly what the first step or two should be.

Believable

In addition to being consistent with your personal value system, you must *believe* you can reach the goal. This goes back to the need to have a positive,

---

The "Guidelines for Goal Setting," "General Goal Setting," "Short-Range Goal Setting Form," and the "Five Years from Now," are reprinted from Phase I and II Workbook and are reprinted here through the permission of the publisher, the Achievement Motivation Program (AMP) of the W. Clement & Jessie V. Stone Foundation. For further information, please write: AMP, Suite 510, 111 East Wacker Drive, Chicago, Illinois 60601.

[1] Adapted from *Choose Success: How to Set and Achieve All Your Goals*, by Dr. Billy B. Sharp with Claire Cox. New York: Hawthorne Books, 1970.

affirmative feeling about one's self. Bear in mind that few people can believe a goal that they have never seen achieved by someone else. This has serious implications for goal setting in culturally deprived areas.

Achievable

The goals you set must be accomplishable with your given strengths and abilities. For example, if you were a rather obese forty-five-year-old man, it would be foolish for you to set the goal of running the four-minute mile in the next six months: That simply would not be achievable.

Controllable

If your goal includes the involvement of anyone else, you should first obtain the permission of the other person or persons to be involved; or, the goal may be stated as an invitation. For example, if one's goal were to take his girl to a movie on Saturday night, the goal would not be acceptable as stated because it involves the possibility that she might turn him down. However, if he said his goal were merely to invite the girl to the movie, it would be acceptable.

Measurable

Your goal must be stated so that it is measurable in time and quantity. For example, suppose your goal were to work on your term paper this week. You would specify your goal by saying, "I am going to write *twenty pages* by 3:00 P. M. next Monday." That way, the goal can be measured; and when Monday comes, you know whether you have achieved it.

Desirable

Your goal should be something you really want to do. Whatever your ambition, it should be one that you want to fulfill, rather than something you feel you should do. We are well aware that there are many things in life a person has to do, but if he is to be highly motivated, he must commit a substantial percentage of his time to doing things he wants to do. In other words, there should be a balance in life, but the "want" factor in our program is vital to changing one's style of living.

Stated with no alternative

You should set one goal at a time. Our research has shown that a person who says he wants to do one thing or another—giving himself an alternative—seldom gets beyond the "or." He does neither. This does not imply inflexibility. Flexibility in action implies an ability to be able to make a judgment that some action you are involved in is either inappropriate, unnecessary, or the result of a bad decision. Even though you may set out for one goal, you can stop at any point and drop it for a new one. But when you change, you again state your goal without an alternative.

Growth-facilitating

Your goal should never be destructive to yourself, to others, or to society. A student recently set a goal to break off fourteen car antennas before 9:00 A. M. the next morning. The goal was certainly believable, achievable, measurable, and so forth. Obviously the group cannot support such a goal. If a member is seeking potentially destructive goals, the group should make an effort to encourage him to reconsider.

GENERAL GOAL SETTING

Success in daily living can be enhanced by *action*—talking about "what I want to do" and doing it are two different things.

The use of goal setting, short range and long range, is a means to *action*. In setting a goal, the following guidelines will enhance the potential of a successful experience:

1. It must be *CONCEIVABLE,* that is, capable of being put into words.
2. It must be *BELIEVABLE* to the person setting it.
3. It must be *ACHIEVABLE.*
4. It must be *CONTROLLABLE,* subject to permitted involvement of others.
5. It must be *MEASURABLE* in time and accomplishment.
6. It must be *DESIRABLE,* that is, something "I want to do."
7. It must be stated with *NO ALTERNATIVES.* (No "either-or")
8. It must be *"GROWTH-FACILITATING"* to self and/or others.

A goal to be accomplished by_____
"I will . . .   (Date)

SHORT-RANGE GOAL SETTING FORM

1. What is your short-range goal?
2. How soon, realistically, would you like to achieve your goal?
3. What present strengths do you possess that will help you achieve this goal?
4. What new strengths might be required to achieve this goal?

5. What values led you to choose this goal?

6. What barriers, if any, do you anticipate that might keep you from achieving your goal?

7. Suggest three ways in which you might manage each barrier to help you achieve the goal.
   1)
   2)
   3)

   _____

   1)
   2)
   3)

   _____

   1)
   2)
   3)

   _____

FIVE YEARS FROM NOW

1. Where I would like to be:

2. What I want to be doing:

3. Which of the above is most desirable?

4. What is the most critical thing that must be done in order to achieve this?

5. What must I do in order for No. 4 to occur?

6. What must be done in order for No. 5 to take place?

7. Three alternative ways to get No. 6 done are:
   A.
   B.
   C.

8. Which of the above alternatives do you wish to act on?
   A.   B.   C.

9. State how the alternative selected is to be measured (time, behavior, or feedback).

10. Whom do you wish to share this with?

11. How will you share this?

12. State a goal to be accomplished TODAY that will begin your movement toward your five-year goal:

Delphi: A Decision-Maker's Dream

Alfred Rasp, Jr.

If you're a typical school administrator, you've probably seen some vague references to the Delphi, a consensus forecasting technique originally used to refine military defense systems. You may be aware that the technique has been applied, mainly at the postsecondary level, to predicting developments in teacher education, educational administration, federal funding, and a handful of other educational areas. But do you know how the Delphi fits into a local school administrator's repertoire of data-collection devices?

To find out, first consider the types of decisions administrators make each day. Some are real decisions, others flip-a-coin decisions. The latter can be made quickly with a minimum of information. Being wrong doesn't matter much with a flip-a-coin decision like whether the staff handbook should be bound or in looseleaf form.

The effects of real decisions linger, however, and when a mistake is made, the damage may be irreparable. That's why real decisions, the kind involving personnel and program improvement, require accurate information, careful consideration, and involvement beyond the decision-maker.

To get such involvement, an administrator frequently employs three techniques: single expert, several experts, and round-table consensus. All three leave room for improvement—the single expert method because one person's judgment simply isn't sufficient input; the several experts method because the individuals consulted have neither the opportunity to provide their most thoughtful input nor the benefit of hearing other responses that might encourage a refinement of their contributions; the round-table consensus because group decisions reflect the special characteristics of group dynamics and their potential distortions more often than objective truth.

Reprinted with permission from *Nation's Schools*, Vol. 92, No. 1, July 1973. Copyright McGraw-Hill, Inc. All rights reserved.

Although each of these approaches has utility in some circumstances, each also has significant limitations for the educational decision-maker concerned with program improvements. The Delphi is a technique for collecting judgments that attempts to overcome the weaknesses implicit in relying on a single expert, a one-shot group average, or round-table discussion.

DELPHI DEFINITION

In a 1959 *Management Science* article, Olaf Helmer and Nicholas Rescher presented the classic definition of the Delphi technique: " . . . a carefully designed program of sequential individual interrogations (best conducted by questionnaires) interspersed with information and opinion feedback . . . " By substituting a computed consensus for an agreed-on majority position, the technique has the advantage of not requiring large groups of people to be called together. It can be viewed as a series of individual conferences conducted in writing and having three main characteristics: (1) each participant contributes at each step of the questionnaire process before seeing the inputs of other participants for that step; (2) while the individual knows his own responses throughout the process, inputs of others remain anonymous; (3) input gained at one step of the process is shared as part of the next step.

As the name Delphi suggests, the goal of the technique is to collect judgments and establish consensus about future probabilities in terms of such variables as time, quantity and/or the desirability of some future state.

Typically, the Delphi uses a series of four questionnaires. The first asks each respondent to provide some initial input on the topic under investigation. The second consists of items developed from the first-round responses, and it requests individual judgments in the form of priority ratings on each item. The third provides the respondent with some average of second-round responses for each item, usually in the form of a median or mode. He is asked to reconsider his own second-round response in light of this information and either to move to the group judgment or to state a reason why he feels a minority position is in order. The final questionnaire provides each participant with new consensus data, a summary of minority opinions, and requests a final revision of responses.

Currently the Delphi process is largely supported and legitimated by assumptions rather than research findings. According to a report published at Syracuse University, two of the key underlying assumptions are: (a) that if participants agree and, by agreeing, move closer to a central position or consensus, then the resulting data is more believable; (b) that anonymous responses such as those generated by the Delphi are more likely to lead to reasonable and objective input than are the activities of interpersonal conferencing.

Although the assumptions are far from demonstrated facts and a number of serious questions remain to be answered regarding the process, the Delphi has been used to gain evidence through the organization of expert opinion on a wide and fascinating variety of topics. These include, for example, forecasts of the number of atomic bombs necessary to destroy the U.S. munitions industry and predictions of breakthroughs in world population growth, space exploration, and prevention of war. In the field of education, the Delphi has helped to determine dates and costs for the implementation of innovations, to define commonly used terms, and to establish targets and goals for a variety of endeavors.

SCHOOL DISTRICT EXAMPLE

To get a look at the Delphi in action, follow this brief hypothetical case study from the Ellenstown schools. The superintendent and staff decided to use a four-phase Delphi survey to collect data from which goals for building better programs could be developed.

A representative sample of local students, staff, parents, citizens and teacher trainers from the state colleges and universities was selected to participate in the survey. A working committee then developed the first questionnaire and mailed a copy to each member of the sample.

Delphi Questionnaire 1

(When you respond to the questions below, think in terms of what conditions are likely to be present during the decade 1975 to 1985 and what the results of the Ellenstown schools ought to be in view of these conditions. Specific statements will be more helpful than general ones.)

As a result of the experiences provided by the Ellenstown School District, students should:

Know _____

Be able to_____

Feel _____

Ellenstown School District should:

Increase _____

Maintain_____

Reduce _____

Develop _____

From the input on questionnaire 1 a second-round instrument of specific items was developed (only two appear in the following example). The questionnaire was mailed, like the first, to all participants.

Delphi Questionnaire 2

(Please circle your priority for each item.)

As a result of experiences provided by the Ellenstown School District, each student should:

low				high		
1	2	3	4	5	6	View competition in all things as healthy.
1	2	3	4	5	6	Be able to read and understand the newspaper.

  The responses to the second questionnaire were then used to calculate a consensus position for each item. Each person who participated in round two received the third questionnaire, indicating both the participant's response and the modal response for each item and giving new instructions.

Delphi Questionnaire 3

(On this questionnaire you will notice that for each item your previous priority is circled, and the priority most frequently selected by other participants is indicated by a square. In light of this additional information, you are requested to study each item again. If you decide that the consensus response indicated by the square does not represent your opinion now, please state your reason in the space following the item. If you state no reason, it will be assumed that you agree with the consensus.)

As a result of experiences provided by the Ellenstown School District, each student should:

low				high		
1	[2]	3	4	(5)	6	View competition in all things as healthy.
1	2	3	4	(5)	[6]	Be able to read and understand the newspaper.

  The results of questionnaire 3 were used to recalculate the consensus priorities and to prepare a minority or dissenting report for each item. For the final round each participant received his own responses, the consensus positions, and the dissenting opinions for each item and was asked to submit a final judgment. (It should be noted that many Delphi surveys omit the fourth round because, frequently, little change takes place between questionnaires 3 and 4 and insufficient additional data is generated to warrant the effort.)

  As a result of conducting the Delphi, Ellenstown's superintendent and staff received valuable data for making decisions about what the goals should be. It included priorities, consensus percentages, and dissenting opinions.

LIMITATIONS OF DELPHI

Though the Delphi can make a major contribution to decisions involving planning, it is not the best tool for all decision-making situations. In the area of personnel choice and assignment, for example, other elaborate procedures are followed and a different style of opinion data is available. In evaluation, performance and outcome measures that go beyond subjective judgment can be used. And certainly use of the Delphi would not be recommended in areas where deductive theory has been developed with proven explanatory and predictive power.

Other limitations: The problems of questionnaire construction are great and ought not be overlooked. Almost every study on the Delphi has testified to an uneasiness regarding development of the second questionnaire. The pull toward consensus is strong, frequently stronger than a position of verified accuracy. And with the exception of the dissenting opinions, the Delphi offers little explanatory power—there's no way of knowing why one response was selected over another or why participants moved to consensus. Also, the Delphi process only provides information; it does not make decisions.

KEY QUESTIONS

A number of key questions should be considered by administrators who might use the Delphi technique.
1. What decision needs to be made?
2. From whom should opinions be collected?
3. What questions can be used to generate a broad range of input on questionnaire 1?
4. How can questionnaire 1 input be used to build questionnaire 2? (The construction of the second instrument is the most important single step in the Delphi survey process and the most difficult. This questionnaire must reflect the original input to a degree sufficient to give participants a feeling that somehow their contributions are included. It must also incorporate a sufficient range of items so that the data for the decision-making base has no serious omissions.)
5. What measure of central tendency should be used to indicate consensus on questionnaire 3? (A decision has to be made to use either the mode, median or mean to represent the consensus position. Since few of the response scales used in a Delphi instrument assume equal intervals, the mean is generally not appropriate. The median is often used in surveys focusing on judgments about time or quantity, and the mode is frequently used in efforts to gain opinions about desired future conditions. In any

case the decision needs to be made in advance because it affects both the calculated consensus and the style of statistical treatment that can be used if further analysis is desired.)

6. How will the priorities, consensus and dissent be used as data for decision-making?

Even in the face of limitations, the Delphi does have strength and utility. It collects and organizes judgments in a systematic fashion. It gains input. It establishes priorities. It builds consensus. It organizes dissent. In short, it cannot be overlooked as a useful and reliable decision-making tool.

New Hope Through Conflict Utilization: A Model for Administration-Staff Confrontation

Charles H. Ellzey

THE CONFRONTATION EXERCISE

After a preliminary contact with the school superintendent or principal, plans are made for the principal-faculty meeting. The consultant contacts the principal to explain the exercise and obtain his participation, and the superintendent asks the principal to call the faculty meeting. The consultant also obtains the support and participation of the school board (if deemed necessary).

The principal convenes the meeting and turns the meeting over to the chairman of the faculty committee or to someone selected to be in charge. The chairman introduces the superintendent, who expresses his strong support of the meeting and of the effort to resolve existing conflicts.

The consultant then establishes operating norms or ground rules for the group, e.g., open and honest expression of feelings and ideas, no "game playing," and careful listening to each other. He then describes the exercise to the group.

The principal meets with the consultant and the superintendent in one room, and the faculty meets in a separate room with the faculty chairman leading this group. After one-half hour, the consultant returns to the faculty and thereafter floats back and forth as needed, to facilitate the work of both parties.

Adapted from "New Hope Through Conflict Utilization, A Model for a Pastor-Congregation Confrontation," *The Center Letter*, Vol. 3, No. 12, December 1973. Courtesy of Charles H. Ellzey and Paul M. Dietterich, editors, and the Center for Parish Development.

Each party answers a set of comparable questions and then returns to share and compare them, with plans for the next steps to follow. This question phase takes about one and one-half hours; the sharing phase takes another hour.

The questions to be answered are as follows (the answers are to be given first in brainstorming fashion and are then to be ranked in the order of most importance):

For the faculty members:

1. What does the principal do or not do that limits the effectiveness of our school?

2. What do we as faculty do or not do that limits the effectiveness of our school?

3. What would we like for the principal to do or not do to improve the effectiveness of our school?

4. What would we be willing to do or not do to improve the effectiveness of our school?

For the principal:

1. What do the faculty members do or not do that limits the effectiveness of our school?

2. What do I do or not do that limits the effectiveness of this school?

3. What would I like for the faculty members to do or not do to improve the effectiveness of this school?

4. What would I be willing to do or not do to improve my effectiveness as principal in this school?

POSSIBLE OUTCOMES OF THE MEETING

Within the faculty group, people discover a diversity of opinions and feelings toward the principal and their school. Full agreement is rare on any item, even though some commonly held points and suggestions do appear.

After identifying the principal's shortcomings, the faculty members shift from blaming the principal to recognizing their share of responsibility for the ineffectiveness of the school. They list ways in which they are at fault and become excited about what they might do to improve the situation.

When the two lists are shared, several common themes emerge that increase the feeling of hope and the sense of potential for working things out together. A few of the possible themes are:

1. It is felt by both the faculty members and the principal that the latter should improve the preparation of his presentations at faculty meetings.

2. It is agreed that the faculty members should increase their commitment and take more responsibility for the operation of the school. It is also agreed that leadership training should be made available for all positions in the school.

3. The board of education is encouraged to take the recommendations and to develop goals and plans for achieving them.

4. The faculty committee is to take the initiative in being a liaison between the principal and the total faculty and will provide for additional sharing meetings similar to this one, which will provide evaluation checkpoints.

The consultant, with the superintendent's support, encourages the principal to develop a support-advisory team for himself to help him achieve his goals, and to be comprised of two-to-four peers and a district office representative. (The principal may choose one other principal, whom he trusts and respects, and the superintendent.) The team may also be given financial assistance from the superintendent's office to improve its functioning.

ISSUES TO BE CONSIDERED

Who should lead a confrontation exercise? It would seem that an "outside" person could best establish a feeling of objectivity and honesty. This could be a district staff person or a consultant who has some skill in working with groups.

How should the decision for such a meeting be made? Someone within the school (principal, faculty member) may want to request help from the district superintendent or his staff.

What size group is of optimum value? In a typical school, thirty-five members may attend the meeting and stay together for the entire session. If a larger group is present, it would be wise to divide into smaller groups of fifteen to twenty, and then to combine the results of their discussions into one statement before joining with the principal. This would require more time for the entire exercise. In a small school the total faculty could be invited; in a large school the curriculum committee or another policy-making group could be involved.

What follow-up process is needed? To keep this experience from being merely a therapeutic or "mud-slinging" event, the next steps for both principal and faculty must be identified, with evaluation checkpoints built in. This will usually take the form of referring the suggestions and ideas, such as planning, goal setting, and leadership training, to a responsible group— the administrative council or other program group. Periodic principal-faculty evaluation sessions may be planned, sponsored by the faculty committee or a similar group.

BENEFITS

Through this confrontation experience, the consultant is asked to assist the principal and faculty in dealing with conflict, the air is cleared, the expression of negative feelings allows for positive feelings and ideas to emerge and be supported, and enthusiasm is high for a renewed commitment and new plans for action. Both the principal and the faculty feel supported and relieved. The administration and staff seem to be on their way toward getting around what might have seemed like unwieldy obstacles.

QUESTIONS FOR REFLECTION

1. Do you as the principal or other school official sense a growing conflict between yourself and the faculty, board, or other agency? Would openly dealing with questions in this exercise clear the air and develop a common sense of direction and new hope?

2. Do you as a member of the faculty, board, or other agency sense a conflict between your group and the principal or other official—one who might be amenable to sharing feelings and ideas as directed by this exercise?

3. Do you feel that such an experience is too risky, or would the probable outcomes outweigh the damages?

4. Are there persons—central staff, other personnel—available to lead such an experience?

Part Four
The Open Classroom and Other
Structural Interventions

Even though humanistic approaches to education can be implemented by any teacher within almost any kind of structure, there are certain organizational and instructional arrangements that are more conducive to humanizing processes. Among the terms used to describe these are: open education, learning centers, free schools, alternative schools, individualized instruction, community schools, mini-courses, and team teaching. Since it is difficult to categorize many of the interventions as distinctly organizational or instructional, they will be discussed in this section as part of one large category.

It is important to realize that the organization present within a particular school does not predict a humanistic emphasis. An "open school" can be more authoritarian and the students treated with less concern—than a traditional school. People are what make the difference in humanizing education. Putting together a combination of individuals with a commitment to a humane approach to education and a structure that maximizes the instructor's student-centered emphasis should have the highest priority.

Buildings can be built with openness and the maximum potential for humaneness, but unless there are staff members who can psychologically tune in to the open structure the program will probably fail. A total organization for openness includes teachers who have interactive skills and a philosophy of education in which the learner counts. The commitment of the school district is to provide buildings and resources that allow the teacher to implement humanistic programs. There should be the same kind of accountability for humanistic programs as there is for skill in content areas. A teacher who does not emphasize human dimensions—valuing, caring, communicating, feeling, and listening—should be held as accountable as the teacher who has a contract to teach mathematics but is unable to do so.

Many humanistic programs have been ill-conceived and short-lived. As a consequence, there is a reluctance on the part of many school districts to become part of a movement that has had a high rate of failure. Part of the reason for the failure of humanistic programs is the view of many that they are a panacea and that implementing these programs is an effortless process. Programs in the affective domain take a lot of work and a high level of commitment on the part of each person involved. There needs to be a long-range plan for humanistic education with staffing, curriculum, space, and in-service programs coordinated to help the schools turn out graduates who exemplify the best in human qualities.

Much of what is related organizationally to humanistic education in the United States has its roots in such developments as the British Infant School, Summerhill, and the Danish Folk High School. Even though it is doubtful that the degree of freedom characteristic of these European models will totally permeate American schools, there is reason to believe that many of the organizational attributes of these schools are applicable to American education.

In addition to the organizational aspect of the school and how it contributes to humanizing processes, there are many instructional interventions—approaches used by the teacher—that facilitate student involvement in learning and assist the student in becoming interested in his effectiveness as a person. It has been pointed out previously that the mere fact that a school is organized on an open basis does not predict a humane learning environment. Such instructional interventions as experiential learning, individualized instruction, inquiry teaching, and gaming are of little value if they become ends in themselves. The process aspect of these approaches cannot be ignored and, again, the responsibility is with the teacher to determine to what extent the interventions actually accomplish what is intended.

In the following section, a number of interventions are discussed with emphasis on the implementation and technical aspect of the particular approach. Since open education, in the authors' opinion, seems to best exemplify a totally humanistic approach, a great deal of attention is given to this dimension. Rather than provide in-depth coverage of the majority of interventions, individual articles give an overview and indicate additional resources to which the reader may refer.

A Beginner's Guide to
Alternative Schools

Sixty districts doing their own thing make it impossible to list *all* the different types of alternative schools. The guide that follows, however, will introduce you to the most common varieties, give you a rundown on each, and steer you to some samples.

COMMUNITY SCHOOLS

These schools set up a managerial system in which youngsters and, often, parents share policy-making prerogatives with professionals. The extent of student-parent power varies considerably from school to school—along with academic programs and almost everything else. Some schools are extremely loose when it comes to requirements and discipline, others tautly run because constituents prefer it that way. The schools seem to have little in common beyond their desire to create a close-knit "learning community" rather than an institutional hierarchy.

Two community schools within the same district—Great Neck, N.Y.—offer a study in contrasts. One meets in the corridor of the main high school, the other in a church basement. Students in the "school within a school" came into a program already designed by the faculty, though kids can suggest program changes at any time. The school keeps strictly to standard curriculum requirements but allows youngsters two days a week for independent study and a required outside "service project"—usually babysitting or tutoring. Students "earn" their diplomas, and attendance is mandatory.

In the church basement—at the Great Neck Village School—teenagers design their own program and courses from scratch. Teachers will assist if called upon. Youngsters also select their instructors, evaluate their own progress, and suggest grades. Though teachers eventually evaluate them, Village students are guaranteed a diploma regardless of their grades.

CULTURAL AND MULTICULTURAL SCHOOLS

In response to the awakening of racial and ethnic identities, some districts have created alternatives with a racial or multicultural emphasis. One of the most notable—and controversial: Berkeley's Black House, which used to accept only blacks. The school's admittance policy, however, smacked of segregation to some Berkeleyites and to HEW's Office of Civil Rights. To avoid threatened federal fund cuts, Black House opened up to any whites willing to acclimate themselves to the heavily racial atmosphere.

As a staff member explains, Black House caters specifically to students "who've experienced isolation, powerlessness, and low achievement at the regular high school. Some are literal dropouts, others psychological ones. The program aims primarily at restoring self-esteem and imbuing students with a sense of adequacy."

Courses focus primarily on black studies, with special emphasis on contemporary themes: black consciousness, racism and black capitalism. Berkeley also operates a bilingual alternative school for Mexican-Americans— La Casa De La Raza.

Another alternative in this category is the multicultural school, like Berkeley's Agora, with a thoroughly integrated student body and staff. Mainly through studies of language, culture and history, Agora tries to foster an appreciation of racial and ethnic differences. Both Black House and Agora students can take any courses they choose at the main high school.

SCHOOLS WITHOUT WALLS

Philadelphia's famous program spawned "sons of Parkway" in several cities, including Chicago, Boston, New Orleans, Cleveland and Madison, Wis. Based on the notion that kids don't need classrooms to learn, this option eliminates stiff costs for new construction[1] and incorporates the resources of the entire community. Parkway offers students over a hundred learning options in hospitals, museums, social agencies, and local businesses. Often courses are quite traditional in both content and learning objectives, but the diversity of locations and experiences has a strong appeal for students.

---

[1]Estimates indicate that Parkway's total budget amounts to less than the cost of the interest alone on a new facility for a comparable number of students.

OPEN SCHOOLS

These schools pattern themselves after the British infant school. The design is distinctive: space divided into subject areas, each one richly supplied with learning resources. Open schools take the nongraded approach and allow children of different ages to work together. Accenting informality, independence and creativity, they encourage youngsters to find their own pace and interest level.

A successful example: the St. Paul Open School, initiated by parents in that Minnesota city last year. Located in an office once used by computer repairmen, the school enrolls 500 students aged 5 to 18. While 17 of the instructors are certified teachers, the staff roster also includes poets, artists, former prison inmates, and a British import who serves as program coordinator. The district also has mustered a regiment of talented community volunteers, winding up with an adult-pupil ratio of 1:3.

One of the newest open schools is Louisville's Brown School, started this past September. The school occupies seven floors of a renovated downtown office building. Since Louisville's performing arts society has its headquarters in the same building, Brown has a built-in supply of teachers for a curriculum that puts heavy emphasis on drama, modern dance, art and music.

The curriculum also laces basic subjects with "vital personal and social issues," such as the environment, violence and human relations. Brown sends youngsters to community sites for some classes and involves them in day-by-day decisions about how the school should run. The 409 students who currently attend Brown were selected much like delegates to the national Democratic convention. Brown officials designed an enrollment matrix to ensure an equitable balance of boys and girls, minority groups, and students from various socioeconomic levels.

LEARNING CENTERS

In addition to separate alternative schools, St. Louis, Minneapolis, St. Paul, and Chicago have set up centers specializing in subject areas, such as the performing arts, urban studies, and communications. Youngsters leave their neighborhood schools to attend a center program either full-time, perhaps for as long as a semester, or part-time during the day.

Administrators in St. Paul have created several centers—in high school buildings and community facilities—midway between the suburbs and inner city. Students from both areas attend the centers for minicourses in subjects like foreign languages, social studies, art and humanities, and career exploration.

A big advantage offered by learning centers, say St. Paul schoolmen: desegregation without forced busing. While the district still has to worry about busing kids from their neighborhood schools, busing is voluntary for everyone involved.

St. Paul students attend half-days at the center of their choice, with elementary youngsters coming every third day and secondary students daily. Center programs run for nine weeks.

Open Education: Is It for You?

Donald Nasca

In the past five years, there has been a lot of furor in this country about the student-centered, activity-oriented elementary program usually called "open education." Schools are adopting it, teaching teams and individuals are trying versions of it, numerous authors are writing about it. But the majority of teachers still have questions. What is open education? Haven't some teachers always used open ed techniques? And others who never use them but are still good teachers? What happened to subject-matter structure, learning taxonomies, cognitive developmental states, and so on—are they out the window? Can I try open ed without completely committing myself? Without administrative support? Finally, is it for me?

Most definitions of open ed focus on a responsive relationship between teacher and child, and a stimulating, varied environment. Concern for the individual needs of students doesn't mean that a child always works independently but that he participates in groups whenever appropriate. It has been found that a wide range of organizational arrangements and physical accommodations can serve as vehicles for open programs. It is also becoming increasingly clear that successful open ed teachers have rather specific attitudes toward learning, and that a realistic appraisal of these and past experiences should be made before drastically altering the classroom environment.

No one approach to teaching, however, is more correct than another; each contains valuable elements that can contribute to improved educational conditions for today's children. This article will try to answer some of your questions and offer strategies from which to pick and choose to suit your unique setting. In this way we can preserve the many educational values emerging from this latest swing of the educational pendulum.

WHAT ABOUT YOUR ATTITUDES?

In open education, teachers must be able to handle a flexible program in which they respond to children rather than direct them. Therefore, a teacher's basic attitudes and beliefs about learning are important. Read the following statements. If you find yourself in agreement with most of them, further explorations of open ed techniques will be rewarding.

1. Learning is personal and every individual is tuned in by a unique set of experiences.

If a child does schoolwork (performing a task or producing a product) only or mainly because he is told to, almost always he will fail to internalize it. He'll fuss more about the paper and margins and writing tools than the task content. The learning that occurs, if any, will be superficial and shortlived.

A key concept in open education is a child's personal commitment. Such a commitment is necessary for significant learning—learning that alters his cognitive structure or changes his behavior. Yet a single topic will rarely generate equal enthusiasm throughout a class nor will the same learning experiences be suitable for everyone. The open ed teacher structures the learning environment to offer a range of options, then watches how individual children respond. Children who become interested are encouraged. Those who don't are offered other options or are coaxed and even directed into assuming responsibility.

2. The teacher is responsible for establishing an appropriate learning environment and capitalizing on student initiative within it.

The range and variety of options should depend on individual children's cognitive levels, interests, ability to make choices, and social development, as well as dynamics of the group as a whole. Teachers sensitive to students' needs will be able to use their responses not only to identify their commitments but also to diagnose skill and ability levels.

3. The process of developing a product is frequently more important than the product.

Elementary children are concerned with immediate experiences and possessions. Long-term goals are too abstract to serve as guidelines until near age 11, and standards of excellence for art, written and verbal communication, quantitative analysis, and scientific reasoning are too remote to mean anything to a younger child. The content of a letter should be more important than its form. The way a child reasons from his own experiences is more important than the objective truth of his deductions. A graph should be examined for its story rather than its preciseness. A child who has these personal successes will much more easily and quickly develop the skills leading to better products when he is able to appreciate them than those held to standards too early.

4. Motivating is more a matter of capitalizing on student interests than teacher initiative.

Open ed teachers recognize the value of providing experiences to motivate learning and plan many of them to assure every child of a starting point for learning. They also search for out-of-class experiences that may motivate further skill development. The child who brings in a hot-wheels car, for example, can be encouraged to measure and record its weight, speed, and size. He can indicate on a map where it came from. If he has a collection, he can arrange them, demonstrate them, compile information about them.

5. Children should be encouraged to express themselves in a variety of ways.

The learning value of any experience is enhanced by expression, not necessarily by the usual verbal or written report but in a wide range of ways. Teachers can encourage variety by responding to suggestions with remarks like, "That appears to be one alternative." "Yes, that's one way to describe your experience (or feelings); can you think of others?" Displays of realia, models, photos, drawings, maps, charts, expressions of emotions in various media are all good possibilities.

6. Working together in small and large groups is an important part of the school day.

Finding personal strength in contributing to the goals of a group is considered an important skill. However, groups are more likely to be formed to accomplish a specific purpose (putting on a play, studying a community) than to receive the same type of instruction or perform the same tasks.

7. Physical space for initiating open programs can vary considerably.

A lot of people think open space is synonymous with open education. Open education is a philosophy, and can be developed in almost any type of space. In fact, a majority of open ed programs are taking place in traditional buildings.

8. Successful ability to use language is based on an appropriate set of concrete experiences.

Before being introduced to terms like "smaller than" or "larger than," a child should have handled, ordered, and compared objects of varying sizes. Before learning to decode the word "water," he should know through experience that water flows, splashes, has weight, and gets things wet.

In open education, the emphasis is on seeing that children receive a rich supply of experiences. It is upon these that the child can build the more abstract skills of reading and reasoning. Focusing too early on word decoding without experiential bases turns children into word-callers and guarantees a reading failure rate of 20 per cent, half of whom never recover.

9. A wide range of manipulative materials should be accessible to children at all times.

In open education, manipulative materials are plentiful and handy, with those for related sets of activities within reach of each other. Manipulatives designed for specific purposes, such as tangrams, attribute blocks, and picture-word matching cards are available when they're needed. Always available are raw materials—modeling clay, cardboard, yarn, scrap—for activities and projects.

10. Children in any one working space may successfully engage in a variety of learning experiences on many levels.

Once an atmosphere of constructive work and responsibility for the care of working areas has been established, children in a working space may be simultaneously engaged in number explorations, writing about a trip, painting a mural, preparing a drama, exploring circuits with bulbs and batteries, quietly reading.

11. Meaningful learning more frequently follows interdisciplinary lines than the traditional subject matter lines.

In non-open situations, a child stops researching a social studies project because it's time for reading; a boy measuring for a science project is stopped for math class. Even the language arts and math skills we consider so important can be more effectively developed through multidisciplinary projects.

Is your reaction one of these? "It's too idealistic." "I could never stand the confusion!" "I can't get enough materials" or "I don't have enough space." "They'd never let me do it." "Children have to be taught skills before they learn on their own." If so, especially the last one, you probably should examine other ways to teach.

If you are still a believer, here are some other ways to test your potential for successfully developing an open environment.

● Engage a child in conversation, then let him take over its direction. Success as an "open" facilitator is shown when a child asks questions or volunteers remarks on his own.

• Next time a child writes something for you, respond to the *content*. Can you think of some other activity to help him improve any weak areas? Try to get the children to write in response to a situation rather than as a specific assignment.

• See if you can get kids interested in working spontaneously with different kinds of materials in a free time—weaving, clay modeling, building a kite or terrarium. Don't give open invitations, but start working on your own project with plenty of materials handy. Mark yourself on your ability to resist giving uninvited suggestions and on the variety of products produced by the children.

• Take a topic from any appropriate curriculum guide and list activities that would help children learn about it. Are the activities multilevel and multidisciplinary?

• For a whole week, give every direction in the first person. Instead of "You may not . . . ," say "I don't want you to . . . ." For 'Sit down, please," substitute "I'd like you to . . . ." If your demands on children decrease through the week, it's another good indication of your potential as an open program facilitator.

HOW TO GET STARTED

By now, you're pretty sure you'd like to try an open program, but your school is organized along traditional lines. No chance. Right? Wrong! There are few if any total schools or districts that have been successfully converted by administrative edict. Only those teachers who possess an "open" attitude or who have the potential for moving toward it can be successful in establishing open classrooms. So program initiation at the grass-roots level is not only possible but necessary. A small initial step that is 100 per cent successful is far better than a large step that's only 50 per cent successful.

You'll need administrative support for your plans, of course, but you'll need colleagues as well. The minimum practicable number of teachers seems to be four, located in close physical proximity. The grade-level mixture isn't nearly as critical. Apparently it is difficult for fewer than that because not only can you be thought "too radical" and ignored, but you also miss the necessary sharing of ideas, mistakes, and successes of the new teaching venture.

Possible transitional steps from a teacher-directed classroom to an open one include setting up learning, activity, or interest centers; developing themes; sharing classrooms; having children work on a contract plan. Check educational magazines for articles. Two books that are realistic and explicit in their suggestions for step-by-step progress are *Schools Are for Children* by Hertzberg and Stone (Schocken, 1971) and *The Open Classroom: Making It Work* by Barbara Blitz (Allyn & Bacon, 1973).

Having enlisted like-minded teachers and selected your starting points—several alternatives are useful—it's time to get administrative endorsement. If you are asked searching questions, don't take it as a negative reaction, but as an interested one. And you'll need your building principal's support not only for your program but to keep the other teachers from feeling threatened.

Having obtained approval for your plans, the next step is to get the support of parents. Although parents frequently become the strongest supporters of open ed programs, in their concern for their children they may at first not only question but challenge this departure from their own school days.

A good starting point is to invite parents to share conversations about "What is an ideal educational program?" "How can we help children develop independence?" or "Why explore an open educational program?" A series of evening sessions with interested teachers, administrators, and an outside consultant may work very well. If there are already successful open classrooms in your area, arrange to have parents visit them. Another strategy is to form a parent-faculty committee to monitor progress and continue open discussions. Interestingly, the free, expressive environment of a good open classroom attracts just the people most likely to be useful in helping to develop and maintain it.

KEEPING THINGS GOING

OK, you took a year to lay your plans, spent a year or two in transition activities. You worked hard and long but you're still enthusiastic. Now you have two more questions to face as you begin to maintain a fully open program: *What about curriculum? What about evaluation?*

You may agree with the Summerhill philosophy that "the child should be the sole source of direction for curriculum." But then there's Bruner's dictum that "each discipline has a formal invariant structure that serves as a basis for learning." There are few if any models to help us see how to develop a program along the Summerhill lines, and the programs generated by the Bruner philosophy are almost certain to be standards-oriented rather than child-oriented. So what do open educators do? The good news is that open ed teachers are finding ways to compromise the two, balancing structure with responsiveness. Evaluation procedures, too, have been made to serve two purposes: as an analysis of children's capabilities and accomplishments to use for future decisions, and as an answer to outside demands for formal marks.

Three steps in developing curriculum for the open classroom have emerged:

1. Identify topics to be emphasized during the year, selecting from state or school curriculum guides, textbooks, and so on.

2. Select activities that will provide children with general experiences in the topics and improve skills inherent in them.

3. Prepare techniques for matching activities to individual children's needs and for generating student commitments.

Here are some specific examples of ways to implement these steps.

The topic is writing a business letter. If you simply assigned this task, you could no doubt get a child to write an acceptable letter. But if the need for him to write a "real" letter came up next week, no teacher would be surprised to hear him say, "I don't know how." So the activities you plan should involve the student in the need to write a business letter. You might invite him to help you with a task that involves a letter, or ask him to make an appointment with a resource person by mail, or encourage him to set up a display for which he needs information or materials from an outside supplier. If writing the letter has personal significance for him, you need not even "teach" him how to write one. He will find out by asking you, another student, or a parent; from a book, a chart, a filmstrip, or a learning packet you have already set up.

Another topic could be measurement—of length, area, volume, weight. Provide such activity-stimulating questions as:

• How many paper clips are needed to make a string as long as your arm? Who has the longest arm? The longest leg? Who is tallest?

• How many body-lengths wide is our room? The hall? The distance from the room to the principal's office?

• How many squares are needed to cover this card? Can you find a way to use fewer squares?

• How many golf tees are needed to balance a wooden block, two washers, a large nail?

Encourage students to describe these real measurement situations and others they've been involved in by writing about them, drawing pictures, making charts. Children shouldn't be required to apply standard labels until they show they have developed to the abstract thinking level. Otherwise, they may be solving word problems perfectly but with little comprehension of the mathematical facts involved.

Activities for the topic of recognizing different sounds could involve questions about a series of tape-recorded sounds. Can you imitate the sounds? Can you find pictures of animals that make these sounds? Where are these sounds made? How can you make different sounds? Again, children should experience and play with such elements as pitch, volume, and loudness before the terms are introduced.

Showing respect for other people's property is a different kind of curriculum topic but one that is as important in the open classroom as business letters or measurement. Walking around another child's painting drying on the floor or picking up a pencil and returning it to the owner shows that the child has acquired a certain value. Such things as these might be suggested to pupils:

• Put a paper of yours on the floor where people walk. How many ignored it? Stepped on it? Picked it up and returned it? How did you feel about what they did?

• What would you do if you found an important looking envelope on the sidewalk? Why? What could happen if you did something else?

• Suppose by mistake you wrecked somebody's project. What would you do? What if it turned out to belong to someone with whom you had just had a fight?

Group discussions and role playing are only two of the ways children acquire values (another is teacher modeling), but these techniques are far more effective than direct telling. As with cognitive skills, general experiences should precede any attempt at labeling.

Your transitional steps and preparation have probably given you techniques you feel comfortable with for matching children's needs with activities. And of course the classroom environment should be such that it encourages children's participation. But, above all, you must be alert to children's interests and ready to work them into activities that will serve your curriculum topics.

It takes practice to weave interests into learning tasks on the spot, but there is a way to rehearse ahead of time through a technique called *mapping*. What you do is think of several typical student interests and write them down, each in a box in the center of a sheet of paper. Take a toy car, for instance, or a baseball card, a trip to Grandmother's, an Indian hero, and so on. Add potential areas of investigation growing from this topic at the end of wheel spokes around the box. *Toy car*, for example, can lead to scale (drawing), manufacturer (location, distribution), toys (types, countries), models (birds, planes, dinosaurs), materials (plastic, metal, relative durability), speed (measurement), transportation (boats, planes, trains), automobiles (the graphing of kind, make, and color). Now, think of how these areas can be used to answer children's needs as indicated by your curriculum and pupil accomplishments. A child who needs measurement experiences, for example, could measure and draw the component parts; or he could be asked, "How fast do you think the car goes?" "How would you find out?" "How fast do real cars go?" "Are there different ways of measuring speed?" The child could be encouraged to develop a chart, a display, or diorama to illustrate his answers to these questions.

Now when a child brings in a toy car, you will be ready to turn it into a learning experience. After a while, you'll find it less necessary to get these down on paper ahead of time, but in the meantime you'll have increased your ability to make such relationships.

Mapping can also be used as a class activity to develop general themes in such a way that child interest will be aroused and commitments made. *Community helpers* or *The American Revolution* can be the theme. The group can record its various facets and then choose which of them they would like to explore. The Revolution could be introduced as a central theme by such a vehicle as a movie, filmstrip, or set of pictures. Students are invited to contribute thoughts, questions, concerns about the theme; a "map" is developed and recorded on the chalkboard. A child who offers battlefields is asked, "What would you do about battlefields?" "That sounds interesting; how long do you think it will take you to complete such a project?"

You may be worrying about how you can be sure the activities you plan are meeting children's needs for certain skills and concepts. But before we discuss this concern, let's reexamine some traditional elementary school practices. An inordinate amount of time is spent in teaching and reteaching things children never really learn, so much so that it's been said most 12-year-olds could master the entire elementary curriculum in six months, provided, of course, they had been exposed to many experiences. One reason for this is that we break down skills into discrete bits and teach them, hoping the learner will somehow then put them all together (although this is exactly opposite the way children learn to speak, walk, ride a bicycle, and so on).

Another reason is something I've already pointed out—teaching labels before experiences. Although individual children may vary at the rate they arrive at different stages, their general developmental sequence pattern remains the same: Activities stage, ages 4 to 7; Product Development stage, ages 6 to 9; Formal stage, ages 7 to 11. Traditional group-oriented instruction and recent trends in testing and accountability have led teachers into the third stage far too early for most children.

You'll find that almost any skill or concept elementary children are supposed to master will fit the activity/product development/formal stage sequence. In open education, we furnish the child with as many activities or concrete experiences as he needs. We encourage him to produce a sharable product, seeking a range and a variety of them. Only at about age eight or nine do we reach the formal stage by giving the language required to label parts and processes, often signalled by the fact that the child's descriptions are becoming excellent approximate labels. These do eventually have to be memorized, a process helped by association, frequent use, and application in a variety of settings.

For example, the first activities in map reading can be crude drawings of the room, home, route to school, or weekend or field trip. These maps can be shared or displayed as part of the description. Finally, formal map symbols and use of professional maps are introduced—but these abstract ideas have been preceded by appropriate experiences.

Thus in open education, the formal descriptions or labels are presented to the child only when he can use them and feels the need for them. Rather than presenting a skill or concept over and over, it need be taught only once.

Now, with these thoughts in mind, how do you plan to meet the needs of specific children at specific times? Remembering curriculum needs and children's general developmental stages, begin to observe how children respond to your planned activities. Does Jim show an interest but then seem to lose it? Who joins in the discussion, and how? Who didn't join the discussion? Does Alice ever put back the equipment she uses? Because planning and evaluation are so close-knit, some teachers record such data in their plan book.

At first you may feel you are trying to keep track of a three-ring circus. But you don't need to record *everything*—it's impossible and not necessary—and also comes easier with practice. It isn't necessary because you not only have individual conferences with children, you also ask them to keep diaries, logs, and perhaps notebooks for math and language projects. A diary or log should be two-way, in which you respond regularly to the content of the entries, at the same time noting (but not correcting) any language deficiencies as a source of input for small-group work. The notebooks can serve to show progress. You may also wish to keep a checklist for each child of broadly defined skill areas such as sequencing, counting, and grouping in math; sharing interests verbally, using letters, using words, copying and writing stories, and so on in language. Only when the child does not demonstrate growth in these broad areas are more specific skills evaluated to identify his difficulties. Specific skills should never be taught otherwise. Children's accomplishments are never analyzed in detail unless they seem to deviate radically from the norm.

Children's individual notebooks, logs, and samples of their work; an occasional notation or anecdote from your records; and perhaps a summary are what you use for formal reports to parents or for other appropriate purposes.

Finally, open education programs are obviously great consumers of space, materials, and people's time and talents. If your building has open or flexible spaces, use them. But if it doesn't? Move the desks—group them, push them up against the wall, replace them with tables. Have children keep their own things in cubbies or on shelves, in plastic dishpans or carryalls. Divide the room into work areas.

As for materials, do all the scrounging you can. Encourage children to bring in their own games and books. Send lists of wanted raw materials home. Ask businessmen for scraps and discards. Put these in containers or totes, labeled so children can find them and put them back (this is important). People resources can be augmented by establishing multiage student groups where older children can provide assistance to younger ones, perhaps by moving some of the older children to a different group and bringing up younger ones—with the additional benefit of keeping you from falling into the mental grade-level trap. Another source of human help is to entice parents either to give general help or to use specific skills in specific projects. In all areas, be flexible, imaginative, and bold. You'll become a real open education facilitator; you may even blaze a new trail.

Week of November 1-5

PLANNING	EVALUATION
Large Group	
1. Read " . . . " followed by discussion to examine alternatives of this theme that will be explored further. (Mon. morning)	Note each child's unsolicited contribution or initial exploration. As, puppet—John; diorama—Mary, Jane, Susan; role play—Mark, Billy, Don.
2. Introduce set of task cards on probability. Require that a minimum of two cards be completed, several be completed, or make the set entirely optional. (Tues. afternoon)	Identify starting points that are carried to completion, i.e., chart on wall lists children down one side and task cards are listed across the top. Task cards completed are checked off by students and spot checks are made by the teacher.
3. Set up a microscope on science table and describe its basic use. (Wed. morning)	Identify language, quantitative and/or social skill deficiencies, i.e., gross inability to describe small objects: Bill, John, Mary, Eunice. Refuses to share use of microscope table: Todd.
Small Group	
Mon., 10:00 a.m. Five children have demonstrated approximate measuring techniques and are ready for more accurate measuring skills.	Skills in these areas are checked off as they are mastered. The skills checklist will vary from school to school, depending on accountability demands. If a skills checklist is used to record accomplishments rather than serving as a guide for teaching, then categories can be somewhat broader than those traditionally found in curriculum guides. Specific skills can be examined when necessary if a child has difficulty demonstrating a broader skill.
Mon., 1:00 p.m. Four children have demonstrated difficulty with sentence structure.	
Mon., 2:00 p.m. Work with volunteers in role playing groups.	
Individuals	
Individual conference schedule for the week. (Also posted for student reference)	Each child comes to this conference with a folder containing work accomplished since the last conference. Student and teacher select representative examples to be included in a semipermanent folder maintained by the teacher. Tasks to be completed before the next conference are also discussed.
Monday, 9:00—Mary	
9:15—Tom	
1:30—Dave	
1:45—Eunice	

SOME DANGERS TO WATCH FOR

Unfortunately many poor practices occur under the name of open ed. Watch for signs of these dangers and take steps to stop them before they become full blown.

1. Complete teacher withdrawal from the role of adult authority—instructing children to "do their own thing" without appropriately structuring the environment.

In some schools "open education" is a label applied to a setting where teachers "allow" students to do their own thing indiscriminately—more a lack of direction and irresponsible action than a definite philosophy.

The teacher has a critical role to play in open education, most aptly labeled as facilitative. The teacher must accept children, respond to individuality, and provide opportunities for fostering social, cognitive, and physical growth. This is not accomplished by withdrawing from a supervisory capacity but by taking on a much more responsive role than frequently encountered in the teacher-directed classroom.

2. Suddenly expecting children to make decisions about their own direction, after having been consistently adult directed.

A "Peanuts" cartoon shows Linus writing a report commenting on his summer vacation while extolling the virtues of returning to school where all important things in life occur. After receiving praise from the teacher, he responds to Charlie Brown's shocked look with, "When you've been around as long as I have, you know what sells."

Conformity and teacher dominance are highly prized characteristics in many schools, and the expected teacher role cannot be withdrawn overnight. Children who have developed a dependency on teacher direction will need help in regaining a sense of independence.

3. Teachers assuming too much responsibility for individual development.

If a teacher increases the number of alternatives but at the same time retains control over which ones children may choose, little independence is achieved and the demands on a teacher's time become staggering. When children are consistently required to confirm each decision, the teacher can devote little or no effort to modifying the learning environment or to recording evaluative information.

4. Inconsistencies between teacher and administrator perceptions of open education.

Administrators who approve a plan to increase openness and then go on to impose traditional achievement standards, especially at the primary level where the emphasis is on *activity*, illustrate a basic inconsistency. Using letter grades in progress reports, grouping homogeneously, exposing children to content specialists on a scheduled basis, restricting learning resources through use of mandated textbook series, and assigning specified content to grade levels are practices that must be changed. Unless both teachers and administrators agree that the traditional structure must be modified, little progress can be made.

5. Lack of staff continuity.

The continuance of any program is dependent upon people. Unless arrangements are made for careful screening of teacher applicants to identify attitudes conducive to an open environment, the program has little chance of continuing successfully.

6. Incorporating gimmicks of open education while failing to recognize its basic philosophy.

There are gross misuses of open ed practices. For example, young children in open ed are encouraged to develop dictionaries of their words as they acquire reading and writing vocabularies; but when this is a class activity with a list of words to be included, there is no relationship to the open ed intent.

Or, teaming in the open classroom is done to extend alternatives available to children; but if each teacher assumes responsibility for a content area, overconcern with curriculum and little responsiveness to pupil interests are almost certain results.

So You Want to Change
to an Open Classroom

Roland S. Barth

Another educational wave is breaking on American shores. Whether termed "integrated day," "Leicestershire Plan," "informal classroom," or "open education," it promises new and radical methods of teaching, learning, and organizing the schools.[1] Many American educators who do not shy from promises of new solutions to old problems are preparing to ride the crest of the wave. In New York State, for instance, the commissioner of education, the chancellor of New York City schools, and the president of the state branch of the American Federation of Teachers have all expressed their intent to make the state's classrooms open classrooms. Schools of education in such varied places as North Dakota, Connecticut, Massachusetts, New York, and Ohio are tooling up to prepare the masses of teachers for these masses of anticipated open classrooms.

Some educators are disposed to search for the new, the different, the flashy, the radical, or the revolutionary. Once an idea or a practice, such as "team teaching," "nongrading," and (more recently) "differentiated staffing" and "performance contracting," has been so labeled by the Establishment, many teachers and administrators are quick to adopt it. More

---

Reprinted from *Phi Delta Kappan*, October 1971. Used with permission of the author and publisher, Phi Delta Kappa. For a further discussion of these assumptions, see Barth, Roland S., *Open Education and the American School*, Schocken Books, 1974.

[1]For a fuller description of this movement, see Roland S. Barth and Charles H. Rathbone, annotated bibliographies: "The Open School: A Way of Thinking About Children, Learning and Knowledge," *The Center Forum*, Vol. 3, No. 7, July, 1969, a publication of the Center for Urban Education, New York City; and "A Bibliography of Open Education, Early Childhood Education Study," jointly published by the Advisory for Open Education and the Education Development Center, Newton, Mass., 1971.

precisely, these educators are quick to assimilate new ideas into their cognitive and operational framework. But in so doing they often distort the original conception without recognizing either the distortion or the assumptions violated by the distortion. This seems to happen partly because the educator has taken on the verbal, superficial abstraction of a new idea without going through a concomitant personal reorientation of attitude and behavior. Vocabulary and rhetoric are easily changed; basic beliefs and institutions all too often remain little affected. If open education is to have a fundamental and positive effect on American education, and if changes are to be consciously made, rhetoric and good intentions will not suffice.

There is no doubt that a climate potentially hospitable to fresh alternatives to our floundering educational system exists in this country. It is even possible that, in this brief moment in time, open education may have the opportunity to prove itself. However, a crash program is dangerous. Implementing foreign ideas and practices is a precarious business, and I fear the present opportunity will be abused or misused. Indeed, many attempts to implement open classrooms in America have already been buried with the epitaphs "sloppy permissivism," "neoprogressive," "Communist," "anarchical," or "laissez-faire." An even more discouraging although not surprising consequence has been to push educational practice further away from open education than was the case prior to the attempt at implementation.

Most educators who say they want open education are ready to change *appearances*. They install printing presses, tables in place of desks, classes in corridors, nature study. They adopt the *vocabulary:* "integrated day," "interest areas," "free choice," and "student initiated learning." However, few have understanding of, let alone commitment to, the philosophical, personal, and professional roots from which these practices and phrases have sprung, and upon which they depend so completely for their success. It is my belief that changing appearances to more closely resemble some British classrooms without understanding and accepting the rationale underlying these changes will lead inevitably to failure and conflict among children, teachers, administrators, and parents. American education can withstand no more failure, even in the name of reform or revolution.

I would like to suggest that before you jump on the open classroom surfboard, a precarious vehicle appropriate neither for all people nor for all situations, you pause long enough to consider the following statements and to examine your own reactions to them. Your reactions may reveal salient attitudes about children, learning, and knowledge. I have found that successful open educators in both England and America tend to take similar positions on these statements. Where do you stand?

ASSUMPTIONS ABOUT LEARNING AND KNOWLEDGE[2]

Instructions: Make a mark somewhere along each line which best represents your own feelings about each statement.
Example: School serves the wishes and needs of adults better than it does the wishes and needs of children.

strongly agree	agree	no strong feeling	disagree	strongly disagree

I. Assumptions About Children's Learning

Motivation

Assumption 1: Children are innately curious and will explore their environment without adult intervention.

strongly agree	agree	no strong feeling	disagree	strongly disagree

Assumption 2: Exploratory behavior is self-perpetuating.

strongly agree	agree	no strong feeling	disagree	strongly disagree

Conditions for Learning

Assumption 3: The child will display natural exploratory behavior if he is not threatened.

strongly agree	agree	no strong feeling	disagree	strongly disagree

Assumption 4: Confidence in self is highly related to capacity for learning and for making important choices affecting one's learning.

strongly agree	agree	no strong feeling	disagree	strongly disagree

---

[2]From Roland S. Barth, "*Open Education*," unpublished doctoral dissertation, Harvard Graduate School of Education, 1970.

Assumption 5: Active exploration in a rich environment, offering a wide array of manipulative materials, will facilitate children's learning.

strongly agree	agree	no strong feeling	disagree	strongly disagree

Assumption 6: Play is not distinguished from work as the predominant mode of learning in early childhood.

strongly agree	agree	no strong feeling	disagree	strongly disagree

Assumption 7: Children have both the competence and the right to make significant decisions concerning their own learning.

strongly agree	agree	no strong feeling	disagree	strongly disagree

Assumption 8: Children will be likely to learn if they are given considerable choice in the selection of the materials they wish to work with and in the choice of questions they wish to pursue with respect to those materials.

strongly agree	agree	no strong feeling	disagree	strongly disagree

Assumption 9: Given the opportunity, children will choose to engage in activities which will be of high interest to them.

strongly agree	agree	no strong feeling	disagree	strongly disagree

Assumption 10: If a child is fully involved in and is having fun with an activity, learning is taking place.

strongly agree	agree	no strong feeling	disagree	strongly disagree

Social Learning

Assumption 11: When two or more children are interested in exploring the same problem or the same materials, they will often choose to collaborate in some way.

strongly agree	agree	no strong feeling	disagree	strongly disagree

Assumption 12: When a child learns something which is important to him, he will wish to share it with others.

strongly agree	agree	no strong feeling	disagree	strongly disagree

Intellectual Development

Assumption 13: Concept formation proceeds very slowly.

strongly agree	agree	no strong feeling	disagree	strongly disagree

Assumption 14: Children learn and develop intellectually not only at their own rate but in their own style.

strongly agree	agree	no strong feeling	disagree	strongly disagree

Assumption 15: Children pass through similar stages of intellectual development, each in his own way and at his own rate and in his own time.

strongly agree	agree	no strong feeling	disagree	strongly disagree

Assumption 16: Intellectual growth and development take place through a sequence of concrete experiences followed by abstractions.

strongly agree	agree	no strong feeling	disagree	strongly disagree

Assumption 17: Verbal abstractions should follow direct experience with objects and ideas, not precede them or substitute for them.

strongly agree	agree	no strong feeling	disagree	strongly disagree

Evaluation

Assumption 18: The preferred source of verification for a child's solution to a problem comes through the materials he is working with.

strongly agree	agree	no strong feeling	disagree	strongly disagree

Assumption 19: Errors are necessarily a part of the learning process; they are to be expected and even desired, for they contain information essential for further learning.

strongly agree	agree	no strong feeling	disagree	strongly disagree

Assumption 20: Those qualities of a person's learning which can be carefully measured are not necessarily the most important.

strongly agree	agree	no strong feeling	disagree	strongly disagree

Assumption 21: Objective measures of performance may have a negative effect upon learning.

strongly agree	agree	no strong feeling	disagree	strongly disagree

Assumption 22: Learning is best assessed intuitively, by direct observation.

strongly agree	agree	no strong feeling	disagree	strongly disagree

Assumption 23: The best way of evaluating the effect of the school experience on the child is to observe him over a long period of time.

strongly agree	agree	no strong feeling	disagree	strongly disagree

Assumption 24: The best measure of a child's work is his work.

strongly agree	agree	no strong feeling	disagree	strongly disagree

II. Assumptions About Knowledge

Assumption 25: The quality of being is more important than the quality of knowing; knowledge is a means of education, not its end. The final test of an education is what a man *is,* not what he *knows.*

strongly agree	agree	no strong feeling	disagree	strongly disagree

Assumption 26: Knowledge is a function of one's personal integration of experience and therefore does not fall into neatly separate categories or "disciplines."

strongly agree	agree	no strong feeling	disagree	strongly disagree

Assumption 27: The structure of knowledge is personal and idiosyncratic; it is a function of the synthesis of each individual's experience with the world.

strongly agree	agree	no strong feeling	disagree	strongly disagree

Assumption 28: Little or no knowledge exists which it is essential for everyone to acquire.

strongly agree	agree	no strong feeling	disagree	strongly disagree

Assumption 29: It is possible, even likely, that an individual may learn and possess knowledge of a phenomenon and yet be unable to display it publicly. Knowledge resides with the knower, not in its public expression.

strongly agree	agree	no strong feeling	disagree	strongly disagree

Most open educators, British and American, "strongly agree" with most of these statements.[3] I think it is possible to learn a great deal both about open education and about oneself by taking a position with respect to these different statements. While it would be folly to argue that strong agreement assures success in developing an open classroom, or, on the other hand, that strong disagreement predicts failure, the assumptions are, I believe, closely related to open education practices. Consequently, I feel that for those sympathetic to the assumptions, success at a difficult job will

---

[3]Since these assumptions were assembled, I have "tested" them with several British primary teachers, headmasters, and inspectors and with an equal number of American proponents of open education. To date, although many qualifications in language have been suggested, there has not been a case where an individual has said of one of the assumptions, "No, that is contrary to what I believe about children, learning, or knowledge."

be more likely. For the educator to attempt to adopt practices which depend for their success upon general adherence to these beliefs without actually adhering to them is, at the very least, dangerous.

At the same time, we must be careful not to assume that an "official" British or U.S. government-inspected type of open classroom or set of beliefs exists which is the standard for all others. Indeed, what is exciting about British open classrooms is the *diversity* in thinking and behavior for children and adults—from person to person, class to class, and school to school. The important point here is that the likelihood of successfully developing an open classroom increases as those concerned agree with the basic assumptions underlying open education practices. It is impossible to "role play" such a fundamentally distinct teaching responsibility.

For some people, then, drawing attention to these assumptions may terminate interest in open education. All to the good; a well-organized, consistent, teacher-directed classroom probably has a far less harmful influence upon children than a well-intentioned but sloppy, permissive, and chaotic attempt at an open classroom in which teacher and child must live with contradiction and conflict. For other people, awareness of these assumptions may stimulate confidence and competence in their attempts to change what happens to children in school.

In the final analysis, the success of a widespread movement toward open education in this country rests not upon agreement with any philosophical position but with satisfactory answers to several important questions: For what kinds of people—teachers, administrators, parents, children—is the open classroom appropriate and valuable? What happens to children in open classrooms? Can teachers be *trained* for open classrooms? How can the resistance from children, teachers, administrators, and parents—inevitable among those not committed to open education's assumptions and practices—be surmounted? And finally, should participation in an open classroom be *required* of teachers, children, parents, and administrators?

Preparing for
Open-Classroom Teaching

Robert P. Parker, Jr.

I am speaking here primarily to students who are preparing to teach in elementary and secondary schools. I hope that some teacher educators, school administrators, and experienced teachers are also listening. If you are at all interested in this business of open classrooms or informal education that we have heard so much about lately, I want to say this: "Yes, it's in this direction that we'll find better ways of helping young people to grow and learn." This kind of vague statement may be encouraging, but it is not very helpful. I would like to discuss here a few things that people can do to prepare themselves for working in freer and more natural ways with children.

First, some assumptions about what I perceive to be the reality of most school situations:

1. Few teachers who try to open up their classrooms for work that is freer, more informal, more centered on human interests and human relationships have had any personal experience with this kind of teaching at any level of their school experience as students. For this reason, they are forced to work out of what I call "an experiential vacuum." You might also call it "flying blind." They know only what they have heard and read, and that is mostly slogans. In effect, they have no cognitive map to use in imagining or predicting what will happen over fairly long periods of time. Thus, teachers give in or quit when their self-doubts combine with criticism from students, colleagues, administrators, and parents.

2. Colleges, including schools or departments of education, are unlikely to provide open-classroom situations for teachers-in-training to experience as learners, let alone to encourage frank, personal discussion and evaluation of the educative value of these experiences.

Reprinted, courtesy of the author and publisher, from *Elementary School Journal*, April 1973, 354-358. © 1973 by University of Chicago. All Rights Reserved.

3. When a young teacher behaves differently from his more experienced colleagues, few of them take his behavior seriously as an alternative way of working with children. They attribute his behavior and point of view to youthful idealism and a lack of experience with "reality." They assume that with time and experience the idealism will disappear and the young teacher will realize that the way others behave with children is, after all, the best way. Do not expect immediate tolerance of difference or respect for your point of view, let alone encouragement or support. If you want these things, you will have to work for them, over a period of time, with the people whom you expect to influence.

4. Once a teacher begins teaching like everyone else has taught for years, it is unlikely that he will ever change his behavior very much. Only an unusual combination of circumstances, both internal and external, can stimulate change in experienced teachers, and such combinations of circumstances rarely happen. So, commit yourself to what you want from the beginning and work at it.

My point is that you must have some real experiences in working, growing, and learning in open, supportive situations. Mostly, you will have to create these situations for yourselves. All the activities that I am about to recommend I have seen teachers doing. Each is designed to help teachers in some way become more creative, more sensitive in their responses to other people and their work, more flexible in developing environments for learning, and more confident of the value of their work in teaching and in other areas. The more of these activities you try over some period of time, the better your chances for growth and learning.

1. Cooperative small-group work is at the heart of a truly open classroom, just as it is at the heart of a true democracy. Therefore, you need to get together in small groups to talk about things: poems, plays, paintings, music, politics. You also need to work on projects in small groups where the group is responsible for everything, from deciding on the project to evaluating its success. You need to experience planning, consensus-taking, idea-developing, decision-making, and leadership-sharing. You need also to analyze audio or video tapes of small-group sessions, yours and others, so that you can begin to figure out what is happening in groups—linguistically, intellectually, emotionally, socially, creatively. It takes time to develop skills in cooperative group work. Don't be in a hurry. Give yourself several months.

2. Find someone who can lead you into creative dramatics, particularly improvisation. This area of group work has tremendous potential for individual development. Through theater games, pantomime, and improvisation you can learn to use more of yourself in situations to become a more potent person. Your awareness of situations and human relationships will increase, your ability to respond more spontaneously to situations will increase, your confidence in your own imaginative powers of planning and

enactment will increase, your sense of development or movement in human affairs will become sharper, and your ability to analyze your own efforts in relation to those of others will increase. Just two warnings: One, don't confuse role-playing with improvisation. Role-playing has a specific problem-solving orientation; the goal is predetermined. Improvisation has no fixed goal. It is open-ended and exploratory, allowing you to take the characters you are developing as far as you can in the situation you have chosen. Two, don't emphasize performance until you have worked together for awhile, or you will negate the exploratory, developing nature of improvised drama.

3. Start a writing workshop. Write things, and share them with one another. Don't allow anyone in—including professors—who does not bring a piece of his own writing. Experiment with a wide variety of forms: poetry, autobiography, fiction, polemic, analysis. Keep a writer's notebook, and fill it with all kinds of stuff that interests you. After the workshop is moving and you have an open and trusting atmosphere, start keeping notes on your own writing process each time you write something. Share these notes along with the piece and see whether you can learn something about the composing process as well as about evaluation of the product. Read poems, novels, essays, letters. Read what published writers say about their own writing processes and habits. *Then,* and only then, think about the teaching of writing and read books about the teaching of writing. Finally, try to publish at least some of your work.

4. Start a creative arts workshop in which you can work in media that are unfamiliar to you. Paint, sculpt, weave, build things with wood, compose with found objects. Set problems and work on them in several media. Come to terms with the feeling of being a complete, fumbling novice at something. Then begin to read and talk about such things as creativity, inductive learning, problem-solving, individualized instruction, and all the other "trendy" notions.

5. Define a deep interest of yours that you are not being encouraged to pursue for a course and develop an independent research project—one that leaves room for short-term goals but that can also be pursued over some time. Learn to be imaginative and to take initiative in seeking out resources for your project. If your interest is serious and carefully articulated, most people will be willing to help.

6. Start a media workshop so that you can learn to manipulate confidently and to use creatively such things as tape recorders, portable television units, still and movie cameras, and computers. Look at this workshop as more than just a self-generated A-V course: see it as a chance to learn creative uses of these media in ways that will be personally satisfying. For instance, you might do a series of audio-taped or video-taped interviews on educational problems—interviews that you actually intend to produce for some kind of public hearing. Or you might do a film essay on "life in classrooms" based on Philip Jackson's book of the same name.

7. Organize a group to go together into a school. In most schools you cannot survive alone as an open-classroom teacher. The sociopolitical structure of most school systems, by its very nature, promotes the isolation and the alienation of teachers from one another. The point is that you must have people with whom you can talk, people who will provide real intellectual and political support for your ideas and your work. Perhaps you might even try your hand at some small-scale political organizing. Teaching, itself, is a political activity, so there is no virtue in your being naïve or powerless. And don't be fooled by unions; they are not interested in fighting for any of the things I am talking about here. You might, for instance, form a small group to investigate what the American Civil Liberties Union is doing in the area of the legal rights of students and then use this knowledge in a specific school context.

There are many more things I could suggest. However, with the help of the bibliography I have prepared, I think the seven activities proposed should suffice as starting points. My underlying message is this: you can and must take control of your own learning, and you cannot wait much longer to begin. I hope that you can gain the support, and perhaps even the participation, of your professors and your institution. Publicize what you are doing: write to teachers-in-training around the country to tell them about yourselves and to find out about them and the interesting things they might be doing. In plain language, do not remain isolated from the things that other students and teachers are doing.

One final note of warning, which you may recognize as Deweyan in its philosophic orientation. If, or as, you experiment with some of the activities I have suggested, or with other activities that you may create for yourselves, do not let yourselves be trapped by the notion that these activities are exercises preparing you for some reality that will come later. Enter into them fully as present sources of excitement, satisfaction, growth, and learning. If you behave in this way, the preparation will take care of itself. Full involvement in present living is the best preparation for future life and future roles. Good luck!

BIBLIOGRAPHY

Books

Blackie, John. *Inside the primary school.* London: Her Majesty's Stationery Office, 1967.

Coles, Robert. *Teachers and the children of poverty.* Washington, D.C.: The Potomac Institute, 1970.

Dennison, George. *The lives of children.* New York: Vintage Books, 1969.

Dixon, John. *Growth through English.* Oxford, England: Oxford University Press, 1969.

Evans, William (Ed.). *The creative teacher.* New York: Bantam Books, 1971.

Friedenberg, Edgar Z. *Coming of age in America.* New York: Random House, 1965.

Herndon, James. *How to survive in your native land.* New York: Simon and Schuster, 1971.

Hodgson, John, & Richards, Ernest. *Improvisation: Discovery and creativity in drama.* London: Methuen and Company, Ltd., 1968.

Holbrook, David. *The exploring world.* Cambridge, England: Cambridge University Press, 1968.

Holbrook, David. *The secret places.* Birmingham, Alabama: University of Alabama Press, 1965.

Jackson, Philip W. *Life in classrooms.* New York: Holt, Rinehart and Winston, 1968.

Jones, Richard. *Fantasy and feeling in education.* New York: New York University Press, 1968.

Kohl, Herbert. *The open classroom.* New York: Vintage Books, 1969.

Maslow, Abraham. *Toward a psychology of being.* Princeton, New Jersey: Van Nostrand, 1968.

Pincus, Edward. *A guide to film-making.* New York: Signet-New American Library, 1969.

Portchmouth, John. *Creative crafts.* New York: Viking Press, 1969.

Postman, Neil, & Weingartner, Charles. *Teaching as a subversive activity.* New York: Delacorte Press, 1969.

Postman, Neil, & Weingartner, Charles. *The soft revolution.* New York: Delacorte Press, 1971.

Rogers, Carl. *Freedom to learn.* Columbus, Ohio: Charles E. Merrill, 1969.

Rogers, Carl. *On becoming a person.* Boston: Houghton Mifflin, 1961.

Rogers, Vincent (Ed.). *Teaching in the British primary school.* New York: Macmillan, 1970.

Silberman, Charles E. *Crisis in the classroom.* New York: Random House, 1970.

Journals

This Magazine Is About Schools. Toronto, Ontario, Canada.

Media and Methods. Philadelphia, Pennsylvania.

Psychology Today. New York, New York.

Individualization of Instruction:
What It Is and What It Isn't

Robert E. Keuscher

There are several generalizations one can make about individualization of instruction today. First, it's "in." Everyone is in favor of individualizing. Second, most teachers will look you squarely in the eye and tell you they are individualizing instruction to some extent in their classrooms. Which leads naturally to the third generalization, that there are easily as many definitions of what individualization is as there are people attempting to do it. Fourth, every major producer of instructional materials and equipment in this country is peddling one or more sure-fire gimmicks to enable teachers to individualize. And last, but surely the most disconcerting, is that very few, if any, of the different modes of individualization or the kits, packages, and programs purported to help teachers individualize, do much of anything for the individual; in fact, they may do much to stifle the learner's initiative, his creativity, and his independence.

INDIVIDUALIZATION IS "IN"

It is easy to account for enthusiasm for individualization of instruction. Primarily, it is a natural reaction against the impersonal, mass-production methods we have been using in education. The idea of a teacher standing before a class of 30 or more youngsters attempting to teach the same lesson to all of them at the same time is preposterous. It defies all we know about the wide range of differences that exist within the group. It negates what we know about motivation, about children's needs, their interests, their creative capabilities. Nor does dividing 30 kinds into 3 groups do anything to make instruction more effective. The teacher must get closer to the individual pupil than that—at least ten times closer!

Reprinted from the *California Journal of Instructional Improvement*, May 1971. Used with permission of Robert E. Keuscher.

If learning is to be meaningful to children they need a voice in deciding what they study and when and how they study it. Children must see the utility of what they are learning. We're a long way down the road from the time when adults (curriculum committees, textbook writers, teachers) can play God, handing down the decisions as to what students must study "from on high." All we've done with that kind of behavior—and educators are beginning to realize it *finally*—is turn kids off, make exhortation the number one task of teachers, and increase classroom discipline problems. Older students are complaining about "relevancy." The younger children would, too, if they knew the word. Far too much of what we have been handing out as required curriculum is not relevant to children at the time we confront them with it. The term "individualize instruction" to me means bringing the decision-making about curriculum closer to the individual learner. Unless he participates in the decisions, the planning, the goal-setting, let's not pretend we are "individualizing" anything. The term just doesn't apply.

TEACHERS DELUDE THEMSELVES

Most teachers recognize the myriad of differences that exist among children, but they have never really faced the possibility of adequately meeting such a great range of diversity. Rather, they tinker with the organizational structure or the assignment requirements and honestly believe they are individualizing.

It is very difficult for most teachers to visualize a classroom where everyone is busy working alone, in pairs, or in groups of three to eight on a variety of projects spanning several subject areas at one time, while the teacher moved freely about the classroom lending a hand here, making a suggestion there, asking an appropriate question or two here, receiving a progress report there. Teachers who work in this manner tell me they have never known their students so well and have never seen boys and girls so excited about schooling.

Teachers have to quit kidding themselves about how individualization takes place. To really do it, they must know their children like they've never known them before. This means listening to students much more than they have previously, observing students more than they have in the past, and permitting students to incorporate their own needs and interests into the instructional program. The teacher will do far less "teaching" in such a program and much more facilitating, or helping learning take place.

MOST PROGRAMS MISS THEIR MARK

With so many different versions of what constitutes individualized instruction, it is inevitable that most individualized programs fall far short of their mark. One thing is increasingly clear to me as I visit so-called individualized classrooms. There is no possibility of attending to the diversity we find there without increasing many times over the number of options available to students. Children must have choices as to what to study and how to study it.

Providing alternatives for students dictates a different kind of classroom environment than the desk and textbook-dominated rooms we now have, most of them so tidy and formal that they bore the teacher as well as the pupils. "Chalk and talk classrooms," one visiting British educator dubbed these unexciting boxes we cage our children in while we talk and they sit passively and listen. And then we wonder why they begin to turn off as early as second or third grade and learn to dislike school!

Learning should be an exciting activity and to make it so, schools have to be exciting places. There have to be projects for children to do, problems for them to investigate, ideas for them to read and write and calculate about, activities that are fun as well as educational, and experiences to whet the interest of pupils of different levels of maturity, of different backgrounds and cultures. There should be books and books and books—not textbooks, but library books—books so plentiful, so colorful, and so broad in their interest appeal that one would almost defy a child not to find several that turn him on. There should be interest areas for science including experiments with plants and animals, a microscope, a dry cell battery or two, mealworms, tropical fish, perhaps a salt-water aquarium, small animals, rocks, shells, insect collection boxes, and a lot of common, inexpensive science supplies.

There should be a mathematics center. Here is a place where students can weigh, measure, time, and graph their data. It contains yardsticks, tape measures, rulers, a click wheel, balances, two or three different kinds of scales, a stop watch or two, and of course things to weigh and balance— beans, pebbles, nuts, blocks. Also found in such a center are paper, yarn, and other materials necessary for pictorial representation of findings.

There should be a language arts center with all kinds of suggestions and incentives to help motivate children to write. An old typewriter or two is a must for this center as well as the materials needed to make hard back covers for the "books" children will write.

There should be a quiet corner for research or just plain reading. A piece of used carpet, an old sofa or rocking chair, and several large pillows can make this area the most popular in the room.

Other attractions might include a junk art area, the "tinker table" where children dismantle old clocks, radios, and electrical appliances that the teacher has picked up at the repair shop where they were about to be discarded. Also one might find a puppet theater or drama corner, a sewing or knitting center, an educational game area.

Where does one find room for all of this? In the regular classroom!

But most or all of the students' desks are removed. Bookcases and tables properly placed divide the room into the various areas and students keep their belongings in tote trays or individual cubby holes in a cabinet along one wall.

Students are encouraged to bring materials for the room. Parents get in on the act. It's surprising what an exciting environment can be built in a short time when everyone pitches in. Surprising, too, will be the different attitude students have about the room when they feel it is "their" room.

It won't take a lot of money to set up a room along the lines suggested. In fact, you will find it much less expensive. The classrooms I visited in Great Britain were simply "rich" with materials for children to work with despite the fact that the expenditure per pupil is only a small fraction of what we spend in this country.

One thing is certain. You will not need to purchase many of the products currently appearing on the market and advertised as facilitating individualization.

GIMMICKS AND PACKAGES AREN'T THE ANSWER

Most materials and programs marketed in the name of individualization do very little over and beyond adjusting the pace with which the student wades through the prescribed assignments. Everyone covers the same material (what allowances for differences exist here?)—some just go through faster than others.

Another indictment of most programmed or computer-assisted materials is that they teach only those facts and understandings that are going to show up on the tests. Both information and answers are decided beforehand by some "all-knowing" person or group of people who, although they do not know, have never seen, nor ever will see the pupil, has decided what he should learn and the manner in which he should learn it.

Let's face it! What programmed materials do is indoctrinate, with no concern whatsoever for the individual's rights in the matter. And they can indoctrinate for any purpose desired. I'm sure that Adolph Hitler, if he were alive and training German youth today, would be using many of the same kinds of materials and methods that are being urged upon teachers in this country as aids to individualization. Proponents claim their programmed materials and methods to be a more efficient way of educating. They may be right, if we are willing to accept the premise that what we are tying to do is get our students to learn a specified, fixed block of knowledge. But is there such a block of knowledge that everyone must have? If so, who determines what that knowledge is? And is our methodology in exposing the child to that knowledge going to accomplish what is intended? I'm fully convinced that in our zeal to teach some children to read through the high pressure tactics of computer assistance, systems approaches, and programming, we may be raising reading scores but turning children so against reading that they will never enjoy it again as long as they live!

Individualizing instruction along the lines of diagnosis and prescription, pre-testing, and post-testing, through behavioral objectives, is a manipulative method of teaching. It stresses what is to be taught and how it is to be taught with little or no regard for the feelings of the individual. He becomes a pawn in the process. There is *no* way we can develop a zest for learning, self-confidence, rational thinking, independence, and responsibility through the programmed approach to learning.

Educators who grasp such methods hoping they'll solve all problems ought to be smarter than that. They should realize that all they are going to reap is more disinterest and alienation. If there is anything children *do not need* at this time, it is more manipulation, more distance between pupil and teacher. Schooling is far too impersonal now. What we need desperately to do today is to *personalize* our teaching.

IT'S WHAT HAPPENS TO THE PERSON THAT MATTERS

Most attempts at individualization fail to do much, if anything, for the individual, his self-concept, his feeling about school. I'm convinced we must start with the learner before we worry about reading or mathematics. If a child doesn't feel pretty good about himself, have some confidence in his ability to succeed, and if he doesn't feel good about school, enjoy being there, look forward to returning each day, find it an exciting, fun place to be, we aren't going to accomplish much with reading or any other content we try to teach. *We must work on first things first.* The child's feelings about himself and about school precede all other concerns.

This cannot be accomplished with a machine, nor can it be programmed. It takes a teacher who gives primacy to the feelings of his children and to the personal development of each member of his class to turn students on to learning. Place that teacher who is personalizing his instruction in the rich environment that every teacher owes his pupils, and learning is going to take place. There is no way to prevent it! Furthermore, creativity will flourish, relationships between students (a great concern to many of the teachers I know today) will become less aggressive and more warmly cooperative, and boys and girls will not only learn to read but learn to love reading!

Personalized teaching (I prefer that term over individualized) is not a program; it's a way of performing in the classroom, based on a set of values about children and schooling. It's not a method; it's an attitude.

Most British schools have moved dramatically in this direction, and I have never seen more turned-on, happy, productive students than those

I saw there on a recent visit. Over there, they call it Open Education and I recall one primary school Head who told me, "It's not a program we have, it's a way of living!"

I think it is a way of life based on a genuine concern for our most precious resource, our children. Whether we call it Personalized Instruction or Open Education or stick by the oft-misused term Individualized Instruction, it is urgent that we educators re-examine our programs with special concern for one question regarding what we are now doing—"What is happening to the person in the process?"

READINGS

Association for Supervision and Curriculum Development. *To nurture humanness*. ASCD Yearbook, 1970.

Holt, John. *What do I do Monday?* New York: E. P. Dutton, 1970.

Howes, Virgil M., Darrow, Helen F., Keuscher, Robert E., & Tyler, Louise L. *Individualization of instruction: Exploring open-structure*. Los Angeles: ASUCLA Students' Store, 308 Westwood Plaza, Los Angeles, Calif. 90024, 1968.

Howes, Virgil M. (Ed.). *Individualization of instruction: A teaching strategy*. New York: Macmillan, 1970.

Kohl, Herbert R. *The open classroom*. New York: The New York Review, 1969.

Rogers, Vincent R. *Teaching in the British primary school*. New York: Macmillan, 1970.

Silberman, Charles. *Crisis in the classroom*. New York: Random House, 1970.

Practical Questions Teachers Ask About Individualizing Instruction —And Some of the Answers

Rita Stafford Dunn and Kenneth Dunn

A rapidly increasing number of schools and universities throughout the nation are focusing attention on developing or adopting improved and creative approaches to the teaching-learning process. Individualization has received more emphasis than other instructional strategies and, in an effort to initiate such a program, the following questions are frequently asked by interested (or concerned) teachers:

1. What does "individualization" really mean?

That each child in your group may:
- assume some responsibility for his own learning, and thus
- become an independent learner, capable of progressing without being dependent on others,
- learn at a pace (rate, speed) which is comfortable for him,
- learn through materials which are related to his perceptual strengths (seeing, hearing, touching, acting out, combinations of senses, *etc.*),
- learn on a level which is appropriate to his abilities,
- relate the curriculum to his major interests,
- learn in accordance with his own learning style (alone in small groups, through media, at night, *etc.*),
- be graded in terms of his own achievement and not in comparison with others,
- feel a sense of achievement and thus be able to develop self-esteem and pride, and

Reprinted from *Audiovisual Instruction*, Vol. 17, No. 1, January 1972, pp. 47-50. By permission of the Association for Educational Communications and Technology.

- select options from among a series of alternatives and participate actively in the decision-making areas of the learning process.

2. How can a teacher do all these things for 30 or more children in a group when she has no assistance?

It's easier with clerical, parental, paraprofessional, or professional assistance, but it can be done effectively by one teacher with a 30:1 student ratio providing that teacher knows the techniques for individualizing.

3. What are the techniques for individualizing instruction?

There are five basic ways of individualizing instruction:
- the contract method (which builds into it a series of excellent small-group techniques),
- instructional packages or educational materials,
- programed sequences (like SRA, IPI or Project Plan),
- work-study programs (like the Parkway School) and/or internships, or
- community contribution programs (such as introduced in Cherry Creek, Colorado).

4. Which of these techniques is used in the British Primary School, the Open Classroom, and the Open Corridor Schools?

These three use essentially similar organizational patterns which rely heavily on the use of educational materials to stimulate learning. "Open Classrooms" are adaptations of the original British Primary Schools, but each class in both of these structures may differ markedly from every other. The "Open Corridor" schools were so named when previously unused corridors were pressed into service to provide more learning areas in older buildings where versions of an open classroom pattern were being tried.

5. Is the British Primary School something which we in the United States should emulate?

No. We should extract and adapt those features which appear to be appropriate to our youngsters, communities and faculties, but the British children, communities, faculties, and systems are very different from ours and their methods are not easily transferable.

6. Then should we discount individualizing through instructional materials?

No. Some instructional materials and many "packages" such as ESS, SAPA and SCIDS in science are excellent, but they should comprise only a portion of an instructional program.

7. *Why?*

Because our youngsters are used to learning in a dynamic, exciting existence outside of the classroom, and any one type of instruction used in all of the curriculum areas will quickly lose the initial motivation of novelty, regardless of the excellence of the method.

8. *Then do teachers in the United States need many methods?*

Yes. Any variation will do, but several effective techniques, each used in selected curriculum areas, will probably absorb our children indefinitely.

EFFECTIVE UTILIZATION

Instructional Techniques	No. in Group	Age Levels	Curriculum Areas				
			Lang.	Math	Sci.	Soc. Stud.	Prob. Solv.
Team Learning	5-8	5-18	•	•	•	•	•
Simulations	5-8	9-18	•			•	•
Role Playing	1-9	5-18	•	•	•	•	•
Learn. Activity Pkgs.	1-6	5-18	•	•	•	•	
Independent Contracts	1	5-18	•	•	•	•	
Team Task Force	3-6	5-18	•	•	•	•	•
Tutoring Teams	1-5	5-18	•	•	•	•	
Learning Circles	5-10	8-18	•	•	•	•	
Brainstorming	5-30	5-18	•			•	•
Multi-Media Projects	1-30	5-18	•	•	•	•	•
Community Contrib.	1-30	12-18	•	•	•	•	•
Working While Learning	1-30	14-18	•	•	•	•	•
Case Studies	1-30	9-18	•			•	•

9. Be specific. Give examples.

One well-designed individualized program would provide contracts in social studies, programed materials in mathematics (supplemented by tapes and films), instructional packages in science, and a combination of these in reading and language arts.

10. I see, rather than rely on any single method, you'd suggest a variety of techniques as part of a total process. With which subject should I begin and with which techniques?

Begin with the curriculum area you like best. Assess the amount of money or materials available and then plan a program around that curriculum. If you've no money or materials, you'll either have to innovate or create materials. Learn some simple small-group techniques before you begin and train the pupils to function independently through these. As the students mature, design an individualized plan for those who appear to be able to assume some responsibility for their own progress.

11. What are "small-group" techniques?

Methods of helping pupils to work independently with their peers. These should be used as a beginning step toward individualization (See chart.)

12. Do any small-group techniques work best with bright pupils? With disruptive ones? With slower ones?

All of the techniques work well with motivated, intelligent and/or creative youngsters. Circle of Knowledge, team-learning, role-playing, case studies, brain-storming, and task forces tend to be effective with most children.

13. I want to individualize. What must I learn to do?

- Diagnose your pupil's academic abilities, perceptual strengths, learning style, major interests, and amount of self-discipline;
- help pupils to assume partial responsibility for their own learning;
- organize the room, the instructional materials, and the program for individualized learning;
- operate varied media effectively;
- win support from the pupils, parents, administrators, and the community;
- write individual learning prescriptions; and
- guide pupils through the learning process.

14. Won't that be a lot of work and won't it take a lot of time?

It will take time, but much of this is merely a reorganization and refocusing of what teachers always do.

15. How can I learn to use the small-group and individualized techniques?

Read about them, observe teachers who use them, try to implement them (preferably with a "partner" so that you may help each other over the rough times), and have an experienced person offer concrete suggestions for improvement after he has worked with you in your classroom with your students. As you progress, you'll improve on the techniques and use them to your advantage.

16. Is individualizing instruction worth the effort it will take?

It's better for the students, and once accomplished, much easier for the teachers.

17. Do students learn more?

Most do, but it has other advantages. It reduces friction, tension and disruption because students aren't forced into little boxes; they may be themselves and move ahead in a way that makes them feel comfortable and worthwhile. It provides feelings of accomplishment for marginal children; it doesn't restrict the learning of the more able ones. It also helps youngsters to become lifetime learners rather than "under pressure" students.

18. Where can I see effective individualized programs?

Write to your own state education department for a suggested list.

19. Where can I get knowledgeable assistance?

Try your own administration; peers; the teachers' association; AECT; the National Education Association; the state education department, the Board of Cooperative Educational Services; the Office of Health, Education and Welfare; local colleges and universities; local professional groups; and the Association for Supervision and Curriculum Development. Also, look for well-reviewed books and articles on individualization.

Techniques for Initiating Independent Study

Joe W. Wilson and Terry Armstrong

Independent study is defined in this article as study chosen by an individual because he wants to pursue it, and in any manner he desires. Independent study as so stipulated is perhaps one of the easiest concepts in education to understand. It is also one of the oldest. A look at the history of American education shows independent study, in a somewhat disguised content, in the early apprenticeships, vocational education, and physical education programs to mention only a few specific instances.

In all realms of the learning situation, the student must either actively acknowledge or passively accept responsibility for the realistic acquisition of learning in order for the endeavor to be successful. The role of the teacher is much more clearly illuminated than that of the learner in the sense of knowing how it happens. Thus, the teacher must be constantly alert and willing to try new approaches to interest students in the learning experience.

A review of recent educational literature reveals that there has been a trend during the last decade, and particularly during the last five years, toward providing independent study programs for students. Not until the sixties was this type of format advocated for all students rather than for "gifted" students only. Most available literature describes organizational and administrative procedures for setting up such programs, or the type of teacher and atmosphere needed to be effective. This information is valuable, but it offers little practical help for the classroom teacher. In this article we offer three successful techniques we have used, not in the laboratory with accelerated students but in the classroom with average students. The ideas are not new or original but we are attempting to present them from a different perspective.

Reprinted by permission from the May 1973 issue of THE CLEARING HOUSE.

The techniques presented are: analysis of discrepant events, presentation of open-ended problems, and problem formulation activities. These terms are not absolute but are our way of categorizing the techniques into some order. These are ways of thinking about initiating independent study. The three methods build on independence—from more structure and teacher direction to less structure and student direction. Analyzing discrepant events is a method useful in preparing students for independent study. Subsequently, the use of open-ended problems and problem formulation activities may be helpful in getting students involved. You may wish to try these techniques which may lead to your developing many more, possibly better than ours for your purposes, and this article will have served its purpose.

ANALYSIS OF DISCREPANT EVENTS

When first attempting to introduce independent study, exercises are beneficial which give students experience in dealing with inductive assignments. Students often lack inquiry behaviors and proper methods for proceeding in an independent fashion.

One method that allows in-class practice of inquiry behaviors for subsequent independent study as well as a focus for additional assignments involves the use of discrepant events. Naturally occurring discrepant events serve as an ideal stimulus for student discussion and investigation. This procedure utilizes either a picture of a discrepant event or the actual on-site setting such as might be encountered on a field trip, television program, or film.

A discrepant event is any circumstance that involves people, living or physical systems, or happenings in a situation that is extraordinary for that particular setting. Examples are difficult to describe on paper but could include a picture of a pine tree growing from a granite ledge, similar fossils appearing in different colored matrices, people behaving in a deviant way such as a riot developing from a peace rally, a play on words, and examples of faulty or misleading advertising. In general, the events are usually those that stimulate students to ask questions and probe for information and answers.

One easy method to give students this experience is by using 35mm. color slides or color lift transparencies taken from any clay base, slick surface color photograph. The use of the color lift transparency for overhead projection of 35mm. color slides provides teachers with an inexpensive, student centered activity that is stimulating and worthwhile.

Using a picture, slide, film or the actual event or an account of the event, the teacher first asks the students to detect a discrepant event from the source presented. It may be necessary to explain what is meant by the term "discrepant event." Usually students will identify a number of alternatives to the situation posed by the teacher. Under these circumstances, the teacher should value every response and list each description on the board or note it in some manner.

Following the identification of the discrepant event, or problem, members of the class, working individually or in teams, list as many hypotheses as they can that they think account for the occurence of the event. Care should be taken to allow time for complete discussion and consideration of the hypotheses formulated. The individual learners or teams are then instructed to select the hypothesis that they feel best tests the problem.

The final activity involves students in the design of an experiment or researching sources to obtain information that would prove or disprove the hypothesis. In a science class the students may desire to design an experiment and attempt to prove or disprove the hypothesis. Social studies students might also design an experiment or research the hypothesis in the library.

Students enjoy these activities. Teachers who have used the discrepant event technique quickly become adept at identifying discrepant events for use in their classes. Success with this technique has been realized in the social studies, science, and English disciplines.

Following exercises which provide students with practice in using primary skills and thinking critically about problems, additional independent study activities are appropriate. These activities should be less structured and involve more active participation on the part of the students.

PRESENTATION OF OPEN-ENDED PROBLEMS

A less structured technique is the use of open-ended problems. Using this approach, the teacher gives the student a problem, provides guidance and assistance when necessary, and places the responsibility for completing the activity in the hands of the individual student. The less help required or volunteered on the teacher's part, the better. The problems are developed and assigned by the teacher; subsequently, the students become active participants in the learning experience. Open-ended problems are particularly useful because, if properly constructed and assigned, a single problem can be completed by students at any achievement level. Reading ability is not a prerequisite for many problems. Thus, the non-reader has an opportunity to excel. If library problems are assigned, they should be constructed so that answers are obtained from several sources.

Teachers find open-ended problems particularly attractive for a number of reasons. The name "open-ended" provides a clue for the most important of these. There are no set ways to approach a good open-ended problem. Students must use their own initiative and creativity to solve the problem. The solution or solutions may come through a variety of different procedures and methods of analysis. Divergence of approach should be encouraged and supported by the teacher. Another prime reason for the acceptability of open-ended problems arises out of the complaint of many teachers of the lack of equipment or facilities found in many schools. If this is the case, it is advisable to develop problems that can be completed with resources common to most homes and communities. A listing of open-ended problems might include but would not be limited to the following examples.

Language Arts:

　　1. Develop a language of your own and determine the rules for parts of speech.

　　2. Determine the etymology of some terms unique to your area.

　　3. Relate your experiences to an author's experiences or situations depicted in a novel.

Science:

　　1. Prove the existence of micro-meteorites.

　　2. Find the center of gravity in an irregular rock.

　　3. Determine the amount of air taken in by an organism over a given amount of time.

　　4. Prove that a system which undergoes more pressure has an increase in temperature.

Social Studies:

　　1. Determine the public opinion on a local issue.

　　2. Change someone's position on a current issue.

　　3. Determine in an unobtrusive way how individuals behave in groups.

　　4. Propose a system of government for a nation of your own design.

　　The foregoing list represents a compilation of successful open-ended activities from three of the disciplines. These are intended to offer ideas about how the problems are stated and ideas about what topics lend themselves to open-ended situations. We trust you will soon decide to begin a long list applicable to your own subject matter area.

PROBLEM FORMULATION ACTIVITIES

A third technique for initiating independent study is problem formulation, a highly unstructured approach. In essence, problem formulation is an exercise which presents the students with a situation affording them an opportunity to solve a problem and, during the process, to identify other problems of interest to them. These individual problems often are those of clarifying internal values, bringing those feelings to a conscious level and allowing the students to realize the logical or illogical basis for holding such. The problems selected for independent study are not teacher-made but are those chosen by students themselves. When working with open-ended problems, the students work individually on teacher-designed problems of their choice. In problem formulation activities the teacher presents a problem which the class discusses and in the process develops additional problems for study independently.

An example of the technique may be explained as follows. "Who's more important, the political party or the candidate?" Students may hold strong opinions concerning a "right" answer, but usually find it difficult to support their opinions without further research. Since this is a global question, one student would not be expected to research the subject in its entirety. Individually or in small groups students will volunteer to search for possible evidence in particular elections from the state level to the national political scene. Others may be interested in historical analysis of the subject from the angle of why political parties originated and survived in early American government. The possibilities are numerous, and regardless of the conclusions students will eventually reach, they will have progressed from subjects of interest through invaluable exercises in research and logical clarification of thinking patterns. Secondary gains are as numerous as those mentioned, and direction for the next topic or subject could already be decided by the students.

When this technique was used in a ninth-grade social science class, it generated much enthusiasm. As would be expected from asking a two-sided question, the class split into two factions, one for the party and the other for the candidate. After bouncing opinion back and forth for a short while, students sought to resolve the question by research. Many aspects were studied and some interesting subjects were covered. One student interviewed the state party chairmen (taped via recorder), asking both the same questions. Valuable printed material was also secured from these men. The class compared this information as well as the tapes, pointing out contrasts and distinguishing opinion from fact. Others corresponded and contacted U.S. senators and governors. Some students worked on this problem for a few weeks; others independently continued research throughout the semester.

Other problem formulation exercises could include examining conflicting accounts of historical events, logically arranging scrambled outlines, or identifying historical accounts such as the British version of the Boston Massacre and Kent State. This list is limited only by one's imagination, ingenuity, and desire to let students learn independently.

REPORTING AND EVALUATING INDEPENDENT STUDY

Students may report the results of their work in independent study through a variety of techniques. Popular methods include video-tapes, cassette recordings, films, oral reports, or conventional themes and reports. Opportunities for various ways of reporting should be encouraged.

Evaluations of independent study range from assigned grades on a percentage or letter grade scale to student assessment of worth via check sheets or questionnaires. Student involvement can be dampened through the use of carelessly designed grading procedures. Our experiences have been that students should have some responsible part in determining their own grades on each problem.

SUMMING UP

Our intent has been to illustrate examples of techniques for initiating independent study which have been effective with the students with whom we have worked. Enthusiastic student involvement in independent study results when teachers (1) provide students the opportunity, (2) provide some motivating activity, and (3) recognize and allow for individual differences among students and classes.

We are reminded of the time when one of us had used a number of activities to involve ninth grade geography students in independent study. The instructor was delighted with the success as most of the students were actively involved. One student who had accomplished little came to the instructor and said, "I have thought about a lot of things related to the subject, but none seem to really grab me." His next statement was "I'd like to make you some new transparencies." For the next few weeks he produced some of the most artistic and creative audio-visual aids we had ever seen. Additionally, he learned a great deal and so did the instructor.

Learning Centers: A Path to Individualized Instruction

Meg Thompson

Learning centers can be utilized in almost any classroom to introduce a multisensory approach to learning. By employing visual, auditory, and tactile experiences, communication, and devices, the teacher can help children to become aware of the many stimuli to which they are exposed and to integrate these experiences into their personal learning processes. As the child develops an awareness of and interest in new subjects and ideas, he is allowed to develop his interests and skills at his own pace. This, in turn, enhances his pride in his own accomplishments and aids him in developing greater independence and self-direction.

In order to implement the learning-center approach effectively, the teacher must believe and communicate the belief that children can select, carry out, and evaluate worthwhile learning activities if they are given the opportunity to do so. By providing open-ended learning materials and experiences, the teacher can stimulate a sense of discovery and inquiry on the part of the students, rather than a passive reception of lectures and directions. The idea is to have the children create and utilize independent and individual sources of learning; it is not to have children finish a task and then wait to be assigned another one. The teacher selects (with the children's input) and provides learning materials and gives guidance and direction when necessary.

SUPPORT

Obviously, the teacher must first obtain the support of the school administration before attempting to restructure the classroom. By demonstrating her understanding of the concepts of individualized instruction and her genuine concern for the students, she may also win the support and cooperation of other teachers who hold views similar to hers. This is an important step; the cooperation and insights provided by other teachers can greatly enrich any learning experience, and particularly one that a teacher may be attempting to initiate for the first time.

It is also a good idea to explain the learning-center concept to the students' parents. They may actually be invited to see the classroom; at this time the teacher can demonstrate how and why the concept works.

SEQUENCING

An important aspect of the individualized approach is sequential development of skills and concepts; experiences are paced so that the child can master one phase before moving on to the next. A balance is provided between quiet periods and active periods, between structured times and free times.

PHYSICAL ARRANGEMENT

The room is physically arranged so that space is provided for quiet areas and for active areas, with well organized traffic flow to and from these areas. The long rows of desks found in many classrooms are pushed aside (or partially removed) so that more space is provided for activity and relaxation areas; space can be conserved, if necessary, in sitting and writing areas.

As in any classroom, good ventilation and good light must be provided. In many areas, the furnishings will be composed of rugs, small rug squares, pillows, chairs, and boxes (for extra tables, etc.).

MATERIALS

Careful and extensive preplanning is necessary to assure that materials (learning aids) are available when they are needed. Often, materials must be ordered well ahead of time.

Because many of the materials provided in the multisensory learning centers will be unfamiliar to the children, the teacher should demonstrate how to handle and use any special equipment that is provided.

PLAN OF ACTION

The learning centers are most effective (or at least most easily accepted) if they are introduced gradually. From the beginning, the children are involved in establishing ground rules for use of the interest centers. A reward system (extra free time, compliments, etc.) may be set up to reinforce the rules established for the use and maintenance of the areas. It is helpful to emphasize that the rules have evolved with the cooperation of the entire class.

Initially, between two and four areas may be set up. Careful instructions are necessary; for example, signs may be put up that identify the various areas and indicate how many children may be in the area at one time.

The areas can be scheduled the same way a reading group is scheduled, or the children can spend time in an area when they have finished their assigned work. If time periods are utilized, the time may be extended to include more and more of the school day until as much of the curriculum as is desired is presented on this more personalized basis.

A plan must be established to check and evaluate progress. Specific evaluative criteria can be used as a means by which the teacher and the students can determine what has been learned in order that new activities can be planned to reinforce, extend, and complement this learning. Some of this evaluation may be in the form of quizzes, tests, interviews, discussions, and recorded observations.

New interest areas may be introduced one or two at a time, at intervals of between one and three weeks, depending on the interests and needs of the class. As each new center (area) is established, the teacher should provide a careful introduction and explanation of the purpose and possible uses of the area and should restate that the children are capable of assuming responsibility for the care of materials and equipment in the area.

TYPES OF LEARNING AREAS

The possibilities for different interest centers are limited only by the interests and imagination of the teacher and the class. Some of the centers that I have provided with some success are:

Art Area

Here you can provide water colors, tempera paints, finger paints, crayons, colored chalk, clay, scrap materials, glue—the list is endless; the purpose is to encourage creativity and free expression.

Math Area

In a *grocery store,* the children can use real money (nickels, dimes, pennies, quarters). They will buy and sell cardboard objects with price tags on them or may actually use small objects (toys, candy, etc.).

A *post office* is another useful math experience. The children experience using money, making and handling stamps, weighing packages, and writing and placing addresses.

In the *"Tick Tock Clock Shop,"* children plan activities with movable clock hands on cardboard clocks.

A *Balance Scale* is also useful for many math activities.

Slim Jim: A large life-sized cowboy is drawn, and math problems are written up and down his body. A child throws dice and then moves his marker an equal number of spaces. The child then must solve a math problem. If he is incorrect, he must move his marker back four spaces. The object of this game is to get around the cowboy's body first. An answer sheet is provided so that children can check their own answers.

Math equations can be taught in numerous ways. Answers can be put on a turkey, with the equations provided as corresponding "feathers." The children then match these up. (The same idea may be applied to a tree and its leaves or a leopard and its spots.)

Science Center

This area can include live animals (we have gerbils, a rabbit, and fish), a terrarium, an ant colony, thermometers, plants, models, magnets, pulleys, wedges, levers, wheels, weather charts—the list is endless.

Social Studies Area

In this area can be maps (including relief maps, globes, etc.), transparencies, magazines, newspapers, photographs, posters, artifacts from different countries, and various items made by the students.

Language Arts

Centers can also be used to teach and reinforce *reading, phonics, writing,* and *listening* activities. Helpful equipment includes a record player, a tape recorder, an overhead projector, a filmstrip projector, and a typewriter. Listening stations and book nooks are popular areas.

The teacher can supplement these ready-made materials with many "home-made" activities. Some of the possibilities are:

Contraction Car

Words are put in an envelope. The children put the contraction on the car door and the matching words on the wheels.

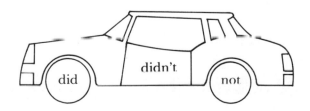

What Am I?

The child puts a stack of pictures face down in front of him. Each picture contains a hole cut out for the child's face. He holds the card up to his face (he can not see picture) and asks the class ten questions such as "Am I a food (person, etc.)," and tries to guess what the picture is.

Concentration

A set of cards is laid face down, and each card is labeled "A," "B," etc. A matching set of cards (the cards may be picture cards, word cards, playing cards, etc.) is laid down and labeled "1," "2," etc. One child calls a letter and a number and the corresponding cards are turned over. If they match, the child scores one point. If they do not match, the cards are turned over again, and a second child takes a turn at matching. (This game is similar to the one played on television.)

Daily Record

Each child (or the class as a whole) keeps a daily (or weekly) record of the activities that have been completed during that time. These records may be in the form of illustrations, such as activities in the form of petals to be added to a flower stem or activities in the form of features to be added to a clown's face.

The Possibilities Are Endless

The possible areas, resources, and materials that can be utilized to encourage interest and exploration and to reinforce learning are limited only by the imagination, needs, and resources of the teacher and the class. Area possibilities include a music center, a housekeeping center, a mystery box, a special-interest table, a help-yourself shelf, and so on. Human resources include persons from different vocations (policemen, farmers, bakers, etc.); parents; representatives of government agencies (conservation, etc.); members of the school system, and so on. The challenge will be a welcome one to most teachers, and the rewards are obvious.

CONCLUSION

Multisensory learning centers can be utilized in the classroom to enrich the learning process. Among the many outcomes of this approach, the most obvious are:

1. Motivation becomes more intrinsic (relies less on external rewards or punishments).

2. Results will reflect the change in emphasis from grade level expectations and competition to individual expectations based on realistic goals for each pupil.

3. A child who experiences success in learning "on his own" finds that there is more to school than just doing what the teacher tells him to do. If he can do something that is important to him, he can experience an amazing depth of learning and learn to capitalize on his own strengths.

4. Children can develop their own ideas creatively since they are free to move at their own rate and accomplish tasks in their own way.

5. The children will show signs of relying on their own judgment and will improve in judgment-making abilities.

6. Children will be less likely to fail.

7. The children will develop a more positive and more realistic view of themselves and others.

8. Special talents and interests will become more evident.

9. Children learn to utilize many sources.

10. By developing independence in children, the teacher will have more time and energy to help individual children.

11. Certain learning habits and attitudes toward learning will change in a positive way.

12. The relationship with parents will be strengthened. It will be one of involvement. They will foster and nurture the efforts of the children.

Experiential Learning

Robert Dow

Experiential education is goal-oriented. This fact alone assures that the teacher-learner is ready to learn, a basic condition for learning. Let me illustrate.

Several "learners" have arrived at the first teaching-learning session of a given course. The first hours are spent dealing with the learners' expectations and learning goals.

TEACHER-LEARNER: Experiential Learning is a laboratory learning process. I use this process here. I do not expect to teach *at* you. I expect that we will learn together. I believe we can teach each other, and that I can learn as a teacher and that you can teach as a learner.

A laboratory setting simply implies that within certain defined boundaries, we can work with several variables, unknowns, in the hope of discovering what these variables can do or mean to us in our lives. This, I hope, makes our learning both relevant and dynamic. In experimentation no attempt at an answer is wrong. We are free to try many things, even what appears to be ridiculous at first. Imagine Alexander Graham Bell thinking that he could talk across distances on a thin strand of wire. Ridiculous!

Now I'd like you to pair off, select a partner, and for the next few minutes discuss your answer to this question: What do you expect will happen in this class?

The teacher-learner pauses for five minutes, as the new learners interact.

Let me break through your discussion and invite you to move into quadrants (fours) of two pairs to continue your discussion, only using a minor shift in emphasis. Now discuss your answer to this question: What would you like to see happen in this class?

Again, there is interaction for five minutes.

Reprinted from *Learning Through Encounter*, by Robert Dow. Used by permission of The Judson Press.

Now bring two quadrants together, with one quadrant seated immediately behind the other. Like this:

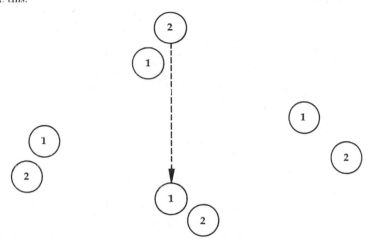

Let me give the first assignment to quadrant two. Your task now is to observe the person who is sitting directly across from you. Carefully consider the three questions listed before you as regards that person:

1. What does his role in his quadrant seem to be?
2. What does his central concern appear to be?
3. How might he be more helpful? Remain silent during the next few minutes. You will have a chance to feed your information to your opposite after six or eight minutes of observation.

Here, the teacher-learner is beginning to initiate several important processes central to experiential education. Question one helps the observer and the observed to begin to look at roles each one plays in a group. This is a process question. Question two allows for a substantive (content) focus. What does he see as the task? Is he doing the task? Question three begins the personal feedback process which, if done gently, becomes a helpful first encounter that leads to personal growth and change.

Now let me speak to the first quadrant on the inside of the circle. You have been discussing both your expectations and your hopes for this course. Right now, I would like to encourage you to focus on what your personal learning goals are to be as they relate to this course. Simply put: What do you want to learn this term in this class? You will have six to eight minutes to discuss this question.

After the six to eight minutes of interaction, ask the observer to work with the observed (in pairs) in order to feed back the information gleaned during the first encounter.

Now, return to the same groups. Do not discuss what your observer told you, but use whatever your observer shared with you as you wish in the next four-minute encounter, as you bring to a close your discussion regarding your personal learning goals.

After four minutes, reverse the roles. Ask quadrant one to observe quadrant two in the same manner as before. Take the time to clarify the assignments.

When this process is completed, have the two quadrants merge into a single group. Suggest:

For the next ten minutes, discuss what you have heard from each other. Using newsprint (or the chalkboard), write down those personal learning goals your group feels are important to everyone in the group. You may have only one, or you may have as many as eight or nine. List them.

Have each group of eight post its list on the wall or board. Together, as a total group, examine all the goals and develop what seem to be the trends, until the group (not by eliminating the personal learning goals, all of which are valid) can highlight some of the more common goals. They should come to some consensus as to what goals the class can bring into focus for the work period that lies immediately ahead.

Having chosen common learning goals and having posted them explicitly, test the group commitment.

Are you ready to dig into this/these area(s) of concern? Discuss together what you expect to contribute to this enterprise and what you expect others to contribute. Be specific.

This discussion can be conducted one to one, or in small groups of eight, or as a total group. It is important that these commitments be stated explicitly somewhere. It would be good to write them down. These commitments are what is known as "contractual arrangement," essential to experiential learning. It is to say, "This I will commit myself to do during this period of time." It is a "buying-in" process that helps the learner to know that the learning to be done is his responsibility, not another's (i.e., teacher's).

In a church setting, this contractual arrangement is often called a "covenant." A covenant agreement generally includes:

1. a contractual agreement between specific persons, in a specific time;

2. an agreement upon objectives;

3. an agreement regarding the frame of reference (beliefs); and

4. an agreement regarding the guidelines (norms) for operation (bylaws).

Any time a new person joins the group, or a member leaves the group, the covenant-contract must be reexamined, and, if necessary, rewritten. Any time the group membership changes, the whole contractual arrangement changes. (This is one reason for every church to rewrite its covenant at the coming of every new minister.)

Now we have the basis for a teaching-learning experience.

There are three primary styles of experiential education: situational, structured, and contrived. Let us examine each style briefly:

Situational

In a very real sense, every experience we have is potential data for learning. Living every day, moving in and out of events and relationships, making and breaking commitments, success and failure, all serve as grist for growth. But most important is to be willing and disciplined enough to stop experiencing long enough to enter the learning process. Again, we are tempted simply to move from one activity to another, without explicit learnings. In every extraordinary situation, and periodically during the routine, someone needs to ask these questions: (1) What happened? (2) What was helpful? What was not helpful? (3) What have we learned that will help us another time?

Structured

Most classroom learning is structured. The classroom may be in the out-of-doors while trekking up Pike's Peak, sightseeing in New York City, or sailing in a sixty-foot ketch across the Gulf Stream from Florida to Bimini. It may be a schoolroom, or the hallway, or the auditorium. It might well be a playing field, or the auditorium stage, or the band rehearsal room. Structured learning can happen in a church school class, in the church council, in a counseling session, or in worship. What the word "structure" implies is not the place, but the deliberate effort of one or more persons to pull learnings from experiences, while, at the same time, he or they may seek to heighten the learning by structuring an added experience. This direction is generally done by the designated, but sanctioned, leader in a given group. But not always. Other leadership can emerge at specific times, be sanctioned by the group, and serve to facilitate significant learning.

What happens? The teacher-learner becomes spontaneously aware of something happening that is not seen directly by either the group or the individual to whom it is happening. In the hope of intensifying the data for instructional purposes, he may use an exercise, such as the action parable.

Contrived

Since 90 percent or more of our teaching forces in public and private schools, in church schools, and in social agencies, tend to develop a teaching style that is contrived ("I must control what *my* pupil is learning"), the experiential learner must be prepared to pull learnings from even these experiences or lose great worlds of knowledge and wisdom. It is amazing, but people can learn under these conditions, not only *in spite* of the teacher, but *because* of the teacher. The real responsibility for learning lies with the learner anyway. To move through a contrived, gimmick-ridden, and controlled "learning" situation *is* an experience. The same questions need to be asked. What happened? What was helpful? What was not helpful? What can I learn (even about teaching) from this experience?

Learning occurs most easily when the learner is conscious of his necessary participation in the process. The joy of this truth is that we can learn from everything; and we can learn the most when:

We are responsible for our own learning;

We learn from our mistakes;

We learn from the mistakes of others;

We make the most out of our present condition.

Experiential education basically requires the development of specific here-and-now skills if a teacher-learner is really going to make it happen.

1. Experiential education encourages a *maximum participation*. First, each learner is responsible for his own learning. Second, each learner is encouraged to get involved since he will learn more by doing than by watching. (This is a serious matter for a learner who has been previously schooled in spectator education.) Third, each learner is helped to discover that the resources he brings to the learning experience are a part of the learning grist. Fourth, all learners are encouraged to build on each other's resources in the hope of finding new learning. Fifth, each learner is respected for who he is rather than for what he knows, freeing him from the congestive anxiety of questioning his self-worth. He knows that when his anxiety level goes up, his learning level goes down.

2. Experiential education encourages *respect for the person*. Contrary to the accusations of those who oppose the small group experiential education process, this style of education develops individuality; it does not deter it. It is a freeing process; supporting the person while he is exploring and discovering for himself new avenues of learning; helping the person to discover his own potential and ways he can develop it; and encouraging experimentation with the right to fail in the hope of growing. Experiential education does not threaten a man's right to be in control of himself, nor his right to control what affects his life. And it guarantees the same rights to others. This respect for the individual is certain only in community, a community where dependence is mature and voluntary.

3. Experiential education *applies the learnings of human development*. The process takes into serious account what the person can be expected to learn or achieve at his particular stage of life. It is fair and yet open to those who can achieve more and to those who, for various reasons, achieve less. The process enables the learner to set his own learning pace and to find his

own primary learning style. (Secondary and tertiary tools do not go undeveloped, but how the learner learns best is understood and fully developed.)

4. Experiential education applies all that we have learned about the *small group process*. The process takes into account not only the level of individual development but the level of group development. Since most of what happens to us happens in relationship to others, an understanding of the small group process helps to achieve a maximum level of learning as well as a maximum level of satisfaction. Successful use of this process requires both a theoretical and an experiential preparation. It also requires an understanding of what strengthens and what blocks group interaction, the roles group participants play, the development of decision-making tools for group life, and ways to develop group cohesion for mutual support and growth.

5. Experiential education leaves room for *shared leadership*. The designated teacher is acknowledged as a learner, too. As participants discover and come to respect their own resources, they are encouraged to use them to facilitate multiple learning in the learning community. No one is encouraged to lead all the time. No one is encouraged to follow all the time. The community moves toward a mutuality that encourages total commitment and a willingness to share.

6. Experiential education is a learning style that permits, indeed, symbolizes, *flexibility*. In a world of rapid change, no one idea becomes *the* idea. No one form holds all the answers. Spontaneity is the key to the learner's development.

7. Experiential education is *personal goal oriented*. It depends on the will of the learner to learn, on his readiness to learn, and on his willingness to apply the learning. The teacher-learner may structure the opportunities for learning but only in the hope of the learner's responding.

8. Experiential education always *deals with living issues*. Even ancient history can be taught with a view for learnings applicable in our lives today. And what other reasons are there for studying it? To pile up knowledge? The teacher-learner teaches relevance, lives relevance, and aims to make the learning relevant for the learner.

Analyzing and Evaluating
Classroom Games

Judith A. Gillespie[1]

People often use games for a variety of different purposes. A child can transform a few blocks into houses, cars, or stick figures and build a community. He can then model the behavior of adults at work and explore community life. Piaget has demonstrated that with a few marbles and fewer rules, children can explore some basic aspects of social interaction. Children rely heavily on imagination to construct their games, yet these games often provide important insights into the real world.

Children, however, seldom develop games about a whole range of serious scholarly topics. Rarely does a child's game explore the reasons for the outbreak of war or the politics of legislative logrolling. Serious games are of a basically different sort. They rely much more on knowledge than on imagination. A serious game is constructed out of a wide range of research and scholarship on a topic. It is based on principles or theories which provide players with explanations of dimensions of human behavior, mathematics, or ecology. These principles or theories constitute the knowledge base for a game.

Building a sound knowledge base for a serious game does not mean that the game need be more complex. Some of the most serious scientific investigations have been based on very simple game-like constructions. With a point, a line, and four rules (postulates) Euclid discovered the basis for geometry as it is taught in schools today. With two symbols, X and Y,

Reprinted from *Social Education*, January 1972, pp. 33-42, 94. Reprinted with permission of the National Council for the Social Studies and Judith A. Gillespie.

[1]Acknowledgments are due to Howard Mehlinger and Allen Glenn of the High School Curriculum Center in Government, Phillip Mow of the History Education Project, Lee Anderson of the American Political Science Association Project, and John Patrick of the World History Project, Indiana University, for major criticism and stimulus of many ideas presented here.

and some basic rules of division, Mendel created the basic knowledge for the science of genetic evolution. Thus serious games, like children's games, can convey a great deal of knowledge from very simple constructions.

Classroom games are a mix between imaginary situations similar to those children so easily and naturally create and serious scientific explorations. They are designed to provide a sound knowledge base for learning and at the same time take advantage of children's imagination. Like the game of marbles and the science of geometry, classroom games are based on simple elements: choice, moves, and rules. The way in which these three elements are put together largely determines what students will learn from playing games and whether they will enjoy them.

The choices, moves, and rules which form the basic structure for games can be evaluated in many ways. The question can be asked: "Are they interesting?" Many games are based on exciting choices such as crisis decisions in national and international politics or decisions about life chances in ghetto situations. Many games also offer interesting moves or activities for players such as controlling large corporations or participating in election campaigns. However, most teachers would not be satisfied with a game that only offered students "involvement" and excitement.

A second question can be asked: "Is the game workable in a classroom situation?" Many games structure choices and activities for a classroom environment. Fewer of these games are accompanied by clear instructions and a manageable number of materials. However, again few teachers would be satisfied with a game that was merely "workable."

Most teachers expect a game to serve some instructional purpose so that students can learn something useful and important from playing. The first two questions are important for the teacher, yet without some reasonable answer to the question, "Does the game have a sound knowledge base?" he has relatively little assurance that the game can effectively contribute to student learning. Very few games actually make this kind of contribution. The choices available to students can be unclear, the activities unstructured, and the rules inconsistent. Often the game is so complex that students cannot determine major influences on their behavior. Because games are subject to these weaknesses, the teacher needs a means for analyzing and evaluating classroom games that will give him reasonable assurance that a game will make a sound contribution to student learning.

Accordingly, choices, moves, and rules will be analyzed here in terms of the knowledge base they create for learning. Six questions through which the teacher can identify the knowledge base of the game are posed. (1) What is the central problem presented in the game? (2) What choices are available to players? (3) What are the different moves or activities provided for players? (4) What are the rules for the game? (5) How is the game organized? and (6) What summary activities conclude the game? Criteria will be developed for each question in order to enable the teacher to distinguish sound from dysfunctional answers. For each question and criterion, various practical applications to games will serve as illustrations. In this way the teacher will be provided with a means for choosing among available games those that have the maximum potential for classroom learning.

QUESTIONS AND CRITERIA: AN OVERVIEW

In a sense, games form a type of snapshot picture of some feature of human behavior. They cannot give a complete view of everything included in a life situation, but they can picture a small fragment accurately. The accuracy of the picture is determined by the whole image that it projects. Just as someone would not judge a snapshot's quality totally by the facial expression of a person photographed, a teacher cannot judge a game by looking only at one component.

Therefore, the six questions about the game are not much help to the teacher singly, but together they provide an accurate picture of the knowledge base of a game. A knowledge base is built upon a problem statement (Question #1). From that statement the essential concepts and principles are transformed into choices, moves, and rules in game play (Questions #2-4). The choices and moves are organized in a way that effectively or ineffectively guides players to learn about the basic concepts and principles (Question #5). The summary activities of a game determine whether or not the game can achieve its purpose in the final outcome (Question #6). Therefore, each question is tied to an important part of the knowledge base of a game. Figure 1 demonstrates this relationship as follows:

Questions	Parts of a Game
1. What is the central problem presented in the game?	Problem
2. What choices are available to players?	Choices
3. What are the different moves or activities provided for players?	Moves
4. What are the rules for the game?	Rules
5. How is the game organized?	Organizations
6. What summary activities conclude the game?	Conclusion

**Figure 1. The Relationship Between Questions
and Parts of a Game**

If the questions are taken together, they provide the teacher with a means for identifying the key aspects of the game as a whole.

Once the teacher has identified significant parts of the game, he needs to have on hand some useful criteria for evaluation. The criteria should serve two purposes for the teacher: (1) they should enable him to distinguish sound from dysfunctional parts of a game, and (2) they should promote a judgment of the total acceptability of the game. In order to accomplish these purposes, criteria need to be developed for each part of the game and for the relationships between parts.

Three criteria are developed for evaluation of the central problem of a game: clarity, conceptual content, and utility. Since the problem is the cornerstone on which the remainder of the game is based, a clear, conceptually rich problem statement will ensure that the game is more than a collection of activities without a sound foundation in key concepts and principles. A problem statement which gives direction about the use which will be made of the game ensures that the concepts and principles will serve a purpose, such as developing a skill or knowledge, which fits the teacher's objectives. If the problem statement meets these criteria, the teacher will have maximum assurance that the game is based on an insightful view of a real-world problem situation and that it can be useful in his classroom.

The choices, moves, and rules that are developed from the problem statement can be evaluated according to the criteria of soundness, consistency, and lack of distortion. To be sound, choices must be carefully grounded in the problem statement of a game. The activities or moves need to present an ordered, consistent sequence of behavior as the result of meaningful decisions. In addition, the rules of the game need to provide undistorted guidelines for behavior which lead players to make sound decisions and act consistently. If the components meet these three criteria, the teacher can make a well-reasoned decision about what students will learn from participating in game play.

The effectiveness of the way activities are organized in the game can be determined by two criteria: Inclusiveness and sequencing. If the players are organized such that only a certain group makes the essential choices in the game, then very few students will really be exposed to the "learning by doing" payoffs of the game. If the activities are sequenced such that students do not have time or opportunity to consider the major learning aspects of the game, then the teacher has very little assurance that the students will learn from game play. Accordingly, the inclusiveness and sequencing criteria give the teacher a basis for judging whether students have adequate opportunity to learn through participation in the game.

Summary activities are designed to bring out what students have learned during game play. The summary needs to be adequately related to the problem statement and the activities in the game as well as to provide some application lesson for students. If the game does not provide adequate summary or application activities, the teacher cannot be assured that the final outcomes of the game will be learning outcomes for students.

The relationship between questions and criteria can be summarized, as follows:

Questions	Parts of a Game	Criteria
1. What is the central problem presented in the game?	Problem	Clarity Conceptual content Utility Relationship to real world
2. What choices are available to players?	Choices	Soundness
3. What are the different moves or activities provided for players?	Moves	Consistency
4. What are the rules for the game?	Rules	Lack of distortion ------------------ Relationship to problem
5. How is the game organized?	Organization	Inclusiveness Sequencing Relationship to choices, moves, rules
6. What summary activities conclude the game?	Conclusion	Adequacy Applicability Relationship to problem Relationship to activities

Figure 2. Questions and Criteria

The figure demonstrates how the knowledge base of the game can be evaluated by this set of criteria. The criteria determine the quality of each component of the game and the relationship between components. In this way the questions and criteria provide the teacher with a means of determining the soundness of the picture of the world that the game creates.

In order to demonstrate how the questions and criteria can be practically applied, several concrete examples of games will be developed. One game in particular will be introduced in order to serve as a concrete example of some sound ways in which an ideal game fits the criteria. The game in finished form would contain a full range of kaleidoscopic materials that a normal game does. It is a simulation about voting behavior in which students take on roles of voters and candidates, attend rallies and run a newspaper, and vote on election day. There are ballots and public opinion polls, money exchanges, and radio broadcasts. In short, the game is typical of simulations of its kind, complex and full of activity. The game can be outlined briefly as follows:

Problem:	On what basis do people decide to vote?
Objectives:	1. Students can determine a general relationship between party identification and voting behavior.
	2. Students can determine how issue position and candidate appeal influence voters in making decisions about voting.
	3. Students can determine the conditions under which a voter switches parties in voting.
Game Play:	Students act out roles as voters, group leaders, candidates.
	Students participate in party meetings, group bargaining sessions, campaign rallies, and voting.
	Students make choices among party loyalties, issue positions, and candidate appeals.
Game Rules:	E.g., students cannot base their vote totally upon one factor in the election if it conflicts with traditional party loyalty.
Organizations:	Number of players can range from 4-48. Total time is 4-5 class periods.
Summary Activities:	Students answer questions about the relationship between party identification, issue position, and candidate appeal.
	Students apply their findings to the most recent U.S. election.

The essential parts of the ideal game are developed in this outline. Other games of various kinds will serve as counter examples in order to illustrate how the criteria discriminate between less well-developed games. Taking both the ideal game and the counter examples into consideration, the usefulness of the questions and criteria posed earlier can be demonstrated through practical examples.

Question #1: What is the central problem presented in the game?

To begin to answer this question, the teacher needs to surface a problem statement from a game. He does this by examining the background information and the educational objectives stated in the teacher's guide, and advertisement, or information from another teacher. Problem statements are not usually developed in the form, "the problem of the game is . . . ," but by reading the background information and objectives the teacher should be able to learn what the central problems of the game are. He then begins to apply this criteria of clarity, conceptual content, and utility to the background information and objectives.

The clarity of a problem statement is important to the teacher's evaluation of a game. Suppose that the teacher is giving a course in American Government which covers the topic of voting behavior. He desires to determine whether the hypothetical game on voting behavior introduced previously will serve his purposes. If he finds in the general description of the game a statement such as, "the purpose of the game is to study about voting," he would know very little about the content or use of the game. The problem is too vague. It does not indicate the kind of voting (legislative, electoral) or the nature of the study (voting procedures, voting decisions).

A clearly-defined problem statement gives the teacher a great deal of information about a game. For example, a game that is based on voting behavior can have several kinds of well-defined problem statements. One problem statement could take the form: What is the process through which people vote in national elections? The problem statement indicates that the game will be utilized to develop a skill: how to vote in elections. The major concepts will include registration, primaries, and balloting. A second problem statement could take the form of the ideal voting game outlined previously: On what basis do people decide to vote in national elections? This problem statement indicates that the game will be utilized to present a body of knowledge—what is involved in a citizen's decision to vote. The game will center around such concepts as party identification, issue salience, and candidate appeal. Thus a problem statement conveys to the teacher both the essential conceptual content and the use that can be made of the game.

If the problem statement is accompanied by a set of educational objectives, the teacher can be more certain of his evaluation of content and utility. Again, with a voting game, a set of objectives might be constructed as follows:

1. Students can participate in a simulated election campaign.

2. Students can learn how to conduct rallies, campaign for candidates, and vote.

3. Students can learn about role behavior of voters and candidates. These objectives tell the teacher very little about the substantive content

or use of the game. He knows that students are going to enter into activities, but he has no way of determining what they will achieve in terms of learning in the game.

A set of objectives which will give the teacher insight into what the game is about and how it can be used might be presented as follows:

1. Students can determine a general relationship between party identification and voting behavior.

2. Students can determine how issue position and candidate appeal influence voters in making decisions about voting.

3. Students can determine the conditions under which a voter switches parties in voting.

These objectives outline the major concepts of party identification, issue position, and candidate appeal. The use of these concepts in the game is also clear. Students will be encouraged to learn about a body of knowledge focusing on voting behavior, not how to vote or who are the candidates in the most recent campaign.

From a clear problem surfaced by analysis of the introduction and educational objectives, the teacher can evaluate whether a game is realistic and useful for the classroom. The degree of realism in a game is determined by a comparison of the problem statement with what is known about the real-world situation. Suppose that the teacher is evaluating a game about international conflict and the essential concepts are war and trade relations. The teacher could easily see that a game on international conflict needed to include the concept of negotiation or diplomacy in order to accurately represent an inter-nation conflict situation. Otherwise the militaristic and economic aspects of conflict are overemphasized. The purpose of the game is not realistic according to the teacher's evaluation because it does not accurately represent the real-world problem situation. A game will never include *all* the necessary concepts to completely identify a real-world situation, but a teacher must be sure that it contains the essential ones. Otherwise students learn an exaggerated or wrong image of the problem situation.

In contrast, the voting game which has as its essential concepts party identification, issue position, and candidate appeal does represent accurately a real-world situation. There are many concepts which are omitted such as media influence or status, but the game does not distort the students' perceptions of the real-world voting situation. According to what is known about voter behavior, the three concepts represent the major forces generally influencing voting decisions.

The teacher can also begin to evaluate the utility of a game based on a clear problem statement. If the teacher wanted to teach students about the basis for citizens' decisions to vote, then the ideal voting game would serve his objectives. However, if the teacher wanted to teach students the process of voting, e.g., how to register, then the game would not serve his purpose. If the game did not state clearly the purpose for which it would be used, then the teacher would be at a loss to determine what the game intended to teach.

Thus the problem statement determined by background information and educational objectives validates the purpose of the game for a teacher. Having made initial judgments about clarity, conceptual content, and utility of the game, the teacher can be sure that the game is fundamentally sound and useful in his classroom. To the extent that the problem statement fails to meet these criteria, the teacher gambles on whether the game accurately represents what he wants students to learn and whether the game will serve the purpose he intends for his class.

Question #2: What choices are available to players?

It is impossible to determine all possible choices that a player could make in even a relatively simple game. In the case of Tic-Tac-Toe, for example, players face 15,120 possible choices of moves by the fifth turn.[2] However, it is relatively easy to determine what *types* of major moves a game contains. For example, in Tic-Tac-Toe, a player makes only two types of choices for any of his 15,120 possible: he can attempt to make 3 X's in a row, or he can block his opponent from making 3 O's in a row. The types of choices, then, will give the teacher a basis for determining the decisional base for the game.

For any given game, the teacher determines the choices that are made by analyzing the major points in the game which change player behavior. In a board game, the teacher looks at how game play is presented and pulls out the major (at most a half-dozen) situations in which players make different types of decisions. It can be a new level the player attains or a new resource he has obtained from a previous turn. In the case of Tic-Tac-Toe there is one type of decision with two alternatives for choice. However, in the case of *Monopoly* there are two types of decisions, one to buy new property or risk paying rent to an opponent on the next round and another to add to holdings after the player "owns" a square. In a simulation, the teacher can just as easily determine the major choices by examining individual roles and group activities. In the voting game, for example, the major activities are party meetings, group meetings, rallies, and voting. By examining these activities, the teacher can determine that party meetings are organized around a decision about party loyalty, group meetings are

---

[2]The case of Tic-Tac-Toe and more general information about the increases in complexity of decision trees as numbers of players and choices increase can be found in Anatol Rapoport's *N-Person Game Theory: Concepts and Applications.* Ann Arbor: University of Michigan Press, 1970, p. 57. His book *Two-Person Game Theory: The Essential Ideas,* Ann Arbor: University of Michigan Press, 1966, provides an excellent discussion of the basic ideas in game theory.

designed to promote given interests on issues, and rallies focus on candidate appeal. Thus the major types of choices in the game are of these kinds.

Once these types of choices are outlined, the teacher can determine whether the choices are sound. The "soundness" of choices is determined by comparing the problem statement and the major choices in the game. Essentially, the choices should capture the full range of each of the major concepts in the game. For example, a game concerned with ghetto poverty whose major concepts include housing quality, educational disadvantages, and lack of semi-skilled job opportunities would not offer "sound" choices if players' moves in the game were determined totally by increases in employment opportunities or, worse yet, totally by chance. Even though the problem statement was clear and rich in conceptual content, the choices would be unsound because players would never be faced with situations involving the essential concepts of the game.

The voting game can serve as an example of a series of sound choices. Corresponding to each major concept—party identification, issue position, candidate appeal—there is an activity in which players participate —party meetings, group bargaining sessions, rallies. In each activity, players make a choice about one or more of the concepts such as whether to remain loyal to a traditional party or switch. The choices are simplified, but accurate representations of the voting problem posed by the game. One choice is not emphasized out of porportion to others, nor is any major concept in the problem omitted.

In general, then, the teacher identifies the choices in a game by analyzing the major decision situations in the game—turns or activities—and determining the different *types* of choices involved. He then evaluates these choices based on a comparison between the concepts delineated in the problem statement, seeking to determine whether or not the alternatives offered in the game adequately involve these concepts. This is an important determination of the soundness of the knowledge base for a game, for it tells the teacher that students will be involved in making decisions which accurately represent all dimensions of a problem statement.

Question #3: What are the different moves or activities provided for players?

When an outside observer looks through the classroom door at a game, his immediate reaction is often "What chaos!" He may see students dispersed around the room participating in seemingly unrelated activities. He may also see students in groups moving pieces on a board in what seems to be mere entertainment. Actually, in a well-constructed game these apparently unrelated activities are all parts of some important game strategy.

The basic strategies in a game are most easily determined after the essential choices have been examined. Once the teacher has identified the *types* of choices in a game, he then determines which choices precede others. For example, in *Monopoly* the decision to own a square occurs before the decision to add to holdings. He then proceeds to link choices together by examining alternative sets of choices. For example, if a player chooses to own a square in *Monopoly,* his next choice can be to add houses. If a player chooses not to own one square, his next choice may be to own another square. As the players move from their first to their second choices, they progress toward an outcome. Outcomes can be defined as winning or losing, as well as achievement of a particular kind of goal which is not measured directly as a "win" or a "loss." A set of choices, moves, and outcomes determines a strategy.

The voting game can serve as an example of analyzing choices and moves. The major choices in the game concern party identification, issue position, and candidate appeal. The sequence of choices is determined by the order of activities: First, students attend party meetings to make some choice about party identification. Second, students attend interest group meetings to argue issues. Third, students attend campaign rallies to make a decision on candidate appeal. The situation is considerably simplified, yet an accurate way of representing real-world choices. The alternatives of each choice are Democrat or Republican. Having identified the major choices and their sequence, the teacher would then determine which set of choices led to "winning" outcomes and which led to "losing" outcomes. He would then have generally identified each of the important strategies or sets of moves in the game.

Once the teacher has identified the major strategies in the game by analyzing the sequencing of choices and the outcomes, he can begin to evaluate the degree of consistency in each strategy. The teacher primarily wants to make sure that winning strategies do not involve inconsistent choices or moves and that one losing strategy is not emphasized over a winning one.

The import of this type of evaluation cannot be underestimated. The teacher uses a game and the students play it in order to learn something about the central problem of the game. If players are forced to make inconsistent moves in order to win, they will not learn from their behavior in the game. If they are forced to lose because that strategy is most available, they will not profit in the gaming situation from "learning by doing."

Therefore, "consistency" is determined by judging whether the major strategies in the game involve contradictory choices or moves. For example, in an economic game concerning money expenditures, winning could be defined as making the most money. The choices involved in a "winning" strategy might include both stock market speculation and investment. If a player had to invest to win the game and every time he invested he was driven into bankruptcy, then the player would lose by a winning strategy— an outcome from which he would learn very little. However, in the voting game, party identification is the strongest factor determining the vote. To win by voting against his traditional party loyalty, a player must have a very strong vested interest in issues and candidates of the opposite party. Therefore, if a player decided to vote Democratic based on a Republican party identification and a weak issue position, he would lose and thereby understand the import of party identification.

Consistency, then, is a fundamental requirement for the strategies in any game. If the teacher is unable to identify the major strategies and evaluate their consistency from a review of the gaming materials, he can be sure that the knowledge base of the game is not well-developed. The strategies in the games are key to the learning experience a game provides. The degree to which a game meets the consistency criterion determines to a large extent whether the game involves learning which is both sound and rational.

Question #4: What are the rules for the game?

Rules function in games much as they do in any other context. The largest deviation in the gaming situation is that one significant rule in the game is often the operation of chance. Rules of chance can determine everything from who goes first to which strategies are followed by players. Any rule, chance or otherwise, is used in a game to set limits on the choices and moves available to players. They are also often used to direct players to winning outcomes. The central evaluation question for the teacher is whether or not the limits set by rules distort the gaming situation.

It's very easy to determine the rules in a game; most are listed in the gaming material. However, it is more difficult to determine the effect of a particular rule on game play. They are often many in number, highly inter-related, and only implicit in game play. A rule of thumb for the teacher is to look first at the major mechanism which begins the first few turns of play—dice, rotation, and simulated conflict—then to turn to these rules which guide the major strategies, and finally to look at the termination rule or how the game ends.[3]

The major criterion guiding the evaluation of rules is lack of distortion. Distortion commonly occurs when a rule overemphasizes a losing strategy. For example, if an international relations game focuses on conflict, the key choices could involve the concepts of war, negotiation, disarmament, and economic security. Rules which made it very easy to go to war

---

[3]Rules can also serve many other functions in games. For a good general discussion of the various functions of rules in games, see the chapter by James S. Ademan, "Social Processes and Social Simulation Games," in Sarane S. Boocock and E. O. Schild (Eds.), *Simulation Games in Learning.* Beverly Hills, Calif.: Sage Publications, 1968, pp. 29-51.

and extremely difficult to negotiate would distort the major strategies of the game out of proportion to the problem situation. Rules must, however, be evaluated in totality, for if the rule which facilitated war was balanced by a rule promoting negotiation, the game would not sacrifice one strategy for another.

An example of misusing the rule of chance is an electoral college game. The problem of the game is to determine how candidates gain electoral votes. The major concept is votes per state, and the major rule for determining states won is the correct answers to random questions about the three branches of government. In this case chance can be effectively used as a rule for determining which questions students must answer, but unfortunately chance also determines which *states* are gained by candidates. In this way, the Democrats can sweep the Midwest and the Republicans the South without any problem. Thus, the chance rule completely distorts the strategic aspects of election campaigning.

Rules are used effectively when they do not distort strategies or outcomes. In the voting game, for example, one of the rules listed is that voters cannot vote based on candidate appeal alone if the candidate conflicts with both a strong traditional party loyalty and a strong opposing issue position. This limits the choices of voters, but it does not distort the major strategy in the game—to find the most consistent base for voting in an election. Used effectively, rules can aid players in achieving winning outcomes and limit the complexity of the game so that students have a better chance of learning from their moves.

If the choices, moves, and rules of a game are sound, the teacher needs to make one final evaluation. He needs to compare these components as a whole to the problem statement in order to make sure that the major strategies and outcomes of the game are consistent with the problem situation. To do this the teacher evaluates the strategies in terms of the degree to which they promote explanations of the problem situation. If a winning strategy maximizes the problem situation and a losing strategy minimizes it, the two parts are consistent.

For example, the winning strategy in the voting game is to vote based on a consistent party identification, issue position, and candidate appeal. In the real-world voting situation in national U.S. elections this is a maximum position for any citizen. As the contradiction in these variables increases, the citizen is less and less likely to vote at all, much less have a rational decisional base for voting. However, if the voting game were to attribute a winning situation to abstention when the three variables consistently favored voting for one party, the game would not accurately represent the problem of voting for most citizens.

Question #5: How is the game organized?

There are two organizational dimensions of a game that are particularly important for evaluation: the organization of players and the organization of activities. The organization of players determines *who* participates in any given activity in a game. The organization of activities determines *how* players participate.

The organization of players can most often be identified by the initial breakdown into groups of a board game and role descriptions in a simulation. The organization of activities is classified by the moves in a board game and the group interactions scheduled in the day-by-day activities of a simulation. Once the teacher has identified these elements, he can begin to evaluate them according to the criteria of inclusiveness, sequencing, and relationship to the choices, moves, and rules in the game.

The organization of players is important to the success of a game in two respects. First, choices change considerably as the number of players in the game varies. Choices made by teams require organization that choices of individual players do not. For example, in the case of a board game with partners, the increase from four to six players can change the moves in the game from straight competition to coalition formation. The problem for the teacher is to determine whether or not the types of choices remain the same over different class sizes. He can apply the criterion of inclusiveness by first determining the least number of players that can possibly play the game, then the highest number of players that can possibly play the game, and finally the number that will be participating in his class. If, for example, the voting game is constructed for 35 players and the teacher has a class of 20, the teacher should determine whether or not the outcomes of the game are the same. If he eliminates 15 Democrats, can the Democrats win the election? If he eliminates 10 Republicans, will the Republican party meeting have any meaning?

The organization of players is equally important in a second respect. The teacher not only wants the choices to remain the same over a wide range of players, but he wants some assurance that *each* player has the opportunity to make choices about the essential concepts of the game. If games are based on strategies and students learn by making strategic choices, each student needs to have the opportunity to choose for the game to be effective. This does not mean that every student must participate in the *same activity* but rather for any given set of activities in a game, each student must have the opportunity to make the *same choices*. In a great many simulations, many students play "minor" roles. The teacher needs to be sure that even a minor role includes the basic choices in a game.

The logical organization of activity is as important to a game as it is to any learning experience. The phasing of activities can be crucial to the success of the game. If the activity rests on some information that the students have developed in a previous part of the game, it must be sequenced so that the information is provided. If the activity needs to be organized in a specific way to highlight the choices of players, then that organization needs to be specified. The logic of choices should be clear in the staging of the game. In a voting game, for example, where players must make choices between party loyalty and issue positions which contradict the party platform, the loyalty must be developed in a set of choices prior to the issue choices. Otherwise, the choice between party and issues is meaningless because the player has not had adequate opportunity to develop a party loyalty.

Thus the criteria of inclusiveness of all players in essential choices and sequencing of activities are of prime importance to the final learning outcome of a game. In a large part, these two criteria determine whether or not a game can maintain its momentum as an effective learning experience throughout game play. In the final evaluation the organizational parts of the game need to be compared to the choices, moves, and rules which form the knowledge base. The game should be organized so that students can give careful consideration to the major strategies in the game.

Question #6: What summary activities conclude the game?

Summary sessions can occur in many forms. Students may be asked a series of questions, organized into discussion groups, or asked to analyze data that they have created in the course of the gaming experience. Whatever form the session takes, it needs to encompass two different summary tasks: (1) summarization and analysis of what is learned, and (2) application of what is learned. Both components are crucial to the game.

The debriefing session is centered around the central ideas of the game. In a sense, the debriefing session represents a "mini" game in and of itself: a recreation of the fundamental structure of the gaming situation. In addition, the session often uses applications such as case studies, suggestions for exploration of reading material, or the student's own experience to draw out and reapply the information learned. Without the application knowledge, the teacher has very little assurance that the learning from the game has any carry-over to other contexts.

The teacher will normally find debriefing outlined in a series of summary questions following a game. The central evaluation question becomes: Does the debriefing session offer an adequate summary and application lesson for the game? The adequacy of the summary provided in debriefing can be most effectively demonstrated by pairing the educational objectives stated in the teacher's guide and the questions provided for debriefing. Ideally, the basic concepts and relationships in the objectives are linked directly into the questions. The degree to which this is true determines to a large extent whether or not the game has the capacity to accomplish its objectives.

One example of an inadequate debriefing tactic employed by a great many simulation designers is to concentrate debriefing questions on an evaluation of the simulation *per se* rather than its conceptual content. The problem is that the objectives of a classroom simulation are not to create a better simulation, but to teach students something about the substance of the problem that the game poses. Substantive questions can be reached indirectly by this method, but it demands a great deal of outside knowledge on the part of students both about the problem and about the development of a game.

A second typical case of an inadequate debriefing structure is a series of questions which focus on the particular moves or choices in the game without an attempt to generalize beyond the player's participation. Students often find it hard to go beyond a particular play through which they "won" the game or one which cost them a winning outcome. However, the objectives for any game extend beyond the particular situation it represents, and the debriefing questions should provide a linkage between the general problem situation and the particular plays in a game.

Ideally, then, a set of debriefing questions could be paired with the objectives in the voting game as follows:

Objectives	*Debriefing Questions*
1. Students can determine a general relationship between party identification and voting behavior.	1. What was the most important factor influencing your decision to vote?
2. Students can determine how issue position and candidate appeal influenced voters in making decisions about voting.	2. What other major factors influenced your vote?
3. Students can determine the conditions under which a voter switches parties in voting.	3. What made some players switch from their traditional parties in this election?

Each objective is matched by a debriefing question which focuses upon the decisions made by each player in the game. The students are then asked to draw generalizations which extend beyond the gaming situation to national elections.

The application component of debriefing often appears in the form of a case study from a very different problem situation. An abstract or a concrete problem can be presented for students to solve. At times, students may be asked to construct their own case, or even their own game, in order to demonstrate knowledge of the game in another context. Either way, the application situation should offer a roughly analogous case to the game. It should contain most of the central concepts used in the game, with some variation. The analogous concepts give the student a basis for determining similarities between the gaming situation and other situations. The different concepts allow the students to contrast the gaming situation with others. The essentially comparative nature of the application material, then, provides the student with a way of transferring his knowledge to another situation in which he can make useful distinctions between the way behavior is the same and varies in different situations.

Thus debriefing becomes a key element in the evaluation of a game, for it is only through the summary questions and applications that the teacher can determine whether the game has the potential to reach its objectives. The problem statement can be clear and conceptually rich; the choices, moves, and rules can reflect the problem accurately; and the organization can provide an effective dynamic for the game; yet without some means of linking the gaming situation to learning outcomes, the teacher has no way to be sure and the knowledge base is effectively transmitted to student players.

CONCLUSION

Each of the six questions has contributed to the identification of an important part of the knowledge base of any game. Through these questions the teacher can determine the central problem on which the game is built, the choices, moves, and rules which provide a transformation of the problem into a gaming situation, the organization which maintains the dynamic of the game, and the summary activities which determine whether its objectives are achieved. The analysis of these component parts and how they interrelate has led to an evaluation of a game as a whole.

The criteria developed here for evaluation are not inclusive. The game may fail as a learning experience for an entire set of reasons which the criteria do not tap. The teacher may not organize the gaming environment well. The students may not understand the game. The instructions may not be clear when the teacher enters the actual playing situation. However, the questions and criteria do give the teacher one major assurance: the game has the *capacity* to teach students a great deal.

Only a rare game will completely and positively demonstrate this capacity to its fullest extent. The criteria are by no means developed for an all or nothing, use or not use, evaluation of a game. Most games, like most students, will fall somewhere in between maximum capacity and failure. The teacher remains the judge of whether the game fails so desperately on one criterion that it should not be used in his classroom. However, if the game or game description does not give the teacher enough information to identify and minimally evaluate its major components, then the teacher is incurring a decided risk using any game.

The avoidance of the risk is important because games can misteach much more easily than they can effectively contribute to learning. The development of classroom games is still in its infancy and a great many reflect the growing pains of unsound if not dysfunctional attempts at producing a finished product which is useful in the classroom. The teacher needs to view games as an intelligent consumer would view a product and pay a great deal of heed to the economic caveat "Let the buyer beware." The questions and criteria represent an attempt to facilitate well-reasoned consumption of classroom games on the part of teachers by focusing on the primary concern which motivates their choice: the capacity for a game to provide a sound and interesting learning experience for students.

Helpful Hints for Your High School's Alternative Program

Ralph T. Nelson

The ESEA Title III FOCUS Project is an alternative program operating at Madison High School in Portland, Oregon. FOCUS serves a population of one hundred students, all with previously identified school achievement and/or adjustment problems. Funded jointly by Title III and the Portland Public Schools, FOCUS became operational in the fall of 1971. The general goals of the program are to:

1. Increase student participation in school activities and decrease the incidence of school absence;

2. Improve student self-concept by providing an instructional program built around student inputs and stressing success experiences and positive feedback;

3. Demonstrate to the educational community that an alternative program can function effectively within the overall structure of a more traditional high school program.

Two year evaluation results indicate that most of the project's specific goals—the majority of which are affective in nature—are being accomplished. On the basis of evaluation data and day-to-day experience, it has been possible for the project staff to assist personnel from several other schools in their efforts to develop similar alternative models.

HELPFUL CONSIDERATIONS

Many details of operating an alternative school project will, naturally, vary from one school setting to another. There are, nevertheless, several gen-

Reprinted from *Educational Leadership* 31(8):716-21; May 1974, by permission of the Association for Supervision and Curriculum Development and Ralph T. Nelsen. Copyright © 1974 by the Association for Supervision and Curriculum Development.

eral considerations pertinent to "transportability" of the FOCUS model which should be helpful to others planning, developing, or operating a similar program. For simplicity, these will be discussed under two headings, "Do's" and "Don't's."

Do's

1. Solicit faculty, parent, and community interest and support for your project early in the planning and development stages. Continue this involvement throughout the life of the project. Perhaps the best method of doing this is to request key persons in the school and community to serve on an Advisory Committee and have them monitor the project regularly.

2. Keep a steady flow of information regarding the project and its goals, procedures, problems, and accomplishments moving toward both school and general audiences. The more familiar the project is, the better its chances of being understood, supported, and extended.

3. Codify all operational procedures which are followed in the project: for example, purchasing, student selection, attendance, and curriculum development. Change is possible only when current conditions are easily identified. Formative feedback can be used only when staff and evaluators know what is happening. For example, an attendance system may prove to be unsatisfactory and revisions can proceed more easily if the staff has a document which identifies each element of the faulty method.

4. Involve the school administration in project activities whenever possible. The school principal will certainly be more at ease with too much information than with not enough information. In addition to being a professional obligation, keeping your administration well informed as to what is happening is just good politics. Remember, it is hard for the principal to defend your "space" if he does not have the data about what you are doing.

5. Involve the other members of your school faculty. There is no way that your project staff, no matter how large or talented, can provide all the resources students will need if they are really encouraged to pursue their learning interests and needs. The cooperation of your colleagues is necessary when you want to send them a student for short-term work in a special area or when you want to borrow a room in order to provide an extra class in the project's daily schedule. Also, your faculty colleagues can provide your project with a tremendous volume of information regarding supplementary materials and services which you can obtain to use with students in the project.

6. Keep a close record on all project expenditures. We would recommend maintaining a second ledger book within the project, if only to keep a rough estimate of what money has been spent and what remains for the

balance of the school year. It is also helpful, from a management point of view, to require everyone to make a written request for purchase authorization, listing items to be purchased, approximate cost, model numbers, and, very important, recommended suppliers. These requests should also indicate the relationship of each item to be purchased with the prestated goals and materials of the class for which it is needed.

7. Allow all members of the teaching team to participate in the decision-making process. There will be, of course, occasions when there is no room for "negotiation" and a unilateral decision must be made by the principal or project director. However, most project decisions can be made cooperatively and it is the experience of the FOCUS staff that the support and involvement of teachers and students on any issue increase in direct relation to the proprietary feelings they have toward the solutions and procedures eventually followed in dealing with that issue.

8. Keep files of interesting pictures, articles, gadgets, etc., which may someday be useful to students. When the curriculum is open, based primarily on the interests and concerns of students, the demand for new materials is tremendous and previously stored materials can be extremely valuable.

9. Utilize student and parent inputs when planning daily, weekly, and monthly class schedules. Problems current in many high school classrooms never occur when students feel they own a share of the action.

10. Encourage students to take part in school activities, sports, drama, music, etc. A primary objective of any FOCUS-type program should be the involvement of students in new activities which allow them to observe, meet, and relate to peers in a variety of settings.

11. Encourage students within your project to plan and present at least one "service" activity for the entire school. This may be an all-school dance, play, variety show, or lunch hour motion picture series.

12. Utilize the resources of the entire community when planning learning activities. A truly magnificent variety of skilled resource persons, interesting places to visit, and "turn on" things to do is available within most urban communities. Also, bring outside people into the classroom as resource speakers, teachers, and consultants. People like to feel valuable and will go to extreme lengths to do something for students when they believe their contributions are appreciated and valued.

13. Maintain an up-to-date list of all visitors to the project and keep them informed of what is happening. (This is a good project for students, particularly those who enjoy writing and dealing with "the public.")

14. Try to keep a feeling of "family" among students and staff members. The project is theirs and they must be encouraged to maintain a strong esprit de corps. This pride will eventually carry over to other areas, particularly feelings of positive identity with the school in general and the community.

15. Keep project rules and regulations at a minimum. A project goal should be to have students learn to proscribe their own behaviors. This is not to say that an "anything goes" attitude should be fostered, but it should be obvious that students do not learn to be thoughtful, independent citizens by being told what to do, when to do it, and how to do it. In short, allow students to make errors and do dumb things—then help them analyze their behavior and recognize that they must live with the natural consequences of their actions.

16. Appoint one member of the team, not necessarily the director, to serve as "resident grantsman." This person should keep on the alert for new sources of financial support. The same type of monitoring should be done in other specialized areas—instructional materials, community services and resources, volunteer personnel, and important professional writings. Try to keep these secondary appointments within the range of the individual's normal interests and activities.

17. Share the goodies. When one member of the team comes up with something that works with a class or an individual student, it should be shared with other staff members. Nurture of the "we" is critical. (It is also a good idea to share new ideas and materials with colleagues on the regular staff of the school.)

18. Acknowledge the contributions of everyone. Students and team members appreciate the support, it may be the only positive feedback they receive during the course of a given day. Additionally, make it a must to acknowledge the assistance given by personnel outside of the project. As has been stated, make people know that their efforts on your behalf are important and valued.

19. Adopt a philosophy which says, in effect, "teachers shouldn't do anything that a student can do." There are limitations, of course, but it is amazing how many things teachers do each day that can be done as well (or better) by students. For example, FOCUS has discovered that students make excellent teachers of other students, that students generally handle sophisticated mediaware better than teachers, that students can "scrounge" materials very nicely, and that students can deliver some very "straight" messages regarding project procedures and practices. One hundred students create a resource bank much too valuable to be ignored.

20. Maintain close contact with the homes of students. Calls on attendance are effective when carried on in a constructive manner. ("Is John sick? We wonder if there is anything we might be able to do.") Similarly, casual contacts, in person or by phone, with parents are effective when approached from a "Let's chat" point-of-view. ("I've been wondering if there is anything you would like brought up at the next parent meeting," or "Have you any observations which might help us make FOCUS a better place for your child?") School becomes a more creditable place in the eyes of parents if they are approached as people with ideas and resources which are valued by the school.

Don't's

1. Avoid selecting staff personnel on the basis of academic credentials alone. Seek out teachers with a variety of interests and skills. A teacher's knowledge of local archeology or his ability to fly an airplane can be more beneficial to a student than his understanding of the principal causes of World War I.

2. Resist all efforts to removed your special project from the school. It may sound great to be offered your own facility, a place where you can operate apart from the constraints of the regular school program. However, it is no service to students when they are isolated and made to feel, again, that they don't fit in with the "others." On the contrary, every effort should be made to integrate the project's population with the general school student body.

Students should be allowed to pursue their own interests and concerns, but they must also become aware that they do live in a larger society and that the society requires some accommodation skills of its members. In a word, "displacement" should be avoided. Don't let your students get shuffled off where they can't be seen and where they can do their annoying things without bothering anyone. Keep them visible and help them to learn the skills that will allow them to enter into viable, productive relationships with the people around them. This *can't* be done if your program is split apart from the mainstream of the school.

3. Never foster the concept of "elitism." Students and staff members must avoid the natural temptation to "overdo" themselves and your project and, by implication, "put down" the other students and programs in the school. Any impact your program makes by way of being a "change agent" in your school must accrue from example rather than from constant reminders to others that they must change. (You may have a good thing going, but don't be ostentatious.)

4. Avoid acting on the spur of the moment in implementing program changes. What you are doing is probably the result of experience or preliminary planning. While changes are always necessary if your program is to be vital, revisions in procedures and methodology should come only after very careful consideration and evaluation. Don't exchange one devil for another. Use some planned method of attacking program problems— force field analysis. Make sure you stay abreast of current literature and use input from other programs and research.

5. Avoid the assumption that a program that is working well for you and your students will work equally as well for all teachers and students. Whatever you are doing probably will not work any better for *all* students and teachers than the system that made you want to establish your type of program to begin with! FOCUS has found it wiser (and more honest) to talk in terms of a variety of program options for students rather than to advocate mass adoption of the FOCUS model.

6. Resist the temptation to "forget the whole thing" when the program seems irreparably snagged and the staff is overwhelmed by physical and emotional fatigue. Based on the FOCUS experience, it would not seem likely that major accomplishments will be attained on a day-to-day basis. Staff members must become skilled in recognizing the small "victories" that occur and learn to "recharge" their professional and personal batteries from the inch-by-inch progress they can observe in their students and in the program's workings.

7. Don't allow your colleagues in the regular program to accept your program for the wrong reasons. Many teachers will support your program because they recognize the need for educational options for students with particular learning needs. There undoubtedly will be others, however, who will deny the philosophical and educational legitimacy of what you are doing while at the same time blessing you for taking the biggest classroom problems off their hands. Perhaps it is realistic to say that support is support, no matter what reasons prompt it, but every caution should be taken to prevent your program from being seen as an educational junkyard, a "fix-it" shop for the school's ne'er-do-wells. (A solid dissemination and PR effort is important, even critical, if your program is going to be accepted and integrated into the normal structure of the overall school program.)

8. Avoid the temptation to bite off more than you can chew. An open school environment provides a variety of new and exciting activities, but it is possible to overextend the resources of the program and wind up in a position in which nothing is done very well. In the long run, it is possible to accomplish just as much and get just as far by "wiggling" as it is by taking huge leaps. (But don't be intimidated by challenges. It is surprising how receptive most administrators and colleagues will be to change if your professional homework is well done and your requests are presented logically.)

9. No matter how sorely pressed, never adopt a defensive stance. The very fact that your project is there makes it creditable. If there are people with objections to your new educational program, let them object. Give them information, invite them to make on-site visitations, listen to their concerns, and acknowledge their right to question and object. If you have done your homework and can cite research and example to substantiate the validity of your efforts, you are on solid ground. You may never win the objectors over, but it is better to have them objecting and friendly than objecting and antagonized by your solid, rational, and fruitless defenses.

10. Never forget the chain of command in your school and district. Spend a few cents more and send copies of all your curriculum materials, brochures, attendance reports, test scores, etc., to every station above you in the district hierarchy: vice principals, principal, curriculum supervisor, assistant superintendent, superintendent, school board members. As has been stated previously, these people can't work for you if they don't know what you're doing. Give them the tools they need to protect your "space."

11. Avoid the pitfall of familiarity. The close student-teacher relationships which develop in your project and on which your program ultimately depends are essentially adult-child relationships. It is very easy to move into a "buddy, good guy" mode of operation which overlooks the important "modeling" role of the teacher. Your project staff consists of intelligent, well-trained *adults* and there is no need for any teacher to view this as a problem to overcome. Warm, effective interpersonal relationships can extend across generation gaps!

12. Work hard to share the power with students. Only when teachers refute the traditional "I teach, you learn" system can a FOCUS-type program achieve real success. This is not to say that teachers should abdicate their leadership role and professional responsibilities; however, it is to say that a program which is built on the concept of self-directed learning can't function without students having a major share in determining what will be taught, who will teach it, and who will evaluate progress and accomplishment.

13. Don't panic when events take a terrible turn. If the staff can maintain a calm, orderly attitude under conditions of duress and crisis, even the worst disaster can be made to appear part of an organized learning activity.

14. Never expect 100% productivity from either students or staff members. A FOCUS-type program which deals principally with the affective realm has to allow room for the weaknesses, shortcomings, and periodic physical and emotional "drains" which affect all human endeavors. The FOCUS staff operates from a philosophic base which says that learning (and teaching) does not progress on an even, steady plan but is, rather, sporadic, alternating between periods of intensity and dormancy. (The trick is, of course, to manage events in such a manner as to keep these periods from occurring at the same time, much as a juggler has three balls going up at the same time as three others are coming down.)

15. Don't think that "team spirit" will compensate for day-to-day resentments and hurts which occasionally crop up between staff members. The sheer intensity of the many expectations and personal agendas which project teachers bring to the program almost guarantees that there will be instances of friction and conflict. FOCUS has found that the wisest thing to do is to let the stress situations flare up, handle them as effectively as possible, and then wait for staff equilibrium to return. Honest confrontation in which one person admits and owns his negative feelings is perhaps the most effective way that FOCUS staff members have found to deal with the relational hangups which appear on the project scene. Additionally, it is helpful for the staff to adopt some "model" for conflict management, a process which the whole group can fall back on when dealing with interpersonal discord.

Starting a Free School:
Red Tape and Hostility

Frank Taylor

Life expectancy: nine months. So reads the prognosis for the average free school founded in the United States since the alternative school movement began to flourish a few years back. Beyond statistics, what are the explanations for this bleak future? They vary, of course, but two of the most popular run something like this: "The staff was nothing but a bunch of hippies, with their pedagogical feet planted firmly on a cloud of dreams." Or, at the other extreme: "What's so 'new' about them? All they've done is repackage the traditional curriculum." Like most shoot-from-the-hip social analyses, both carry a grain of truth—but still widely miss the mark. For the American free school is far more often bled white by battles for survival against petty bureaucrats, red tape and local hostility than it is paralyzed by fevered debates over teaching philosophies and curriculum issues. In most communities, alternative schools are feared outsiders, enigmas in a time and place that do not happily tolerate enigmas.

What follows here is the case history of the founding of one free school. It happens to have been located in Stafford, Connecticut, but what happened to us has happened, varying only in detail, to free school founders all over the country. We want to tell our story both to help explain why free schools really have such a hard time staying alive, and in hopes that it might be of help to others contemplating such a venture.

THE FIRST HURDLE

In the winter of 1970-71, our church group invited Dr. Len Krimerman, from the nearby University of Connecticut, to speak to us about the growth

---

Reprinted by special permission of LEARNING, The Magazine for Creative Teaching, January 1975. © 1975 by Education Today Company, Inc., 530 University Avenue, Palo Alto, California 94301.

of the alternative school movement. The discussion that followed his talk was animated, and later in the week, some of us began to talk about the possibility of opening our own school. It started out as one of those "why-don't-we?" dialogues that usually come to nothing, but as winter turned to spring, it became obvious we were onto something more lasting. We had developed into an identifiable group—a group with a purpose. Most of us were in our 30s, had children in several different nearby schools, and were earning around $10,000 a year. Our members included two public school teachers, two former teachers turned housewives, an insurance man, a waitress, a bank employee, a policeman and a couple of people working on postponed college degrees. Most of us had been friends for several years, and most had been unsuccessfully active in attempts to prod the local government into greater concern about the environment, more openness of government operations and improvement of our local schools. Our post-Krimerman discussion established that we also shared a deep-rooted dissatisfaction with the unimaginative, dull, structured and callous education our children were getting.

We studied Holt, Goodman, Kozol, Dennison and the rest of the "romantic educators" and visited established alternative schools to see exactly what was involved in the process of creating the kind of school we wanted. We held public meetings to discuss the options open to us in nearby towns and on the campus of the nearby university. Gradually, we began to believe we were going to succeed.

In April, we had an appointment with a representative of the state board of education. He did not seem to have heard of the alternative school movement, but he had suggestions: keep small—start with only a grade or two; don't try to include both elementary and secondary students in the same school; check with local health, sanitation and fire officials before you consider building. As an example of a "good" private school, he pointed to a school for extremely emotionally handicapped children. It had wonderful facilities and charged tuition of $25,000 a year. At the end of our interview, he asked me to step outside of his office, out of earshot of the three female representatives of our group. Then he repeated everything because, he said, "you know how easily women get things mixed up, and I want you to really see the situation." But he gave us the forms we needed to acquire legal status and we felt we had cleared our first major hurdle.

ESTABLISHING SUBCOMMITTEES

We now decided to proceed simultaneously on several fronts. One committee went to work on construction plans. (A strong minority wanted a novel building—a dome or an A-frame—anything that would announce to a passer-by that something novel was occurring here.) Other committees dealt with philosophy, bylaws and curriculum, and out of their combined efforts came another decision to run a six-week summer pilot program to find out what's involved in working with a group of kids on a day-to-day basis.

At about this time the local government became interested in us. We set up a variety of work centers in the two first-floor rooms and basement of a church. There were some real drawbacks—the lack of a playground being a major one—but it began to feel like a good place to be. Then one morning, two strange men arrived, announced they were sanitation inspectors and closely examined what we were doing. They said they were responding to complaints from the neighbors, and although they offered no details, we assumed that the conversion of the church from a building empty 95 percent of the time to a center of considerable activity was the reason for the complaints. The men closely examined our facilities and then notified us that they were inadequate, that we could stay in operation only through the summer months. With no place to house the school, we were forced to send our students back to public school in September. At the end of more than eight months of meetings and planning, about all we had to show for our efforts was a conviction that we had come a long way and would eventually get where we wanted to go.

With the advice of the man from the state office of education still very much in mind, we decided to go through official channels and get the church quarters properly inspected. Under our auspices, a committee from the church board of trustees met with the town fire inspector and his assistant. In one relatively brief evening session, the two officials presented us with a staggering bill of particulars. We could not use the building for a school, they said, because the doors were too small, opened the wrong way, did not contain "panic bars" and were not made of steel. Moreover, the bathroom was too small, was not properly ventilated and, in any event, was inadequate, since we needed two. The fire alarm bell was too high, too difficult to see and not loud enough. The windows were too far above the ground, the water had not been tested for purity, the building lacked proper exits, and there were two floors above the one we wanted to use. The furnace was not enclosed in a separate room with fire-rated cement blocks and a fire door. The furniture, drapes and carpets were not fireproof. It took only 20 minutes for the inspector and his assistant to provide us with a list of nearly 50 reasons why not only this building but almost any existing structure in the entire area would not be acceptable. We pointed out that, in fact, the nearest public school building possessed virtually all of the same flaws. That, said the inspector, was an exceptional case, and besides, the building wasn't going to be used much longer.

THE "EVERYWHERE SCHOOL"

Our construction plans now shifted. If we were going to stay in the immediate area—where, incidentally, all of us lived—then we were either going
to have to build from scratch or totally renovate an existing building. Carl
and Carol Rickards, members of the group since its first days, suggested
that we convert their two-car garage and move the school there. Back to
town officials we went to find out what we would have to do to bring the
garage up to standards. In addition to everything they had required at
the church, they told us that the garage's existing carrying beam would
either have to be boxed or replaced with a steel I-beam. Then, tongue-in-
cheek, they suggested that we simply put the school in the Rickards' house,
since it was built of concrete. Their last bit of advice was to the effect that
they could not give us a building permit until we had given them a detailed
set of construction plans and specifications.

Once again, we decided to move simultaneously on two fronts. One
subcommittee began work on specification writing and building design
while the rest of us set out to open an "everywhere school" for those children from our group who were warring most openly with the public schools.
My wife and I filled our old station wagon with kids and school materials
and drove each day to a different home. (We put 25,000 miles on that old
wagon in less than a year.) Classes were held in three different homes, but
we also took the children to factories, forests, parks, museums, other
schools, libraries and anywhere else learning could take place.

The arrangement was enjoyable at first but soon proved tiring, requiring a great deal of coordination and planning. And eventually, we found,
the kids yearned for a base. They needed a place to put their things, build
with them, and find them there again the next day. So we began to use the
same homes a couple of days in a row, a move that soon attracted the attention of officialdom again. The first visitor to arrive was a state policeman
who wandered around for a few minutes, saying he was "just checking for
somebody." (I have lived in my present house for more than five years,
and the only policeman who ever came there arrived on a day that we were
holding school.)

GARAGE RENOVATION

At about this time, the building subcommittee completed plans for renovation of the garage. We tore off the front, removed the tar from the driveway, dug deep footings through stone ledge, dug a trench for the water
line, installed and connected it, poured the footings, designed a septic field
and began its construction. At every interval, the inspectors found little

faults with our plans. In fact, we worked for more than two months before we were granted official permits. (The delay should not be interpreted as leniency. This is simply a small town, one which is not known for its efficiency.)

With cold weather and frozen ground approaching rapidly, it became important for us to get all our digging done. We received approval for a septic system including five 50-foot-long trenches radiating out from the tank. We finished digging them the day before Thanksgiving and felt we had triumphed. But over the holidays, a heavy storm hit. At one point, the snow depth reached 14 inches, and then it began to rain. By Sunday night, the open trenches were filled to the brim. Monday morning brought clearing skies, but it also brought the inspectors, who promptly condemned the septic system and suggested there might be no way to put in an acceptable sewage system. We were beginning to feel that somewhere, somebody had it in for us.

For the first time we went outside our own group for help and retained a local contractor to design a system that would pass inspection. In December, we hand-dug another test hole through frozen ground, four feet by four feet and five feet deep. The town sanitarian still had doubts, and at this point notified us that we would have to install a 1,500-gallon septic tank, considerably bigger than we had been led to believe would be necessary. Why?

"For peak periods," he answered.

"What the hell is a 'peak period'?" we asked.

"Times like recess, when all the kids go to the john at once."

"You don't understand; we don't have recess. We don't make the kids wait all day to go to the bathroom. They go when they need to go, just like people."

"Doesn't matter. Schools have 'peak periods,' and you'll have a bigger tank or no school."

By now, the contractor had finished a plan that would "hold up in any court." We broke the macadam out of the freshly paved driveway again and dug a 150-foot ditch to a nearby field, where we excavated a hole 40 feet square and 3 feet deep. A honeycomb of pipes was laid in the excavation to form the leach field, and the hole was then filled with 8 truckloads of crushed stone and 17 truckloads of gravel. The system, said our contractor, was adequate for a 30-unit apartment complex. We were still greatly relieved when the town approved it.

PERIOD OF BENIGN NEGLECT

Construction on the building continued. On orders from the inspectors, all stairs and ladders to the second floor were removed. And to satisfy our own desire for plenty of natural light, we dismantled an entire wall and installed three double windows. The final wiring and plumbing work we handed over to professional contractors. In frigid January weather, the electrician finished his job and requested the electric company to run the necessary wire in for power service. We waited more than two weeks for that installation.

With the power finally in, it seemed to the inexperienced eye that we were finished. The building was reasonably airtight, the walls were insulated, the electricity and heat were functioning, the rough plumbing had been installed, and overhead lights illuminated the room. We had the warm feeling of a job well done. Happily, the town seemed to be ignoring us, and we basked in its benign neglect.

But all that had gone before came to seem easy in comparison with the job of installing Sheetrock. We had received a good price on 4-by-12-foot sheets of fire-rated Sheetrock, but they proved to be incredibly heavy. We wrestled with them for more than a month, piecing together scraps to save money, taping, puttying, sanding and puttying again.

Now the town developed an active interest in the school again. We were conducting classes in the Rickards' home, where the garage renovation was also underway, when two building inspectors showed up. They immediately disqualified the Rickard house for classes because it had a second floor, ignoring our protests that once they had suggested we use it because of its concrete construction.

So we moved the class to my house, which contains a 15-by-20-foot room with three sliding doors. In a couple of days, the inspectors appeared in response to alleged complaints from neighbors, although I only have one neighbor within sight of my house. They said we couldn't teach children at our house because of the exits, because the water had not been tested for purity, and because we had no sterilizer for washing dishes. They gave us a short grace period, and then placed our house off-limits forever.

By this time, our group paranoia was acute, but we managed to locate friendly homes in three nearby communities and another hideout in our own town. We met at the Inner College of the University of Connecticut a couple of times, and the kids went to the Boston aquarium, several factories, a wildlife sanctuary, libraries, museums, and various other available public facilities. Every time we began to feel even remotely comfortable, we found ourselves on the road again. One day one of the cars broke down, and the teacher walked to a nearby house to phone for help. The inspectors were at the house in half an hour. Obviously, our need for a permanent base was becoming urgent.

MORE REGULATIONS

In this atmosphere, more regulations caught up with us. Although the school enrollment would be very small, we had to have two bathrooms. Moreover, state regulations prohibited the use of secondhand fixtures. So we had to hustle out and buy special flushes with elongated bowls, each fixed at a special height from the floor. And last, the bathroom doors had to open out into the main room and could carry no locks.

In all fairness, let it be stated that many of our problems arose from our own ignorance of specific regulations and the red tape involved in enforcing them. Sometimes we made elaborate plans and spent heavily in time and effort, only to discover that some anticipated hurdle was small. On the other hand, what seemed likely to be automatic frequently became astonishingly difficult. Every official inspection proved to be complicated. Because most of the inspectors had other jobs and were not available during the day, we tried to have someone available after hours at the construction site. If that person were away for a moment, an inspector would invariably show up and leave because no one was there. Frequently we waited a week for an inspection only to be told something like "I'll have to read the regulations again."

Part of our difficulty was also bred in rumor and gossip. Several people told us that a school board member had publicly declared, "We're going to crush that school." We were also told that public school officials were in communication with town authorities about ways to "close down that school." We never pinned such reports down, but they served to keep us edgy and uncertain.

Our last big struggle was with the fire marshal. He required that all our wiring be enclosed in metal conduits and that heat sensors, a bell, blinking lights, illuminated exit signs and fire pull boxes at each door low enough for the smallest child be installed. Eventually, we also had to install an emergency system in the event of a power failure.

With the help of a friendly carpenter and the blessing of good weather, we finally reached a stage at which we could paint the interior of the building. Because our money was running low, we decided to sponsor a fundraising event and rented the auditorium of a local public school for a performance by a professional puppet group. Everything went beautifully. While some of us finished up the painting job, the kids and staff handled the details of the puppet performance. Within 30 minutes of the end of the show, the chairman of the school board received five telephone calls condemning him for allowing those "Communist, hippie homosexuals" to rent space in a public school. The consistency with which the callers used the same phrases indicated that "Communist-hippie-homosexuals" may be a new trinity of hate and resistance to change in small conservative towns such as ours.

CERTIFICATE OF OCCUPANCY

But we moved ahead, and by early spring we had a building we were sure was ready for occupancy. All three inspectors appeared and quickly found the following tentative flaws: 13 windows in a one-room school were possibly not enough; the windows might be too high; there seemed to be six square inches too little glass in the bathroom. We should test the flammability of the paint we had used on the cement floor. Finally, we were forbidden to use overstuffed furniture or rugs that could burn, were instructed to acquire both water and chemical fire extinguishers by purchasing them from the fire marshal, and we had to install emergency lights, replace the main jack-pillars with lolly columns, and taper off the cement at the sills more smoothly.

The cement work, fire extinguishers, lolly columns and emergency lights were all in place in a week, and we asked for a new inspection. The response was that there would be a delay because the state was probably going to come up with some new requirements.

We called our group together and quickly agreed that to the best of our abilities, we had conformed to the guidelines. We knew the building was superior to many, and perhaps most, of the public schools in the area. So we simply decided to use the building without an official certificate of occupancy. For several days, we hardly dared breathe. What were they thinking, planning, doing? But nothing happened, eventually the suspense dissipated, and we developed what has become our normal pattern of schooling. In mid-June, one of our members went down to the building inspector's office and picked up our certificate of occupancy. We framed it and hung it on the wall.

In some respects, it was an anti-climax. There was no big, dramatic final confrontation. If anything, we had simply outlasted the opposition. And while they still may not see things precisely our way, neither do they harass us any longer. However grudgingly, we have become accepted on the local scene.

Even more encouragingly, all the members of the original group who still live in the Stafford area are still together, still fully supportive of our school and its programs. There is irony in that fact: without the hassling we faced in our founding days, we probably would never have become the cohesive and determined group that we did.

The Minicourse: Where the Affective and Cognitive Meet

Arthur D. Roberts and Robert K. Gable

During the last 14 years we have seen an unprecedented effort to initiate curricular reform in the public schools. Major curriculum projects have produced programs, materials, and content reform in most of the subject matter areas. However, there is a very real question about the success of these efforts. Charles Silberman, in *Crisis in the Classroom,* suggests that "the reform movement has produced innumerable changes, and yet the schools themselves are largely unchanged." Both Silberman and John Goodlad, dean of the UCLA Graduate School of Education, conclude from their studies that our schools are much the same as they were 20 years ago in spite of the greatest knowledge explosion in history.[1]

Silberman, speaking for many observers, feels that the greatest weakness in American education is the failure to develop "sensitive, autonomous, thinking, human individuals." This weakness results largely from a false dichotomy in the schools between the cognitive and affective domains, between thinking and feeling. People must be educated not only to think but also to feel. It is only through a combination of the two domains that we can apply what we have learned in order to create a more humane world.[2]

Obviously, no panacea is available to integrate the cognitive and affective. However, one recent curricular innovation that offers modest hope at the secondary level, as well as a break from the lock-step Carnegie unit, is the minicourse. Minicourses are short-term courses, offered for less than one semester.

Reprinted from *Phi Delta Kappan*, May, 1973. Used with permission of the authors and publisher, Phi Delta Kappa.

[1]Charles E. Silberman, *Crisis in the Classroom*. New York: Random House, 1970, pp. 158, 159.

[2]Ibid., p. 196.

The origins of the minicourse can be traced to the widespread student unrest at the end of the 1960s and the demand for more curriculum relevance. In the spring of 1969 the students of Walt Whitman High School in Bethesda, Maryland, ran a 1-week experiment in free-form education during which there were no required classes, no grades, and no traditional class groupings. A list of 242 subjects was drawn up and 150 guest lecturers, including many of Whitman's most talented students, were asked to participate. Whitman students were then asked to sign up for the subjects they wished to study; these ranged from European archaeology to science fiction. Many of the "courses" were action-oriented. Students interned at local and regional planning offices, worked at newspapers or stores, served as student aides in classes for the handicapped, helped U.S. senators with their mail, and so forth.

It was from this experiment and subsequent variations that the minicourse movement was born. It can accurately be called a grass-roots curriculum development. Many teachers colleges have worked with practice teaching modules or minis in their training programs, but the subject matter orientation of the high school mini is original, not borrowed.

No accurate census has as yet been taken to see how many U.S. and Canadian high schools have developed minicourses, but we are familiar with programs in New York, California, New Jersey, Massachusetts, Pennsylvania, and Connecticut. In the fall of 1971, each of 28 Connecticut high schools reported that it was involved in some kind of minicourse program. This number represents, roughly, 8% of the high schools in the state. Undoubtedly, large numbers of schools are developing unpublicized programs. Interestingly enough, however, there are no published research studies other than polls of student opinion on the minis, and there is very little information about them in the professional literature.

The time and timing of minicourses, thus far in their development, varies considerably from school to school. Some schools simply tack the minis onto the existing curriculum for a week or two at any convenient time. Others follow the Whitman model, while still others hold minicourses in unscheduled time blocks at the end of the school year or at the end of a semester. Other schools see minicourses as best suited to lunchtime, study halls, or the final period of the "normal" school day. An increasing number of schools, however, seem to be scheduling minicourses in a 9- or 10-week block of time. In this arrangement the school year consists of four minisessions rather than the traditional two semesters.

A curriculum built of minicourses is usually far broader than the traditional curriculum. It is not unusual for a single department, English or social studies for example, to offer as many as 40 to 50 minicourses, compared with seven or eight when the Carnegie Unit reigned supreme. Students are given a great deal of freedom to choose from this wide range of offerings.

Guided self-selection with few if any prerequisites is usually possible within any given subject matter area. Some areas—English is a good example—may require an introductory skill course such as expository writing, communication, or creative writing (note that the element of choice is still in operation). Once this requirement is met, however, the prevailing model seems to include unlimited choice. For example, instead of taking sophomore English, a student might take "Mythology and the Bible," "Mass Media," "Poetry for the Nonpoetic," "The Plays of Eugene O'Neill," or "Literature of the East." Instead of American history, the student could choose from among such offerings as "The Creative Impulse in America," "Man's Role in Nature," "Military History of the U.S.," "Political Cartooning," et al.

The titles of minicourses themselves are exciting. The following list is representative:

Art
Discovering Art in the City
Printmaking

Business Education
Fundamentals of Data Processing
Personality Development
American Market Economy

English
The Me Nobody Knows
Reading, Writing, and Rhetoric
Fantasy
Sportswriting
Coming of Age
Problem Novels
Alienation in Society
Media's Message
Language: Roots and Shoots
Spiritualism, the Occult, and Witchcraft

Social Studies
The Depression
Isms
Future Shock
American Inventiveness
Criminology
Comparative Religions
Constitutional Law
Film Study
Practical Politics
Archaeology
Russia: From Tsars to Commissars

The above list suggests that minicourses lend themselves to certain subject matter areas more readily than to others. This is no accident. Without question, minicourses are most popular in subject areas, such as English and the social studies, which encompass several diverse disciplines, and are less so in areas such as science, which do not. Although science is as complex and multifaceted a subject area as either English or the social studies, it tends to be more sequential, building on a disciplinary base such as biology, chemistry, or physics. Once a student has been given a base on which to build, however, there is considerable room for the study of minicourse material, ranging from meteorology to astronomy.

Minicourses offer a number of positive advantages that are both cognitive and affective in nature. In the cognitive realm students have the opportunity to study a greater number of subjects in greater depth. It can be argued, for example, that many of the broad survey courses that are taught, notably in the social studies and English, are often superficial and redundant. By the time a student takes high school American history, to cite one example, he may have studied some of the content three or four times. A wide range of minicourses offers the opportunity for challenging, in-depth study of a particular subject. In areas where it is felt that there must be a common core, minicourses can be used for enrichment. In either case, the curriculum offers more challenge and the opportunity for sophisticated study.

In the affective domain choice is a key word. Students choose at least four separate courses in which they are interested each year. Students can pick what they really need or want to know and can skip that which is unnecessary. This is a natural selection process, and it can be very healthy for the curriculum. Students literally vote for curriculum development when they make their choices. Subjects which are outmoded or irrelevant can be discarded, revised, or drastically altered. Basic process skills can still be taught in those subjects which remain.

Students also reap some fringe benefits. They may study with many different teachers; repeat only a quarter's work, not a full year's, if they fail a course; and choose work in areas where they need specialized help in developing skills.

Teachers have a rare opportunity to involve students in their own learning. Students may assist in the creation of courses in which they are interested, or quite possibly teach a course themselves if they have a unique ability. Teacher/pupil cooperation is especially apropos if a major affective outcome that we seek is a change in both student and teacher attitudes. School should be a place of involvement, not a prison for a captive audience. As Herman Ohme has suggested, this is what "relevance" is all about

—the creation of a desire to learn through individual involvement and responsibility.[3]

It will be argued by some authorities that high school students already have the right to choose their curriculum; but in fact, once the college-bound student has met the traditional college prerequisites, he has very little room left for choice. We know from Piaget that the child is the principal agent in his own education and mental development. Minicourses can broaden students' experience and give them the opportunity to do things that they normally would not do. Students who study what they are interested in can also legitimately be held responsible for how well they do—more so, at least, than students who are prisoners of a set curriculum.

Teachers are also given a rare opportunity in a minicourse curriculum. Most college and university education is based on highly specialized courses. The average teacher rarely gets a chance to teach either what he really knows or what he is really interested in. By specializing, teachers have an opportunity to display their talents rather than merely "cover" large blocks of general material. Not only can they utilize their subject matter competency, they can also select courses that reflect their special interests. Thus for student and teacher alike the opportunity "to do their thing" is there, but without the flabbiness that this catch phrase often connotes, since the structure and rigor of a subject matter field are still maintained.

Affect as it relates to teachers should not be minimized. Curriculum developers have learned the lesson in recent years that curriculum change has little chance unless teachers are interested in innovation and see it as important. There is no such thing as a "teacherproof" curriculum. Teacher interests, needs, and motivations must all be taken into consideration if there is to be real improvement in the curriculum.

The limited evidence thus far suggests that both teachers and students develop a positive attitude toward the minicourse curriculum. Note this teacher comment:

> This is the first time I've ever taught kids who wanted to be in my subject. . . . All of us were surprised by which students signed up for what courses [sic]. Freed from the stigma of homogeneous grouping, many of our not-bound-for-college seniors elected to take the more intellectual minicourses. Used to their apathetic performance in general classes, we were amazed by their sophisticated handling of difficult subjects in mixed discussion groups. They sometimes outdid the brightest seniors in their penetrating observations about Bergman's *The Virgin Spring* or his *Smiles of a Summer Night*.[4]

---

[3]Herman Ohme, "Steps Toward Relevance: An Interest Centered Curriculum," *Journal of Secondary Education*, November, 1970, pp. 229-304.

[4]R. R. Hayward, "Maximum Results from Minicourses," *Today's Education*, September, 1969, pp. 55-57.

School authorities in Westfield, New Jersey, report that a curriculum combining 9- and 18-week courses in the social studies has been favorably received by its student body. Students found no difficulty in changing to the new curriculum; many were able to get to know their teachers better; roughly a third got higher grades; and more than 75% rated the program as above-average or excellent.[5]

Finally, the minicourse also offers some general curricular possibilities. Traditional departmental lines which are often more difficult to breach at the high school level than at the college level may take on less importance. Minis may start in one department and end up in another as teachers discuss them and work together. There is reason to believe that there is less emphasis on grades in a minicourse curriculum. People are studying what they are interested in and grades are not as important. This fact may well lead to a blurring of the traditional teacher/learner concept as the two groups work in a climate of real interest, talent, and enthusiasm.

All of these real or hoped-for advantages, of course, assume that minicourses are more than year-long courses broken down into four quarters. There are real and potential disadvantages as well. Teachers may try to compress too much into a mini. The result could well be an extensive tobacco auction.

Scheduling can be a major problem, especially when a school first attempts a minicourse program. The problem can be overcome, as the successful operation of several schools demonstrates. Computer assistance is helpful. Schools report success with 85 to 90% of students computer scheduled the first time through. Experience can and does improve this average.

Another possible disadvantage is the large number of preparations a teacher may be required to make during a session or school year. If assignments were truly based on interest, this would not be a great problem; but if teachers are arbitrarily assigned to sections that they *must* teach, then minicourses could be more of a burden than the traditional semester or year-long course. Some teachers also fear that they may not get to know their students as well as in the longer time block, but others who have taught minicourses argue vehemently that this is not so.

One criticism of the minicourse curriculum that can be currently offered is that it has not been adequately evaluated. Before the minicourse bandwagon rolls too far, we should find out whether it in fact fulfills its promise. The question can only be answered by experimental research under controlled conditions. Evaluation would have to include measurement of yearly changes in both the cognitive and affective areas for two groups of students randomly assigned to a mini or traditional curriculum model.

---

[5] Donald J. Gudaitis, "Minicourses: Are they Useful?," *Clearing House*, April, 1972, pp. 465-67.

One must ask about the cognitive aspects of the new curriculum. We do not seek to create highly motivated idiots. Are there significant gains in cognitive skills after one has been exposed to minicourses? Certainly we would expect the gain to at least equal the gains achieved under the traditional curriculum. But what cognitive skills does one evaluate? Traditional comparisons of achievement performance are not valid, because the two curricula do not contain identical content. Moreover, there are other significant questions that need to be answered before meaningful curriculum comparisons can be made. For example, does exposure to a greater variety of subject matter help the individual to develop the ability to define a problem, select pertinent information for the solution of a problem, recognize stated and unstated assumptions, formulate and select relevant and promising hypotheses, draw valid conclusions, and judge the validity of inferences? Watson and Glaser have defined these statements as the ability to think critically.[6] It is also reasonable to expect that the new method should generate skill development in other areas besides critical thinking. Since vocabulary building, reading comprehension, and reading speed are important indicators and prerequisites for future academic success, they too should be evaluated.[7]

The limited number of practitioners who have been involved in teaching a minicourse curriculum are quite willing to testify that positive changes in attitude occur among their students. Students are thought to enjoy the minicourse subject matter more than they did the traditional curriculum. Is this testimony valid, or simply the result of enthusiasm for something new? Research is clearly needed to answer such question as: Do students experiencing a minicourse show greater changes in attitude toward subject matter,[8] or motivation to learn,[9] than students experiencing the traditional model? Also, do minicourse students have more positive end-of-the-year attitudes toward teachers than a comparable group of traditional-course students?

These questions must be answered. Judging from what we know now, however, the minicourse curriculum has several advantages that recommend its use to the American high school. The disadvantages seem to be fewer and less important. A curriculum based on minicourses may well be a positive step in the search for learning experiences which give weight to both the affective and cognitive domains. Nevertheless, we can't yet be certain whether minicourses are genuinely a positive addition or merely another fad.

---

[6]Goodwin Watson, and Edward Glaser, *Watson-Glaser Critical Thinking Appraisal.* New York: Harcourt, Brace, and World, 1951.

[7]*Cooperative English Tests.* Princeton: Educational Testing Service, 1960.

[8]R. K. Gable and A. D. Roberts, The Development of an Instrument to Measure Attitudes Towards School Subjects. Paper presented at the Northeastern Educational Research Association Annual Meeting, Boston, 1972.

[9]J. R. Frymier, *JIM Scale.* Columbus, Ohio: The Ohio State University, 1965.

Team Teaching: Familiar Ideas in New Combinations

Jon Rye Kinghorn and Barbara J. Benham

Let's face it: team teaching *sounded* like a good idea, but it has never really worked as well as everyone hoped it would. It's time to admit that, and get on to the business of finding new ways to encourage interdisciplinary education—ways that *will* work.

Why did team teaching fail? There are several reasons. First of all, most teachers couldn't (or wouldn't) find time for the group planning that was required. It just didn't happen.

In many cases, teams never really found smooth ways of interrelating material from several subject areas, or of sharing the blocks of time allotted to them.

Frequently, instead of creating harmony, teaming simply aggravated personality clashes that sometimes brought classroom processes almost to a standstill. Most teachers are so used to having autonomous control of their classes that teaming crated real anxiety for many, as they tried unsuccessfully to readjust to the new way, which required sharing of control and responsibility.

But the main flaw in the team teaching concept is that it always remained an innovative idea superimposed upon a basically unchanged, traditional school situation; this inherent conflict made team teaching a self-defeating process right from the start. Even grouped into teams, teachers still performed their duties in basically traditional ways, deciding what, when, and how the students should learn. All too often the teachers would do 80 per cent or more of the talking, while students listened, and were expected to absorb what was "taught." All too seldom were students given a chance to actively learn something for themselves—and rarely, if ever, were the students given the chance to decide *what they* wanted to study.

Reprinted by permission from the February 1973 issue of THE CLEARING HOUSE.

No wonder, under such circumstances, teachers have spent so much time and effort wondering how to get students "motivated."

Teachers are trained professionals who have a great need to feel pride in their work, and throughout the years, the teacher-training institutions have given young teachers the type of instruction that led them to feel most pride in what they were able to do in a traditional, self-contained classroom setting.

Can we design a new kind of interdisciplinary program that will combine the potential for pride of a self-contained classroom with the flexibility and individualized instruction that was always hoped for, but never quite achieved by the team teaching idea? We can, but it will require three or four really basic changes in how we view ourselves as teachers and the students as learners. But the changes, though basic and ultimately far-reaching, are not difficult—and the results would be worth it.

What we want to suggest is an interdisciplinary approach to teaching and learning that is integral, not superimposed.

● Let's think of ourselves as *resource people,* available to any student who needs us—no longer will we be the instructor-in-the-front-of-the-room, giving out the knowledge-we-think-all-students-need.

● Let's alter the traditional role of the guidance department; let's make every teacher an advisor, with 20 advisees—and let's let the *students* choose whom they want as their adviser.

● Let's stop telling the students what they need to study; let's start asking them what *their* goals are, and what they need to study in order to reach those goals.

● Let's break away from thinking of our subject areas as unchangeable large blocks of time—courses lasting a whole year, or even a semester, really have no inherent superiority over courses that would be more specific and of a shorter length. Why, for example, couldn't a Chemistry teacher teach a six-week course in Food Additives? Why couldn't an English teacher offer a nine-week course in The Gothic Novel?

If we can make these four basic changes, we will have altered the traditional school situation in ways that will then make a truly integral interdisciplinary program possible.

When teachers serve as advisors to students who like and admire them, the teachers will have a more realistic picture of what their students want and need to study during their high school years. And if teachers can think in terms of short courses instead of "American History" or "Biology," the curriculum can be flexible enough to respond to those student wants and needs. And credits pose no real problem—students simply accumulate credits by the quarter instead of by the semester or the year. Michael, for example, may still take a whole year of English—but it would be sub-divided, according to his choices, into four nine-week courses: *Early American Authors; Grammar and Basics; The Gothic Novel;* and *Ibsen, Shaw, and O'Neill,* for example. And he might have a different teacher for each one.

Of course, it will take some time for both students and teachers to make these conceptual changes. Students, in particular, are liable to be wary: "You mean I can *choose* what courses I want next quarter? I don't believe it!" But in a short time, most of them will get the idea. And what Physics teacher wouldn't be happy if 10 students came and *asked* him to teach a four-week seminar on the Theory of Relativity?

And what teacher, in any subject area, wouldn't be pleased to have a class of students who were there because they had chosen to be there; wanted to be there?

At this point, a word of warning: we are not suggesting that students be offered a smorgasbord of exciting electives at the expense of "the basics." Instead, there would no longer be a distinction between the two, since all courses would be "elected" by a student, after serious consultation with his advisor. Nor would a student be allowed to take only those courses that appeal to him on some whimsical basis. Instead, the focus will be on what the student realistically knows that he needs to take, in order to get where he wants to go. And so if a student hopes to become a medical technologist, he knows that he must take certain amounts of Chemistry, Biology, and so forth—whether or not he feels particularly attracted to these courses.

Students are capable of being very hardheaded about what they need to study, if given the chance; and most, with the proper guidance from their advisor, will take a balanced load that will prepare them well for college or other forms of career training. In addition, they will feel more involved with their schooling if they are given this chance to control its direction, to some extent, themselves—instead of being expected to sit quietly and absorb material that others have decided is important.

So much for the basic changes in attitude and in organization; now, what about this new interdisciplinary approach that could succeed where team teaching failed?

Not only does the school need to have built-in ways in which students can define their individual, long-range goals; in addition, each teacher can, with little difficulty, let each student in the class set his or her own goals *for that particular course.* This, to some extent, will lead to the creation of subdivisions and smaller groups within the class, making individualized instruction more of a reality and making it easier for the teacher to act as a *resource person* rather than as the omnipotent and All-Knowing Instructor. For example: in a Biology short course on Land Reclamation, three students might want to focus on deserts, and four might want to explore re-forestation. These would form natural small group study units. Perhaps one student will be fascinated by the different kinds of erosion patterns in different kinds of soil—with the help of his teacher, he might design an independent study unit for himself, listing his objectives and the ways in which he plans to meet those planned objectives.

In addition to this new flexibility within the short course itself, teachers can create a new interdisciplinary program by setting up *natural links between their courses,* and encouraging students to develop their *own* connections between the various subject areas. For instance, Janice is taking a Math short course on the Economics of the Poverty Cycle. She is also taking a Social Studies short course on Migration Patterns. With the help and encouragement of both teachers, she is going to interview several families of migrant workers and write a paper on her findings that will tie into both her Math and Social Studies courses. In other words, Janice's Math and Social Studies courses become resources on which she will draw in order to prepare herself for her project. She may also find that she needs some specific knowledge about how to conduct a good interview; realizing this, she may go to yet another teacher who can give her that information. This is a good example of what we mean when we talk about helping students to see teachers as a resource people.

One excellent way that teachers interested in encouraging interdisciplinary studies can link their courses together would be through the development of a common theme around which several of the short courses would be based. For example, a group of teachers in different subject areas might try basing their courses for one nine-week period on the theme "Life in the Year 2000." Ideas for short courses are easy to develop when one has a theme—here are a few possibilities:

Math: Tax Structures
Science: The Oceans
Social Studies: The Cities
English: Utopias
Humanities: Architecture Circa 2000 A.D.

Any student taking two or more of these common-theme courses would be strongly encouraged to develop his own links between them and, because of the common theme, this would not be difficult. An architecture project, for example, might become interrelated with the Social Studies course on The Cities or with the Science course on The Oceans, and so forth.

A great psychological advantage of this approach, for the teacher, is that it is voluntary. No one need feel pressured to be part of a "team," and yet, for those who are interested in trying such a program, the flexibility is built in—while the necessity to share the same group of students for the same block of time, as in the old way, is avoided.

Finally a new form of the "team" concept begins to emerge from this kind of program idea. As the students, with the advice and help of their advisors, choose their courses each quarter, it can be said that the student chooses a team of teachers that can best help him get to where he wants to go that quarter.

A "team" of teachers, in other words, becomes something that the student chooses to best suit his needs—*not* a group of people assigned arbitrarily to an equally arbitrarily derived group of students.

We suspect that teachers would respond with relief and interest to this new interpretation of "team" work—and that students would respond with real excitement to the opportunity to have more real control over the direction of their lives. Now, let's stop saying the Emperor's new clothes look fine: let's stop pretending that team teaching has been working when it hasn't. It's high time we found something that does work—that avoids the problems that have plagued team teaching for the past ten years, and begins to chart a new course towards true interdisciplinary learning for students.

Part Five
In-Service Programs

In a school that wants to move toward a higher level of humanistic functioning, there must be an integration of various components into a total program of staff development. With a stabilization of enrollments and a smaller number of new teachers in most school districts, those individuals currently employed as teachers become the focus of attention. To facilitate maximum effectiveness in staff development, an ongoing and well-planned program of in-service education needs to be developed. The same kind of leadership that has been emphasized for many years in curriculum development needs to become a part of staff development. The employment of specific personnel to be responsible for the coordination of in-service programs is an essential first step.

If a school district is to have a humanistically oriented in-service program, the planning of such endeavors should be shared by representatives from all groups within the school community. Ideally, a committee responsible for in-service planning would include representatives from different levels of staff, from administration, and, if feasible, from parent and student groups. (Since the eventual consumer of most change within a school district is the student, it makes sense to have this group provide input.) In addition to planning in-service programs, the committee should be involved with evaluation, both in terms of immediate feedback from participants and evaluation of any long-range impact that in-service programing has had on the quality of learning within the district.

In-service programing is not intended to be a complete molding of a teacher's approach to working with students. It is, hopefully, an opportunity for the teacher to obtain supportive skills, an encouragement for teachers to seek additional learning opportunities, and a way to provide specific help with problems such as discipline, defining objectives, and identifying important resources. To enable teachers to identify areas of individual need, a school system must develop a method of communication through which administrators and supervisors help teachers identify staff-development objectives. It is also of paramount importance that teachers feel free to let their supervisors know what their interests are in the area of staff development.

Opinions vary as to whether programs of the type described in this section should be offered to all members of a school staff or only to those who are interested. It is our experience that programs differ considerably in terms of the level of commitment necessary as a prerequisite for participation. For a majority of humanistic or affective approaches, a considerable investment is necessary. It is our feeling that beyond introductory sessions made available to an entire school staff, the intensive, in-depth training should be only for those who volunteer and who philosophically can accept the program as having value for them as teachers.

Staff for in-service programs can be obtained from a number of sources. University personnel are available on an ongoing basis to develop and present the programs, as are private consultants, government employees, and employees from other school districts. With the wealth of personnel available to assist schools in presenting meaningful in-service programs, staff selection need not be made in a haphazard manner. Considerable investigation of the credentials of personnel to be used should be undertaken. Many self-proclaimed experts exist in the area of in-service and pre-service programing. Requiring a resumé and recommendations may be one way of determining if the applicant has had formal training and experience in the area in which he will work with members of a school staff. For example, a consultant selected to present a workshop on Parent Effectiveness Training should show evidence of participation in an officially sanctioned P.E.T. group.

Careful planning and scheduling is important in in-service programing. Frequently, programs are scheduled at times that are inappropriate for maximizing participant learning. The authors have been asked to conduct short (two- or three-hour) in-service programs during the last week of the school year or on the day before a vacation period. With vacation foremost in the minds of participants, it is extremely difficult to assist them to tune in to the materials presented. The scheduling of workshops should provide an opportunity for immediate integration into the teachers' daily functioning or at least the potential for an evaluation based on the here-and-now data of their teaching situations.

Included in this section are six examples of programs that have met with success in the schools and universities in which they have been tried. Fisher presents a theoretical model for in-service programing made up of seven areas to be examined: what the individual brings to the classroom, what the facilitator brings to the classroom, the group setting, the interaction process, conditions necessary for learning to occur, establishment of the process for continued learning, and maintenance and utilization of new learning. Hillman describes a "confluent" model; it emphasizes that the consultant must spend considerable time in the district in which he hopes to effect change. French focuses on nonverbal communication as it relates to the pupil, the environment, and the teacher. An in-service model presented by Lansky utilizes sensitivity training and participatory learning as key components. Myrick and Moni present an approach in which developmental consultation becomes the focus of programs that are presented to teachers. And, slightly different from the other articles is Crispin's outline of a transactional analysis laboratory model for teaching T.A. concepts to pre-service and in-service teachers.

A Teaching-Learning Theory for Results in In-Service Education

Delbert W. Fisher

Specialization and technology have had 10 years of rapid growth in hospitals.[1] This rapid growth has affected in-service education within the hospital. Education is no longer a luxury; it is a necessity in order to equip employees with skills necessary to perform their duties adequately.

The emphasis on specialization has led to an increase in in-service education programs, not only for nurses but for all employees in the hospital. It is becoming increasingly evident that, although specialization is necessary, the mere transmission of specialized skills does not insure quality care. A program geared solely to skill training is *mechanical;* it is concerned only with tangible behavior patterns that result in objectively measurable outcomes. Training programs limited solely to the transmission of skills are based on a partial concept of the hospital employee.

Physical service is essential to the alleviation of physical malfunctions, but the physical malfunction occurs in a complex human being with many needs. People served by the hospital (patients) have physical, psychological, social, and spiritual needs. High quality care can be realized only if the healing function takes into account the complex combination of tangible and intangible needs. The healing goals are realized by the transmission of a "caring attitude" and by the employees who serve the patient.

NEED FOR SPECIALIZATION

People who work in hospitals also have many complex needs. One of which may be an increase in knowledge or skill within a specific area. Just as the

Reprinted from *Training and Development Journal,* August 1974, with permission of the publisher.

[1]Editors' note: Although this article was written for hospital in-service training, its principles are applicable to educational settings.

healing function goes beyond treating the physical malfunction to treating the total patient, in-service training must go beyond eliminating the lack of a specific skill to treating the employee as a *total* person.

The educational danger of specialization is that it compartmentalizes knowledge. It trains to meet a specialized need and fails to see the total person or the total situation. An in-service program that approaches employees as objects to be taught a specific skill will have difficulty in helping the hospital achieve goals of total healing. In-service education must convey an appreciation of the employee behind the job-related skill to that of caring for the employee as a person.

EDUCATION THEORY

An in-service education department that wishes to obtain satisfactory results needs a theory of education for guidance in developing its programs. This theory must incorporate both the elements of adult education (hospital employees are adults) and, if the learning takes place in groups, it must also include elements of group learning. There is nothing more useful than a well-developed educational theory. To train for results, careful examination of the existing educational theory being applied must be made.

An in-service education theory programmed for results should involve two basic assumptions concerning the processes of learning and change:

1. The teaching-learning process is a human transaction that involves the instructor, the employee and the learning group in a set of dynamic interrelationships. In-service education is a human relations problem. The instructor and learner are, together, engaged in a learning situation for change. The relationships among the learners and between the instructor and the learners have a great deal of influence on the final product.

2. The target of in-service education is change and growth in the individual manifested by his or her behavior.

These two assumptions form a basis for re-examination of a teaching-learning theory for in-service education. They indicate the need to combine teaching procedures, group work skills and an understanding of the motivational, emotional and cognitive characteristics of the instructor and learner so that creative conditions for learning and change occur.

SEVEN AREAS OF EXAMINATION

There are seven areas that must be examined in developing an in-service education theory for results:

1. What the learners bring to the classroom (in addition to lack of knowledge or lack of a specific skill).

2. What the instructor brings to the classroom (in addition to subject knowledge).

3. The group viewed as a setting for individual learning to take place.
4. The interaction process.
5. Conditions necessary for learning and change to occur.
6. Establishment of the processes for continued learning.
7. Maintenance of change and utilization of the new learning in the life of the learner.

What the Learner Brings

What are the employee's perceptions about the need for learning and change? How deep is his or her dissatisfaction with the present situation? Are the pressures for change external or have they been accepted internally?

What are the employee's expectations for the learning experience? Does he or she expect to remain passive, or expect to be involved in the learning process? What kind of acceptance does the learner have of the instructor and of the learning situation?

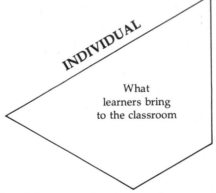

INDIVIDUAL

What
learners bring
to the classroom

What kinds of fears are in the employee—what will happen if he or she fails to learn the material? What threats to his or her self-image are present if he or she opens up to consideration of present inadequacies in knowledge or behavior? Is he or she aware of these?

Adults have self-images and are more resistant to change and to accepting knowledge from others than are children. Adults easily turn threatening knowledge into abstractions, thus removing the need to modify any behavior that is a threat to the self-image. Self-perceived threats to the learner as a person become real blocks to learning.

Venture Into Unknown

For the employee, in-service education means venturing into the unknown, leaving the tried and safe way even though it might be unsatisfactory. Fear of the unknown causes resistance to change. Emotional issues, if they are not adequately reduced, will limit learning to a temporary change—what is learned will not alter the learner's basic behavior.

Hospital employees in in-service education are adults. Malcolm Knowles identifies four characteristics of every adult in a learning situation. These must be given consideration in preparing in-service programs.

Four Characteristics

1. The adult brings a self-concept of a self-directing person. If he or she is not treated as a self-directing person in the classroom, the adult learns if the penalties are great enough, but there is a subconscious resentment and resistance to the situation and learning does not occur as readily nor does it affect lasting behavioral change.

2. The adult brings many life experiences to the learning situation. These experiences make him or her more settled in ways, habits more firmly rooted, and tends to be more closed to new concepts. These facts must be dealt with in planning in-service programs.

3. The adult is time-conscious. He or she learns today what will be used tomorrow. The adult is situation-centered in his or her approach to learning. He or she must experience the relationship between what he or she is learning and how it will help on the job.

4. The readiness of the adult to learn is tied to a social role. He or she must be experiencing a need to change in a present situation and have a desire to put effort into learning.

The employee comes to the learning situation as a *total* person. He or she comes as an adult with a self-image, varied life experiences, time-consciousness, and with a defined social role. When only part of the learner is understood and approached, what he or she experiences does not penetrate very deeply into his or her being and actions.

What the Instructor Brings

The instructor brings far more into the teaching-learning situation than subject knowledge and skill in organizing and presenting material.

First, the instructor must bring an *awareness* that the teaching-learning process is a delicate human transaction requiring skill and sensitivity in human relations. The effective instructor is engaged with the learners in a learning group in which, together, they experiment in new pathways of thought, behavior, and planning for use of new behavior.

The instructor must be aware of the complex process of *human relationships* that exists in the classroom. These relationships involve the anxieties of the learner, the threat of the instructor as a judge, the mixed feelings of the learner about his or her dependence upon the instructor.

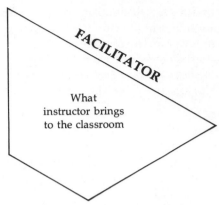

What
instructor brings
to the classroom

Second, the instructor as a partner in the teaching-learning situation needs to be aware of personal needs and motivations. To what extent do his or her needs to control others, to maintain a dependency, or to seek love and affection, distort his or her helping function in the classroom? Knowing one's own motivations and their possible consequences for others better enables the instructor to keep personal motivations under direction and control.

Third, the instructor must have the ability to *accept the learner as a person*. Acceptance means ability to respect and listen to the learners in their present state of development. Acceptance does not mean approval, but acceptance is the entry point for a helping relationship.

Setting for Learning

Most in-service education takes place in group situations. The dynamics of the classroom is at the heart of the teaching-learning process. Group influence can be a powerful force in supporting the learning process.

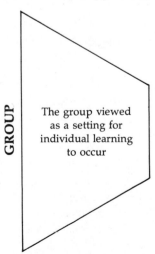

The group viewed
as a setting for
individual learning
to occur

As instructors become skilled in recognizing the emotional aspects of group behavior, anxieties, hidden motives, problems of authority, they are better able to help the learners help each other. The dynamics of group forces are present in all group situations. If the instructor is not aware of, or is unable to use these dynamics constructively, they often work against the instructor and against learning.

Interaction Process

An in-service instructor needs to be aware of the consequences of any *interaction* on all the members in the learning group. Interaction among the group may be as valuable for learning as the interaction with the instructor.

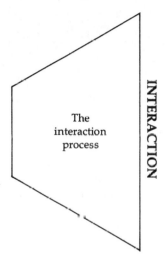

The interaction process has two basic purposes: first, it establishes a climate that reduces anxieties and defensiveness in the learner and helps the learner be open to learning; and, second, it brings about learning and change.

Adults need a supportive climate in the classroom. The interventions of the instructor are of critical importance in developing this climate. The instructor must take the initiative in shifting the balance of motivation for learning to the learner and reducing a dependency on the instructor.

Conditions Necessary

Adults learn more effectively when certain conditions are present in the learning situations. Adults, because of their self-image, previous experience and resistance to change, need an environment that is supportive of

self-diagnosis, experimentation and practice. Adults must be active participants. As long as the thoughts, feelings and behavior needing change do
not surface, learning is hindered by feelings of anxiety, inadequacy and
defensiveness.

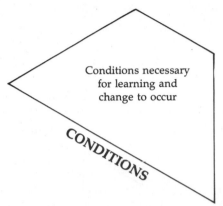

Learning is much more than filling a void with information. It is a
process of internal reorganization of complex thought patterns, perceptions, attitudes and skills, and of successfully testing this reorganization
in relation to the problems of the real situation. A diagnosis of the present
inadequate behavior is the basis for the reorganization process. This diagnosis goes beyond the skill deficiency to include motivation, anxieties, defensiveness, insecurities and perceptions.

Adults not only need to be part of the diagnosis involved in the plan of
action, but they also need relevant, accurate and acceptable feedback on
how well they are progressing toward the new behavior. Adults need constructive feedback following exposure in trying new behavior. Feedback
helps the adult readjust the self-image.

Instructors are tempted to be the sole person giving feedback. This
leads to dependency. Adults learn more effectively when a climate is established in which supportive feedback comes immediately from peers,
self-evaluation of the skill attempted, and the instructor.

Continued Learning Process

As adults become more aware, through an effective teaching-learning
transaction, of their own anxieties and resistance to change, they are better
able to reduce them and enhance the learning and change. Adults need to
become more accepting of themselves in the classroom situation and thus
gain more internal security. As this is achieved, learning is more effective.

A basic purpose of in-service education and of all teaching-learning
situations is to first help the person open up for learning by being able to

bring his or her desires, problems and needs for learning to the surface and to listen and accept feedback about personal problems and behavior. The second purpose is to help the employee gain methods of analyzing and utilizing knowledge from daily problem-solving to continue his change and growth.

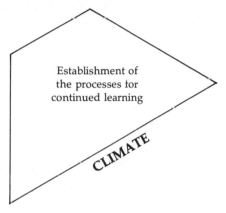

Maintenance of Change

Instructors need to realize that the presence of an adult in the classroom does not necessarily imply a commitment to learning and change. The adult must have the opportunity to experiment with the new behavior, to test it for results, and to become comfortable with it. Unless this process of internalization of new knowledge happens, the learning is compartmentalized and remains outside the individual. The motivation to change must be supportive enough to overcome the resistance to change.

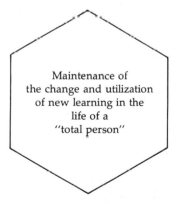

There are several steps that are useful in building the supportive elements:

a. Help the learner diagnose the forces of resistance to change.

b. Help the learner assess personal potential strengths and weaknesses in terms of change.

c. Help the learner plan in applying the new knowledge to the real situation.

d. Help the learner locate support areas away from the classroom situations.

e. Help the learner plan for a continuing system of learning. Implementation of a supportive climate gives the adult confidence to use experiences to internalize new learning and change.

CONCLUSIONS

An in-service educational program that is geared to achieve results aimed toward achieving the hospital goal of "total healing" must be based upon an educational theory that involves the total person. A "robot in" and a "robot out" will not increase the level of quality care.

An effective theory for in-service education needs to incorporate the seven areas of the teaching-learning process. It also calls for developing in the instructor a sensitivity to and an awareness of skills of interacting effectively with the learner and the learning group. Instructors need help in gaining a self-awareness of how their behavior is perceived by others. They need practice in diagnosing human relations and group problems, and experience in sharpening sensitivity to what others are feeling and trying to communicate. Awareness and sensitivities are primary with teaching procedure skills secondary.

Effective in-service education programs need instructors who develop programs based on a teaching-learning theory, a theory that incorporates elements of adult education and group dynamics. Programs built upon such a theory will produce results.

REFERENCES

Bradford, Leland P. The teaching-learning transaction. *Human forces in teaching and learning.* National Training Laboratories, 1961.

Knowles, Malcolm S. Gearing adult education for the seventies. *The Journal of Continuing Education in Nursing,* Vol. 1, No. 1, May 1970.

Lippitt, Ronald, Watson, Jeanne, & Westley, Bruce. *Dynamics of planned change.* New York: Harcourt, Brace and Co., 1953.

Thelen, Herbert A. *Dynamics of groups at work.* Chicago: The University of Chicago Press, 1954.

Wright, Sr. Rebecca, SSM. Accountability: the key to training effectiveness. *Hospital Progress,* March 1974.

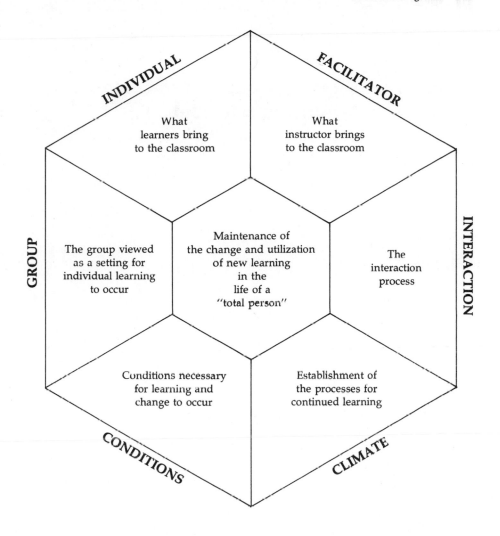

In-Service Training: A Confluent Education Model

Aaron W. Hillman

PURPOSE

The purpose of this article is to describe a Confluent Education model for educational in-service training based upon experience. It is not meant to influence teaching practice directly nor to offer guidelines for the supervision or training of teachers. The purpose is to describe, not prescribe. Yet certain implications for supervision and teacher in-service training as well as "standard" approaches to the same arise from this description, and merit consideration.

It will also serve to introduce the concept of confluent education and some aspects of its methodology.

THE GREAT TRAINING ROBBERY

As a secondary school teacher of some years standing, I have been directly involved with what might be called "traditional in-service training." It was relatively hit-and-miss and as far as I can ascertain its effects were minimal. It can be characterized as "The Man With The Briefcase From Out Of Town" motif who is "An Expert In His Field." I shall also be quick to confess that I have been, and am, one of those people.

The educational consultant is generally a "fly in-fly out" person. He arrives on the scene with some fanfare and advance publicity and "does his thing." Immediately upon accomplishing that thing he disappears into the sunset.

Reprinted from *The New Campus*, Association for Field Services in Teacher Education, Vol. XXVI, Spring 1973, pp. 31-36. Used with permission of the author.

What "follow-up" is made is little, if any. Such follow-up does not have the man's expertise, unfortunately. We as teachers, seem reluctant to accept anyone, administrator or teacher, who lives and works locally, as any kind of an authority. As I said, you have to be from out of town in order to be an authority . . . and carry a briefcase . . . and fly on airplanes.

It can also be pointed out that the decision for the consultant to come in the first place is almost invariably made by one man at the top of the administrative ladder and/or by The Board itself. The persons involved are directed to attend this experience which they did not have a part in deciding.

Such attendance is generally on the teacher's "time." Very little thought is given to stopping classes in order for teachers to participate in training. Teachers should be grateful for the fact that a decision has been made that a consultant will come and enlighten them and that such decision was made for them. They are not.

Of course, students are even less involved than the teacher. Supposedly they will benefit after the consultant has come and done his thing, and the teachers take this thing and improve themselves, and then come back into the classroom and improve the students. Students should be eternally grateful for this state of affairs. They are not.

The educational consultant, my colleague as I see him now, usually "presents" his knowledge. The word "presents" is precisely the word I wish to use. The consultant does not offer an experience. The teachers are spectators at the latest spectator sport. It is deadening on both ends. Of course, this consultant does this bit for a rather nice amount of money. He deserves this, I know. I know I deserve what I get. If you have it, flaunt it. If you can get it, it obviously means you are excellent in your field and if you transmit this to teachers they will be excellent too.

In the above paragraphs I have indulged in a real "ain't it horrible" session. I have exaggerated to a certain extent but, so it goes, there is a lot of truth in exaggeration. Traditional in-service training in terms of expense and results is a "Great Training Robbery." We don't get what we pay for.

I am going to propose a different type of in-service training that *may* offer an alternative to the situation. This type is the result of a new direction being proposed for education, as well as the results of some of my own in-service training educational workshops. Of course they were in no way like the ones described above. Almost.

CONFLUENT EDUCATION

The following statement pertains to children specifically but it also applies to every human being of whatever age or whatever status or occupation in life. For our purpose listen to the implications it has for teacher in-service training.

Given any behavioral objective, there are always conditions attached to the attainment of that objective which could ultimately influence not only the attainment of the objective but also, very intimately affect the way the child feels about himself, his peers, and learning in general. Thus, it seems to me that much could be gained by making explicit those areas which affect what a child learns and how he feels about himself as a learner.[1]

This writer, Dr. Richard Jamgochian of the Graduate School of Education, University of California, Santa Barbara, is speaking about the *affective* side of man's nature. That is, the emotional context of whatever is being presented or whatever is happening. Affective refers to the feeling or emotional aspect of experience and learning.[2]

One of the greatest properties of the human being is that they can experience emotion. These feelings are intangibles. They can't be touched as the chair can be touched. They can't be seen as words can be seen. This *affective* side of man's nature is one polarity of confluent education. Its opposite is the term/concept *cognitive*.

That which is *cognitive* is factual knowledge taught at any particular time and, as prescribed in our curricula, is a series of ideas and/or concepts and the background to support them. *Cognitive* also refers to the activity of the mind in knowing an object; to intellectual functioning. It can also refer to the subject matter that is to be learned.

Confluent Education is the system of education which attempts to merge the cognitive and affective domains in the moment and act of teaching. For information concerning its origins and development see the work of Dr. George Isaac Brown in the book *Human Teaching for Human Learning*.[3] Meantime, listen to how he describes this education.

Confluent Education is the system to integrate the Appolonian and the Dionysian, the Age of Enlightenment and the Romantic Period, head and heart, mind and body, howsoever the basic polarity common to all may be hallmarked, so that like two brooks flowing together into one stream, each merges into the other, losing its boundaries to a greater whole. Confluent Education

---

[1] Richard Jamgochian, "Humanism and Behavioral Objectives." Occasional Paper No. 1, DRICE, Development and Research in Confluent Education, University of California, Santa Barbara, California, 1970, p. 6.

[2] For further information and definition of terms and their working relation to education see Benjamin S. Bloom (Ed.), *Taxonomy of Educational Objectives* (Handbook I, Cognitive Domain), 1956, and Krathwohl, Bloom, and Masia, *Taxonomy of Educational Objectives* (Handbook II, Affective Domain), 1964.

[3] George Isaac Brown, *Human Teaching for Human Learning*. New York: Viking Press, 1971.

is essentially the synthesis of the affective domain (feelings, emotions, attitudes and values) and the cognitive domain (the intellect, the activity of the mind in knowing).[4]

In terms of this paper the models to be proposed as the alternative to "The Great Training Robbery" are based on the elements and concepts, goals and objectives, of confluent education. It is essentially a model in confluent education that proposes a "gestalt"[5] in school in-service training.

TWO MODELS FOR SCHOOL IN-SERVICE TRAINING

As was mentioned previously, the author, in addition to other work, is an educational consultant. The two models for school in-service training to be described are almost verbatim from two in-service training workshops that I led. They are verbatim to the event [sic] that the outline is what actually happened. I am not proposing to list any of the techniques used or the names of any of the individuals involved.

The models, it should be noted, developed *after* I arrived on the scene and as time progressed. There was a general consultation before I was hired but that only covered what expectations the educational department had and what they wanted. So the models are "after the fact." I find this is a good way for me to work in that I can arrange the workshop according to the circumstances of the place, time, and situation, rather than as I *imagine* them to be.

These models are for a series of days. It is the antithesis of the quick speech or three-hour workshop. What is developed is knowledge of the area, the school, its people, the curriculum, the consultant and what he has to offer.

The genesis of these workshops was an experimental program financed by the Department of Education, Province of Manitoba, Canada, and my involvement came about through previous work I had done for the Vancouver, British Columbia, school board as well as my connection with the development and research program in Confluent Education.[6]

---

[4]George Isaac Brown, "Human is as Confluent Does." Occasional Paper No. 9, DRICE, Development and Research in Confluent Education, University of California, Santa Barbara, California, 1971, p. 3.

[5]Confluent Education has a theoretical base in Gestalt psychology and Gestalt therapy, and the work of Dr. Frederick S. Perls. See (a.) Perls, Hefferline, and Goodman, *Gestalt Therapy*, 1951; (b) Perls, F. S., *Ego, Hunger, and Aggression*, 1960.

[6]For information about the program contact John Ekstedt, Coordinator, Confluent Education Project, Box 219, Minnedosa, Manitoba.

Cranberry Portage: Model 1

The Setting. Cranberry Portage, Manitoba, is a small town in north-Manitoba. The school is named Frontier Collegiate and consists of grades 9 through 12. It draws students from a widely dispersed area with the result that the school maintains dormitories for those students who live too far away to commute regularly. The students are generally Indian, part Indian, and Caucasian. The curriculum is what may be termed a general traditional "academic" form. The emphasis is on the academics with little chance to learn vocational skills.

The First Day. [7] Spent the time getting acquainted with the school and its people. After short introductions to the administrative staff I was left to my own devices (something I insist on). I visited the library, talked to students, looked into classrooms, visited a counselor, observed interactions between students and students and others, and talked, individually, to teachers and to non-credentialed employees. After school, I met with the Science Department teachers for an hour and discussed curriculum. In the evening I met with the houseparents at the dormitories with the principal of the school. We discussed problems of the houseparents in relation to the children in the dorms, the relationships between houseparents and students, students and teachers, houseparents and teachers, houseparents and administration, houseparents and community. Practical advice was given on these problems *plus* we engaged in small exercises that illustrated ways of working with other people. Demands were made by the houseparents as to wanting to get involved in teacher's and administrator's meetings, as well as any in-service training that was arranged.

The Second Day. This day I took over two classes for work and demonstration. Spent one period talking with students. One period a teacher was ill and so I became a substitute teacher in a ninth grade English class for a period. Again, I visited the library, talked to students at various places, discussed with teachers their problems, and observed teaching of some teachers. In the evening I spent another three-hour period working with the houseparents and also visiting students in the dormitories as well as in the hallways. During the day I met with the English Department to discuss curriculum.

The Third Day. The day began the formal part of the workshop. School was suspended for two days and all staff and faculty met together. This workshop included teachers, administrators, houseparents, and a student who

---

[7]The arrival was most unique; I came in via ski-plane and landed on a frozen lake, where I was met by an Indian lady and a dog sled and team. We mushed into town, about a mile, in sub-zero weather.

came to observe. After an introduction to confluent education and a review of what we might anticipate, I began to work experimentally with the group. The participants were taught verbal skills, questioning skills, personal communication skills, how to work with behavior problems, and how to correlate cognitive and affective learning, while working with colleagues they scarcely knew (even though they live in a close community). I also presented the formal theory that lies at the base of confluent education. The total number of hours corresponded to a normal school day. At the end I made no attempt to "sum-up."[8] After the day's work we met informally for specific help in various lessons and/or courses.

The Fourth Day. The fourth day was a repeat of the third day with one major exception. For the last two hours we had a formal question-and-answer session as well as feedback to me as to whether the workshop was valuable, and if so, to what degree. Plans were also made for follow-up meetings by the staff and faculty (with the houseparents being definitely included in any and all planning and workshops). For the last event we made it a point to contact each person present and to express our appreciation of one another.

Commentary. The situation here was unique as to its setting but then, so is every situation. Sameness is a mistaken concept; it doesn't exist. There are certainly patterns, but situations are not the same. The major point for me is that as many facets as possible in the situation were covered and/or represented. Teachers do not work in a vacuum any more than administrators do. When we *try* to work in a vacuum we foster suspicions and fail to deal with cross-school or community problems. Nothing develops suspicions and resentments like a lack of knowledge of one another and what we are doing.

Basically Model 1 is a four-day workshop based on the following pattern:

1st Day. Getting acquainted. Familiarization with territory.

2nd Day. Learn to know the problems and needs.

3rd Day. Work with theory and methodology through experiential means.

4th Day. Continue work with theory and methodology through experiential means; have an evaluation of what was learned by the persons in attendance; gain feedback through a question and answer session; have a closure that influences future work; plan for feedback and follow-up by those on the scene.

Note here is [sic] that the coordinator for my visit (not an administrator) was the locus and focus for the follow-up and feedback work.

---

[8]One of my high school students said to me: "Don't sum-up, Mr. Hillman! Every time you do you stop people from thinking!" I thought it was good advice.

An important point for us to learn is that the administrator needs only to assist, not to direct (a good teaching method for any teacher to adopt).

Tanner's Crossing: Model 2

Tanner's Crossing is an elementary and junior high school in Minnedosa, Manitoba. Minnedosa is a large town in central Manitoba. It draws students from the town as well as from the surrounding countryside but there are no dormitories or "live-in" students at the school. Next door to Tanner's Crossing School is a local secondary school and there is another secondary school some miles away. Tanner's Crossing School is an ultra-modern school with at least half of the classrooms in open area concept.

The First Day. Spent the time getting acquainted with the school and its people. After short introductions to the administrative staff I was left to my own devices. I visited the library (a circle in the center of the open classroom!), talked to students, looked into classrooms, observed teaching, visited a counselor, observed interactions between students and students and others, and talked individually to teachers and to non-credentialed employees. At noon there was a catered and sack lunch for the faculty. I was introduced, made a few brief remarks, and spent the rest of the time discussing various aspects of their teaching. In the afternoon I visited more classrooms. After school, two teacher-study groups met (there were several such groups within the school). I met for an hour with each study group, listened to their work, spoke briefly to them, and in general discussed their accomplishments, needs and presumed failures.

The Second Day. The two local secondary schools' facilities and administrators had an in-service day. I conducted an in-service workshop much the same as I had done on the third and fourth days of the Cranberry Portage model. (School was suspended this day.) In the evening a volunteer group of teachers and administrators met with me to discuss curriculum and new methodology in education. While I was the leader-consultant in this later situation, I led it into a "give and take" discussion about what each one was doing in the classroom.[9]

The Third Day. This was an unusual but most satisfying day. I was back at the Tanner's Crossing School and (1) gave a demonstration lesson to a 5th grade language arts class, (2) gave a demonstration lesson to an 8th grade mathematics class, (3) gave a demonstration lesson to (and with) 90 third graders all at the same time (one hour and fifteen minutes). During lunch I met with more teachers. After lunch I met with a group of young people

---

[9]Members of the local faculty have skills that they could teach to other members of the faculty. Also, they can be made a part of the consultant's program.

and their teacher in a class for "slow learners." The school had a voluntary group of young people in a continuing human relations workshop and I met and worked with them for an hour after school (TV taped). During the evening of this day I made a speech and did demonstration lessons for the community. It had been advertised that it was an open meeting and was specifically for the town's people. Among the persons attending was the President of the School Board who became enthusiastic over the workshop and subsequently attended the teachers' phase of the workshop.

The Fourth Day. I began a formal workshop with the staff and faculty of Tanner's Crossing Elementary and Junior High School. School was suspended for two days and the staff and faculty met together. This workshop included teachers, administrators, a school board member, the dean of education from a local university, and some visiting teachers. After an introduction to confluent education and a review of what we might anticipate, I began to work experimentally with the group. The participants were taught verbal skills, questioning skills, personal communications skills, how to work with behavior problems, how to correlate cognitive and affective learning, how to live better in their personal lives. Meantime I presented the formal theory that lies at the base of confluent education. This consumed a normal school day. At the end I made no attempt to "sum-up." The evening of this day was unusual in that I went with some teachers and administrators to see the town's hockey team in action and was introduced to the team and the townspeople at the game.

The Fifth Day. The fifth day was a repeat of the fourth day with one major exception. We had a formal question-and-answer session both in small groups and as a total group. Feedback was given to me as to whether the workshop was valuable and if so to what degree.[10] Plans were made for follow-up meetings by the staff and faculty. For the closure, I led the group through a speech concerning literature and affective teaching that I had made to the National Council of Teachers of English.[11]

Commentary. A totally satisfying experience to me, and the feedback then and since has confirmed my belief as to the value of the experience. This model represents a total involvement and the exceptional model that I would hope in-service training could become. All facets of the school and the community were included in the training. Theoretical and practical

---

[10] At the end of the workshop I was presented with an autographed hockey stick and a puck from the local team. This was the culmination of the feedback session and much appreciated by me.

[11] Aaron W. Hillman, "The Lord of the Rings: Affective Approaches to Teaching Literature." Occasional Paper No. 10, DRICE, Development and Research in Confluent Education. University of California, Santa Barbara, California, 1971.

work was initiated and follow-up measures were taken.[12] This is teacher (and school) in-service training that contains a *how,* and a *what,* as well as a *why* (theory).

RECOMMENDATIONS

That the confluent education approach be utilized as an effective way of conducting in-service training (getting all segments of a school community involved).

That "one-day" or "one-night" stands be avoided. It takes time to develop understanding.

That teachers, administrators, students, other school elements, and community representatives, be included in the planning for any in-service training.

That staff and faculty within the school system be utilized not only as leaders within an in-service workshop but to conduct in-service workshops. There is always great talent on any faculty.

That in-service training be done through individual schools rather than through district-wide facilities. A huge number diminishes the amount of effective work that can be accomplished.

That students, especially, be included in all aspects of in-service training.

In closing, I wish to add that the workshops as conducted were relatively inexpensive. They required no additional facilities and little more of others' time. They did require commitment to learning and teaching and a willingness to drop a day or two of classroom time.

If a consultant is too busy or too "big" to spare you more than an hour, or a speech, he is not worth the price. It seems to me that only through knowing one another and working together can we truly effect change.

---

[12] A follow-up session for both schools was held during the summer vacation period. This was a two-week intensive workshop for volunteer teachers and administrators. Fifty-six were in attendance.

Analyzing and Improving Nonverbal Communication: A Model for Inservice Education

Russell L. French

During the past ten years, interest in the analysis of nonverbal communication and interaction in the school setting has increased markedly. Research in this field has come into its own, and a number of school systems and universities across the country have attempted to incorporate research findings and developmental activities into both preservice teacher education and inservice professional growth programs. Many creative teacher educators, supervisors, principals and teachers have developed their own successful strategies for dealing with nonverbal communication in preservice and inservice settings. The model delineated here should not be interpreted as necessarily the only or best model. It is one model that has proved useful in (1) focusing the attention of teachers on significant aspects of nonverbal communication, (2) bringing to the analysis of nonverbal communication a number of tools (observation systems, visual aids, activities) which bring clarity to abstract concepts, practicality to theoretical notions, and structure to diversified activities, and (3) developing longitudinal in-depth studies of nonverbal communication in the classroom. The model is presented here because the reader may find it helpful in developing professional growth programs and because it may motivate him to develop other formats more useful in his particular situation.

THE MODEL

Examination of nonverbal communication in the classroom teaching-learning situation suggests four major areas for focus and study:

Reprinted from Russell L. French, "Analyzing and Improving Nonverbal Communication: A Model for Inservice Education," *Theory Into Practice*, College of Education, The Ohio State University, Volume X, Number 4 (1969).

1. Pupil Nonverbal Messages;
2. Nonverbal Environmental Communications (messages communicated by use of space, time and other environmental elements);
3. Teacher Nonverbal Clues;
4. A Curriculum in Human Communication.

These areas together with introductory and background material constitute the five content phases of the model.

Three experimentally-based assumptions have governed our structuring or sequencing of the phases in professional growth programs. First, self-assessment (analysis of one's own behavior) is threatening to an individual who has engaged in few structured self-assessment activities. Second, study of the communicative qualities of the environment suggests change from present environmental settings and practices; change also threatens most of us. Third, planning for teaching and learning activities centered on communication cannot be accomplished until the teacher has adequate background to undertake the task.

These three assumptions indicated that we should begin inservice education in nonverbal communication with a general introduction followed by analysis of pupil nonverbal messages, since this area might be least threatening to the teacher. The next phase could be examination of environmental communications. Analysis of teacher nonverbal cues becomes the fourth phase, and developing curriculum experiences and instructional strategies for expanding pupil knowledge, attitudes and skills in communication provides the fifth and culminating phase of the program.

To implement the model, a variety of tools, activities, and strategies must be integrated.

IMPLEMENTING THE MODEL

Phase 1. Introduction and Background

Obviously, the teacher cannot study nonverbal communication unless he knows what it is. In most inservice projects, it is necessary to begin with a general introduction to the field of communication. Fundamental concepts, common assumptions about teaching and the definition of nonverbal communication need to be presented and examined.

A few nonverbal games or encounters borrowed from sensitivity training can provide a good introduction to nonverbal communication. Galloway's recent monograph[1] has proved to be useful in this context as have

---

[1] Charles M. Galloway, *Teaching is Communicating: Nonverbal Language in the Classroom.* Bulletin No. 29. Washington, D.C.: The Association for Student Teaching, 1970.

the writings of Hall[2, 3] and Goffman.[4] Most teachers find the current best seller *Body Language* by Julian Fast[5] both entertaining and enlightening. Presentation, discussion and illustration of both human and nonhuman communicative elements are essential at this time.

Phase 2. Analysis of Pupil Nonverbal Messages

Student nonverbal behaviors are important because they offer a means of perceiving the student as an individual. Further, we know that children learn early in the educational process that they are not supposed to communicate verbally the things which really matter to them. Real feelings, values and emotions are not appropriate content for communication in the institutions we call schools. However, we usually do communicate our needs, feelings and values nonverbally.

One procedure that effectively sensitizes teachers to pupil nonverbal behavior in their own classrooms is the presentation and illustration of the categories of the Student Behavior Survey[6] followed by videotaped or filmed observations of children in the classroom setting and a specific assignment such as that provided in Appendix A.

If inservice time is sufficient and teachers are committed to the task, learning about and using an observational system such as the Student Behavior Index[7] can be valuable. Roderick, Love and Moyer (The University of Maryland) and Schusler (The University of Kansas) have also developed observational devices that should prove helpful in developing teacher awareness of pupil messages.

Good films or videotapes of pupils in action are valuable tools with or without the use of some of the observational systems or strategies outlined.

Phase 3. Analysis of Environmental Communications

Messages are sent to and received by human beings through the use of time and space. Light and dark communicate. Color, geometric design,

---

[2]Edward T. Hall, *The Hidden Dimension*. New York: Fawcett World Library, 1966.

[3]Edward T. Hall, *The Silent Language*. New York: Fawcett World Library, 1966.

[4]Erving Goffman, *The Presentation of Self in Everyday Living*. New York: Doubleday and Company, 1957.

[5]Julian Fast, *Body Language*. New York. M. Evans Co., 1970. Distributed by Lippincott.

[6]Russell L. French, "Individualizing Classroom Communications," *Educational Leadership*, November 1970, pp. 193-96.

[7]Larry R. Parker and Russell L. French, "A Description of Student Behavior: Verbal and Nonverbal." Unpublished paper, The University of Tennessee, Knoxville, 1971.

surroundings, and organizational structure communicate. Whether or not we are products of our environment, we cannot deny the meanings we find in it. Teachers need to see their classrooms and schools in this context.

Holding inservice meetings in diverse settings (an open-space school, a round school, a box-design school, a school with carpet, one with oiled softwood floors) with appropriate discussion of surroundings and their impact on the individuals gathered can be a valuable means of studying environmental communications.

Presentation of slides or films depicting different types of schools, varying classroom arrangements and furnishings, and variations in light and color schemes can be effective in alerting teachers to communication problems in their own classrooms and schools. Videotapes that show alternative ways of using time and space provide excellent focal points for discussion.

Teacher sensitivity to environmental communications is increased even more when the aforementioned activities culminate in a specific assignment such as that which appears in Appendix B.

Phase 4. Self-Assessment: Analysis of Teacher Nonverbal Behaviors

If we assume that the teacher is the dominant influence in the classroom, teachers obviously must give attention to their own nonverbal behaviors. A variety of tools are available to assist the teacher in the self-assessment process.

Using a "buddy" system for observation or videotapes, teachers can develop awareness of recurring and/or outstanding behaviors. An assignment utilizing this strategy constitutes Appendix C-1.

As a second and more sophisticated step, participants can use one or more observation systems in conjunction with videotape or buddy observations. Galloway's initial nonverbal behavior dimensions are useful here as is the IDER system[8] and other systems described in *Theory Into Practice*.

Videotapes and many commercially produced films lend themselves to analysis of teacher nonverbal behavior with or without the use of observational systems. Examples are those in the General Learning Corporation package on microteaching skills, Holt, Rinehart and Winston's *Critical Moments in Teaching* series, and Science Research Associates' *Inner City Simulation Laboratory*.

Following the showing of General Learning's film on the use of silence and nonverbal cues, an assignment such as that appearing as Appendix C-2 might be made.

---

[8]Russell L. French and Charles M. Galloway, "A Description of Teacher Behavior: Verbal and Nonverbal. Unpublished paper, The Ohio State University, Columbus, 1968.

Phase 5. Developing Curriculum in Human Communication

Study in the area of human communication and particularly nonverbal communication makes one painfully aware that we spend a great deal of time teaching children to read, write and compute, but little if any time consciously teaching them to communicate with and interpret the communications of their fellow human beings. This condition represents neither humanistic nor affective education. Davitz[9] has clearly documented the need in this area, emphasizing the significance of the child's development between the ages of five and twelve. A host of other researchers in anthropology, sociology, psychology and education have pinpointed the same need from their various perspectives. At this point in our professional growth project, it seems natural to engage teachers in the development of curricular experiences and instructional strategies designed to help children learn more about human communication and the communicative devices used by themselves and others.

Since most teachers can be quite creative in developing curriculum experiences for the students they teach, our typical inservice approach involves a roundtable discussion of what they are now doing in this area and what they might like to do followed by an assignment similar to the one provided in Appendix D.

Typically, teachers and their students have been very creative. Their resources and explorations have integrated a number of disciplines, activities and experiences.

Throughout the educational process, from nursery school to doctoral programs, we are engaged in teaching people. Content, of necessity, must be secondary. How can we teach people better? How can we improve the educational process? One answer may be found in the nature of our human interactions and communications. The problem for many of us is one of teaching teachers. Perhaps the model presented here will be useful in addressing that problem.

APPENDIX A: AN ASSIGNMENT IN ANALYSIS OF PUPIL NONVERBAL CUES

This assignment follows our discussion of pupil nonverbal behaviors. It should help you gain useful additional information about several students in your classroom.

1. Select three (3) of your students about whom you want to know more. They may be problem students (discipline, learning problems, etc.) or they may be students whom you just don't feel you know well.

---

[9]Joel R. Davitz, *The Communication of Emotional Meaning.* New York: McGraw-Hill, 1964.

2. Over the next week, observe *each* of these students closely for a total of *no less than twenty-five minutes.* Obviously, you can't give your entire attention to any one student for twenty-five minutes at a time, but find opportunities in the classroom, on the playground, in the cafeteria, etc., when you can consciously shut out everything and everyone else for *three to five minutes.*

3. After each observation period, record specific behaviors in whatever categories seem appropriate on the Student Behavior Survey. If what you saw doesn't fit any of the categories provided, create your own categories.

4. After you have observed each of the three students you selected for twenty-five minutes (total), review his Behavior Survey asking yourself these questions:
   a. What do I now know about this person that I didn't know before?
   b. How can I use this information to reach and teach this student?

STUDENT BEHAVIOR SURVEY

Pupil Name _____

Dates and Times of Observation (Each pupil to be observed for no less than twenty-five minutes) _____

Teacher (or Aide) _____

BEHAVIORS OBSERVED

   I. Need Expressions

  II. Distress Signals (Anxiety Cues)

 III. Expressions of Boredom

 IV. Expressions of Involvement

  V. Verbal Substitutions

APPENDIX B: ASSIGNMENT IN ANALYSIS OF ENVIRONMENTAL COMMUNICATIONS

This assignment results from our discussion of environmental communications. Perhaps it will help you become more aware of environmental communication problems in your classroom and school.

1. *Change some physical aspect of your classroom or some aspect of your teaching day.* You might choose to rearrange the classroom furnishings, reorder the content you're teaching, use class time differently, try teaching from one or more different positions in the classroom, introduce something new into the environment (music, colorful objects, carpet in one area of the room for independent study), or

you may want to move your teaching and learning into new surroundings—outside the classroom or outside the school.

2. After planning the change you wish to make, *try it out for at least one week.* One day or two days or even three days will not provide sufficient time to prove the change successful or unsuccessful. Both you and the students will need time to adapt and adjust.
3. At the end of the try-out period, evaluate the success of your experiment:
   a. Write a brief description of the change.
   b. Describe how students reacted.
   c. Describe how you reacted.
   d. Try to respond to some key questions: Has the change improved the atmosphere of my classroom? Has it had any effect on my teaching? Do students seem to be learning more, demonstrating more interest, more enthusiasm?
   e. Make a decision about what to do next—continue with the changed routine or situation, modify it, try something else, go back to the way things were before.

APPENDIX C-1: ASSIGNMENT IN ANALYSIS OF TEACHER NONVERBAL CUES

This assignment follows our discussion of teacher classroom impact and teacher nonverbal cues. Perhaps it will help you gain additional feedback about your nonverbal behavior and the ways in which others perceive you.

1. Select another teacher in your building with whom you feel comfortable.
2. Make arrangements to have him observe in your classroom *twice* during the next week. He should observe for *at least twenty minutes* on each visit. You will be expected to visit his classroom twice, also, observing for no less than twenty minutes on each visit.
3. During the classroom visits, observers should focus their attention primarily on the teacher. Note recurring or particularly noticeable nonverbal behaviors. As these occur, write a *brief* description of what you see.
4. After the two classroom visits, observers and those observed should plan a time to share observations. Try to provide the teacher you observed with a written record of what you saw.

APPENDIX C-2: ASSIGNMENT IN ANALYSIS OF TEACHER NONVERBAL BEHAVIOR

You have seen the General Learning film on teacher use of silence and nonverbal cues. In the film the teacher conducts a lesson for almost five minutes without saying a word. We do not think that this approach is the right way or best way to teach, but an attempt to teach *without talking* certainly makes us aware of our nonverbal cues and their impact on students. For that reason, we make the following assignment:

1. During the next week, try to teach portions of two separate lessons *without talking.* Try to teach nonverbally for at least five minutes in each instance.
2. After each experiment, take time to write down your observations:
   a. How did you feel during this interlude?
   b. How did students react?
   c. What occurrences or personal behaviors or particular student reactions stand out in your memory?
   d. What did you learn from these experiences?

APPENDIX D: ASSIGNMENT IN DEVELOPING CURRICULUM AND INSTRUCTION IN HUMAN COMMUNICATION

We have spent much time in studying human communication, particularly nonverbal communication as it influences the teaching-learning situation in our classrooms. We are all aware of the complexities of human communication, the distortions which occur, the problems which result. Our most recent study and discussion has indicated that most teachers in most schools spend little time in teaching students about human communication and the communicative devices of themselves and others. It is hoped that this assignment will reveal new content and teaching strategies for your classroom.

1. Plan a unit (two or more lessons or experiences) focusing on human communication for students in your classroom. Be sure to identify specific objectives to be achieved, strategies for achieving them and the measurement technique or instruments to be used in assessing the accomplishments of the objectives.
2. Teach the unit.
3. Evaluate the unit. Based on the measurements obtained, student feedback, and your own feelings about the content and approach as it developed, make some judgments about the content and format of the unit.
   a. Did your students accomplish the objectives?
   b. Were the instructional strategies appropriate to the objectives and the students involved?
   c. Did students enjoy this study? Did they get deeply involved?
   d. Did you enjoy the experience? Did you get deeply involved?
   e. How should the format or content be changed if you teach the unit again?

f. Would you teach the unit again?

g. What other units or experiences in the area of human communication would you like to develop?

Note: Use any materials, experiences, or instructional strategies you wish, but think creatively. Commercial television, movies, creative dramatics, advertising, architecture, art and music all provide possible resources for the unit you wish to develop. You can probably think of many others.

Microdesign for Training Conveners

Richard Schmuck and Philip Runkel

The following is a two-day sequence of activities for training participants to conduct effective meetings. The learning model for this training consists of a recurring cycle of five activities: (1) modeling by the trainer, (2) experiencing a simulated meeting, (3) debriefing the simulation, (4) short lecture and/or handout to present concepts, and (5) discussing applications of the concepts. In brief form, the two-day outline is as follows:

First day:
   Building an agenda (3 hours). Using communication skills such as paraphrasing, describing behavior, checking feelings of others, taking a survey (3 hours). Evaluating a meeting (2 hours).

Second day:
   Convening a group and task and maintenance functions (3 hours). Practicing meeting management skills (3 hours). Practicing meeting management skills (2 hours).

Here is the design in detail:

I. Building an agenda.
   A. Modeling the agenda-building. Describe your task of building the agenda for these two days.
   B. Experiencing agenda-building.
      1. Each participant writes on a side of a 3 x 5 card one goal he wishes to achieve during these two days, and on the other side two re-sources he will contribute to this group.

Reprinted from the *Handbook of Organization Development in Schools* by Richard Schmuck and Philip Runkel, Mayfield Publishing Co., 1972. Courtesy of the Center for Educational Policy and Management, University of Oregon.

2. In turn, each participant conducts the group for ten minutes by leading discussion on an agenda item.

C. Debriefing the agenda-building.
   1. What behaviors facilitated or inhibited involvement?
   2. What behaviors decreased or increased anxiety?
   3. Were the group's resources brought out? What behaviors helped or did not help bring them out?
   4. Were the goals and priorities clear to all participants?
   5. Were the agendas realistic? Did convener attend to constraints of time, space, etc.?
   6. Was newsprint used effectively?

D. Short lecture on agenda-building. Describe how to involve participants in setting an agenda so they feel that their interests are represented; discuss guidelines for structuring an agenda around the problem of the meeting.

E. Discussion on agenda-building.
   1. Discuss use of process checks for clarifying which type of inquiry group is engaged in.
   2. Discuss need for skills to encourage bringing out and clarifying ideas for keeping meeting at maximum effectiveness. This leads into next section.

II. Using communication skills.

A. Paraphrasing.
   1. Modeling paraphrasing. Describe paraphrasing and its usefulness by recalling one or two incidents from some earlier session where an effective paraphrase was used and helped procedures.
   2. Experiencing paraphrasing in trios.
      a. Ask each person to think of an idea or a concept related to his job that he has had difficulty in communicating to someone else. Write it down on a 3 x 5 card.
      b. Form two trios in which each person in turn will experience each of the following roles:
         1) Communicator: tries to express the idea he wrote.
         2) Receiver-helper: paraphrases at various levels.
         3) Observer-helper: takes notes on which paraphrases are most helpful and why.
      c. Run through cycle in each trio as follows:
         1) Communicator states idea.
         2) Receiver-helper paraphrases.
         3) Continue 1) and 2) until communicator believes that receiver fully understands the idea.
         4) Observer reports his observations and trio discusses.
         5) Switch roles and repeat 1) through 4).

6) Switch roles again and repeat 1) through 4).

3. Debriefing (in total group):
    a. What behaviors by a communicator facilitate or inhibit effective paraphrasing?
    b. What behaviors by a receiver promote defensiveness or facilitate clarification on the part of a communicator?

4. Reading (instead of short lecture) about paraphrasing. Hand out sheet describing the skill.

5. Discussion of paraphrasing.
    a. Subtleties of the skill—easy to paraphrase, difficult to do it well.
    b. Two-way nature of skill—need for active listening by both sender and receiver.
    c. Misuse and misappropriate use of skill—e.g., putting people on defensive or using paraphrasing as a forum for persuading group to your own position.

B. Describing behavior
    1. Modeling behavior-description.
        a. Describe some behavior noted earlier in the day. Contrast the description with a statement or two about the same behavior which are not descriptions.
        b. Describe some behaviors that are occurring right now.
    2. Experiencing behavior-description. Hand-mirroring.
        a. Form into pairs. Pick someone not in your previous trio.
        b. Directions: stand face to face, looking each other in the eyes at all times. Put up your hands, in mirror fashion, and, without touching fingers, move your hands in unison. This is a nonverbal exercise, so remember, there is no talking during the exercise itself.
            1) One person leads.
            2) Other person leads.
            3) There is no designated leader. (Move directly from 1) to 2) to 3) for a minute or two each—without discussion.)
    3. Debriefing.
        a. In pairs: describe behaviors you enjoyed or did not enjoy.
        b. In total group:
            1) What behaviors distinguished parts 1), 2), and 3) for you —what behaviors by you, by partner, and by both of you made each experience different?
            2) Describe behaviors you noticed in other dyads. What did you infer from these behaviors? Ask others whether your inference was accurate.
    4. Reading about describing behavior:
        a. On consensual validation: criterion for whether you are, in fact, describing observable behavior.

      b. On acceptance vs. change: describing behavior should not imply that the other must change.

      c. On use of skill to develop own sensitivity.

      d. On pitfalls, cautions, and need to attend tactfully to feelings of self and other.

C. Checking feelings of others.

   1. Modeling perception check:

      a. Refer to instances when you have acted on your inferences of how the group was feeling; e.g., calling a coffee break in response to perceptions of boredom or fatigue.

      b. Cite examples of maladaptive actions based on faulty perceptions that were not checked.

      c. Check your perceptions of how group members are feeling right now.

   2. Experiencing checking feelings by means of the five-square puzzle:

      a. Appoint one member to assist you as observer to note behaviors.

      b. Instruct remainder that they will perform a task involving acting on perceptions without being able to check them verbally.

      c. Observe group performing task.

      d. Debrief group.

        1) Follow sequence of a) describing a behavior, b) checking perceptions of how various people felt during that behavior, and c) paraphrasing those reactions to insure that they are clear.

        2) Some perceptions you may wish to focus on (perhaps for use as observers' guide):

          a) Willingness to give away pieces.

          b) Feeling divorced from struggles of the group.

          c) Unwillingness to give away pieces.

          d) High or low involvement in the task.

          e) High frustration or anxiety.

          f) Turning points concerning the amount of cooperation.

          g) Rule violations.

        3) How falsely confident did you feel about acting on perceptions you could not or did not check?

   3. Discussion.

      a. Projection of own feelings onto others.

      b. When is checking a perception likely to threaten?

      c. Describing own feelings and constructive openness.

      d. How to be sure you are checking perceptions helpfully.

D. Taking a survey.

   1. Modeling taking a survey.

a. Describe the skill.
b. Survey the group to determine whether tonight's session will last two hours or three hours.
c. Make a consensual decision.
2. Experiencing the survey. Ask each participant to write on a 3 x 5 card some question he has on how meetings "back home" should be run. Have each participant then survey the group for its opinions.
3. Debriefing.
   a. What kinds of questions (statements) are best suited to a survey?
   b. How did it feel to respond to the survey as contrasted to how it would have felt if someone had announced a unilateral decision or simply taken a vote?
   c. What are some other ways to encourage participation?
4. Reading about taking a survey.
5. Discussion on taking a survey.
   a. When is a survey appropriate for purposes of policy development?
   b. What behaviors inhibit an effective survey and how can we avoid these?
   c. Hand out a Post-Meeting Reaction Sheet (PMR).
   d. Ask group to fill out PMR referring to entire day's activities.
   e. Collect responses.
   f. Collect data and prepare a summary.

III. Evaluating the effectiveness of meetings.

A. Modeling evaluation.
   1. Review data from PMR sheet.
   2. Point out usefulness of debriefing (refer to earlier activities).
B. Experiencing evaluation.
   1. Ask each participant to write on a 3 x 5 card an evaluation question pertaining to an aspect of the day's activities.
   2. Collect data from all participants (i.e., have entire group answer each person's question).
C. Debriefing the evaluation.
   1. What kind of question provides what kind of information?
   2. What kinds of questions are difficult to answer or ambiguous?
D. Short lecture on evaluation of meeting. Describe uses of evaluation instruments to conduct better meetings in the future and as a tool to find out present orientations of participants.
E. Discussion of the evaluation.
   1. What modes of evaluation are best suited to different purposes at our back-home meetings?
   2. What times for evaluation are best for us?

IV. Convening a group.
  A. Modeling convening. Ask participants to list behaviors that have differentiated your role from theirs. Distinguish between task and maintenance functions.
  B. Experiencing convening.
    1. Choose six discussion topics and write them down on 5 x 8 cards.
    2. Hold six fifteen-minute micromeetings, revolving role of convener. (Each convener gets a 5 x 8 card.)
    3. During each micromeeting, each participant receives a 3 x 5 card describing an unhelpful membership role:
      a. Self-aggrandisement: presents credentials and name drops.
      b. Makes long speeches or gives too many ideas.
      c. Speaks in abstractions and uses jargon.
      d. Withdraws.
      e. Skeptical or sarcastic.
      f. Dominates, cuts off others. For each microdiscussion, the group is to consider itself a committee for policy development, responsible for submitting a report to a person or group of high authority.
  C. Debriefing convening.
    1. What behaviors of the convener facilitated or inhibited the progress of the meeting?
    2. How can a convener diplomatically handle unhelpful behaviors of members?
  D. Reading about guidelines for the convener.
  E. Discussion on convening.
    1. Convener as encourager of helpful behaviors.
    2. What taskmaster functions are appropriate for the convener?

V. Practicing meeting management skills.
  A. Experiencing management skills. Each team is given sixty minutes to prepare to run a sixty-minute meeting using the other team as participants. Each group should choose a real problem for the simulation. The simulation should include:
    1. Setting an agenda.
    2. Using communication skills.
    3. Evaluating the meeting via debriefing and other activity.
    4. Playing out the role of convener.
  B. Debriefing about skills after the simulation.
    1. How effectively did the planners accomplish the four skills listed just above?
    2. How could the workshop have been more effective?
    3. What behaviors during planning helped to organize resources and facilitate success of the meeting? You may wish to use some of the following techniques and procedures during this debriefing:

    a. Passing a ball to the speaker.
    b. Time tokens.
    c. Fishbowl.
    d. Buzz grouping.

READING

The reading that follows sheds light on the dynamics of meetings. We have reduced the excerpt considerably from its original source. The interested reader should go to the original piece for more details.

Participants' Satisfactions with Meetings: Research Findings

Barry E. Collins and Harold Guetzkow. *A social psychology of group processes for decision-making.* New York: Wiley, 1964, pp. 188–209.

Collins and Guetzkow summarized findings from many investigations on aspects of meetings that can produce satisfaction for members of work groups. Note that the more satisfying meetings are not necessarily the more functional or valuable to the organization. Some types of tasks almost guarantee that the meeting will be dissatisfying, even though it makes progress on the task.

    ... satisfaction in decision-making groups is produced by the rewards associated with interaction in the conference.... (P. 195.)

    Several measures in the field study of 72 conferences in business and government reflect the heightened satisfaction produced by success on the group task. The larger the percentage of agenda completed in a meeting, the more the participants are satisfied with it. Satisfaction is also higher in meetings where the agenda topics are completed with dispatch. The longer it takes to reach a decision on the substantive topic, the lower the satisfaction. Meetings in which the observers rated the problem-solving as orderly, efficient, and rapidly paced also showed higher member satisfaction. Shorter meetings leave the participant more satisfied than long ones.... (Pp. 197–198.)

    Satisfaction was significantly lower in meetings which dealt with problems requiring integration. As the difficulty of the problems confronting a conference increases, we find an alteration in a number of other variables which were related to satisfaction in the field study of 72 conferences. Signs of strain appear in almost all aspects of the group functioning. More difficult problems are more time consuming, and conferences faced with such problems find themselves with considerable unfinished business at the end of the meeting. This is obviously one source of lowered satisfaction, since members are more likely to be satisfied with meetings in which the problems are disposed of rapidly and completely. (P. 199.)

The Teacher as Learner: A Model for In-Service Training and the Classroom

Leonard M. Lansky

The teacher said angrily, "I don't believe in expressing strong feelings in a group; that's irrelevant to education. Anyway, why are we spending so damn much time on these silly exercises. . . . "

Six men are sitting around a table putting worms on fishhooks. Small groups at five other tables are doing the same thing. All six do it rather quickly and one says, quite angrily, "Hell, I know how to do this. What has this got to do with this workshop?" Another replies immediately, and a bit excitedly, "That's just what my kids say about multiplication. . . . "

It is late at night, and several tired people are discussing a puzzle they had just assembled by sharing the pieces with one another without being able to talk or communicate with direct signs. One person says, "You know, we finished last, but I don't feel we did poorly, because we learned so much from the way we had difficulty in working together. I wonder if kids in the classroom feel this way. I guess we would have got an F for taking so long, but I don't feel we earned one." Another says, "I wonder why we find it so hard to share. I worked in vain with the pieces I had for over five minutes before I even thought of looking up to see who might use the pieces I had. . . . "

A teacher says, in an almost incredulous tone, "I found out others have similar problems in the classroom and that some of my ideas could help them. I didn't know that." Another replied, "I have more choices than I realized. But I'm not so sure that I'm ready to try much that's different. In fact, I wish I didn't know about some of them."

These incidents occurred during in-service workshops for teachers of mathematics or geography. The teachers were active learners. So were

Reprinted from *People Watching*, 1972, Vol. 2, No. 1, by permission of the author.

the staff, college teachers, and public school teachers in these fields and social psychologists like myself. In this article I will present a brief history of the idea, its rationale, and a description of what has come to be called the "content-oriented workshop" (Lansky, 1972a, 1972b).

SOME HISTORY AND RATIONALE

It all began about five years ago in a three-day workshop for 18 to 20 geography teachers who were to be part of the teaching trials of the High School Geography Project (1971). That project is only one of many such post-Sputnik efforts brought together by professional associations, federal agencies (National Science Foundation, Department of Health, Education, and Welfare), and interested college professors and teachers who wanted to change how their subject matter was organized and taught in the primary or secondary schools.

The workshop was to cover several units. One, on manufacturing (Lansky & Stafford, 1967), requires students to define manufacturing and then to go through a role-playing activity in teams, each representing a management group deciding where to locate a new plant.

My role was to try out some notions from sensitivity training to help the teachers *experience and talk about* how pupils might respond and how they (the teachers) might respond to a classroom in which the students were responsible for teaching one another and for coming to their own conclusions about the objectives and general principles in the lessons. The manufacturing unit was designed for such an approach to the classroom. Although I had consulted with Stafford on the role-playing activities in the unit, I could not intelligently discuss its content. Nor did I want to tell the teachers about the unit for fear that they might then tell students about it, an outcome we did not want. For years psychologists and educators have been telling education students and teachers about participative methods, but few teachers use them—they don't know how. Not only have they had no practice, they've never seen them tried. In my opinion, several recent curriculum reforms have faltered, in part at least, because teachers have not been taught the skills for teaching inductively. Another roadblock to new methods is that pupils at all levels, like other people, resist change. They, too, do not go along easily with attempts at new teaching methods in the classroom (Runkel, Harrison, & Runkel, 1969). These resistances persist despite the accumulating evidence (Gage, 1963) that the average group of pupils can and will learn, on the average, the same amount, as measured by a standardized test, no matter what teaching method is used. My most important assumption was that teachers can, if they know how and are supported, focus their energies on helping students to achieve additional educational goals: learning to learn; communicating effectively; taking responsibility; examining values; thinking critically; developing self-awareness, respect for themselves and others, and the like. However, teachers need new skills and practice to move more rapidly toward these aims.

Sensitivity training stresses these other goals; it emphasizes increasing the individual's choices. By sharing your perceptions of others, by hearing others' perceptions of you, and by seeing how you and others function in a group, you become more self-aware and thus, in theory, see that you have more choices and may even exercise them. The t-group, a group whose task is to look at how a group grows and functions and how each person functions in it, is the main device of sensitivity sessions—or was at that time. Other devices are exercises structured to bring out specific features of human interaction, such as one-way/two-way communication, sharing, group problem solving, and stereotyping. Today, descriptions of such exercises are available for teachers and others (Borton, 1970; Mial & Jacobson, 1970; Nylen, Mitchell, & Stout, 1967). At the time of the geography workshop, however, these were neither readily available nor well known.

I reasoned that a few such activities and talking about them might help teachers see the advantages of changing their roles in the classroom. Hopefully, in the allotted four hours, with the help of the geographers to answer questions about content, we could also go through one activity, an early segment where the entire class attempts to define "manufacturing." If some workshop time were also available from other units, the teachers might get additional practice listening, sharing, and "dealing with" one another and the staff in new ways—ways directly relevant to the HSGP curriculum and methods. One cost of this strategy, however, would be less time for geographic concepts.

The results were exciting, confusing, and—in retrospect—predictable. Some teachers preferred the communications sessions; others, those on content. All agreed that there was too little of everything. Four hours were (and are) not enough to get a feel for or understanding of any two- to four-week unit. Teachers who were themselves insecure about their knowledge of geography tended to want more content. Their learning needs and goals for the workshop focused on concepts. For some, whatever the strategy suggested by the HSGP authors, the materials would be taught in the usual manner. For those who already knew considerable content, the ideas about teaching were upsetting and enlightening. They openly discussed their lack of skill in using role playing and similar methods and in responding to the resistance they expected from many students. Several teachers suggested—we agreed—that the entire group's responses to the workshop paralleled what they might expect from fellow teachers and students at home.

The workshop helped the staff. It pointed up the complexity of communicating the new curricula to teachers. We had talked about the issues;

now they became real. Teachers needed (and need) time and help in learning content *and* teaching methods, especially communication skills. Thus, we recommended that future in-service training focus on demonstrating, practicing, and discussing those skills and feelings that are integral to successful implementation of the HSGP curriculum. At that time, however, we did not have a design for such an in-service program.

Using sensitivity training in "education" or for educators was not, of course, a new idea. I knew of two models being developed by the National Training Laboratories. In one, a sensitivity laboratory was designed for teams of college administrators, teachers, and students in which the focus was on improving communications among team members and helping them plan strategies for change back home. That model seemed inappropriate for learning to use a new curriculum.

The other model was quite different. Traditional sensitivity training was the initial or "warm-up" phase of a two-phase in-service management development program. The second phase concentrated on new content materials, for example, in the Internal Revenue Service, on new accounting procedures. However, the two phases were very distinct. The sensitivity notions were not used in teaching the content. The sensitivity trainers did "their thing" and left. Then content experts taught the new materials in traditional ways.

George Immerzeel, a mathematics educator at the University of Northern Iowa, had come across the second model in his search for in-service methods for introducing some "new mathematics" to teachers of "slow learners." The model had been used for mathematics workshops with two interesting results. The teachers reported that the sensitivity sessions were most valuable to them, but that they did not get any help in carrying over the ideas and skills of the sensitivity training to teaching mathematics in the classroom. Immerzeel's efforts, too complex to go into here, led to the first deliberately designed content-oriented in-service workshop (Lansky, 1972a). Our learnings on that occasion paralleled those in the geography workshop. There was considerable tension, confusion, conflict, and excitement plus sufficient success to go ahead with the idea.

Later that academic year, 1967-68, there were several workshops for geography and mathematics teachers. Since the first one, there have been more than 20 programs with geography or mathematics teachers or teams of teachers, supervisors, and other administrators. The programs have varied on several dimensions. The populations have included public school and college teachers, persons responsible for designing summer institutes in mathematics or geography, and others. Some workshops have included teams from the same district, school, or departmental program; some have been for strangers. The length has been from 2½ days to one week as a total package; others have been segments in a larger training program extending over a quarter or summer; still others have been part of a staff's planning a program for others.

THE WORKSHOPS THEMSELVES

The programs are hard to describe. The brief episodes at the beginning of this article give the flavor of some activities. Perhaps the terms "confusion," "conflict," "confrontation," "collaboration," and "choice" can help.

Confusion

The confusion begins with the first session. There is a general welcoming, introduction of staff, discussion of "nuts and bolts"—schedule and the like—a statement of goals, and an activity. However, the content of these sessions is strange to many. Staff are introduced by first names, usually without any listing of credentials. The schedule lists only "work" and "meal" times rather than specific topics—participants are told that the activities are to be planned in response to what happens *and* their active participation. The goals sound a bit strange—sensitivity to students and fellow teachers, communication skills, sharing our successes and failures, and examining how we feel and what we do here as a potential model for our classrooms.

These messages are not understood, and the opening activity adds to the confusion. One favorite activity is asking the teachers to share their goals for the workshop. Rather than just writing them down or listing them in a large group, small units are formed in which one person states his or her primary goal following which the person to the left *paraphrases*—says in different words—what was heard. The entire group of six or seven then assists the two persons in clarifying the goal. After both are satisfied, the paraphraser states his goal and the next person paraphrases. The activity continues until all have done both, stated a goal and paraphrased. Periodically, the group stops to ask what it has learned about paraphrasing, about communication, about stating goals, *and* about one another. The activity ends with a "fishbowl": a representative from each group sits in a circle in the middle of the room. The representatives work while the others observe. The center group's tasks are to share what happened in their groups, to assess the entire session, and to discuss their own feelings and experiences in the fishbowl. Here, in a simple exercise, a group of teachers share their goals, practice some communication skills, and begin to share their feelings toward their subject matter, the communications activities, and one another. But the activity and the reactions are not that simple. Many participants are confused and frustrated.

The frustrations mount as the workshop progresses. There seems to be almost no attention paid to content. In addition, even when there are content materials—lectures, demonstrations, or whatever —the focus is on the communications activities that precede, accompany, or follow the curriculum materials. All activities are "processed," examined for their impact on participants and their relation to the classroom. Given these events, many participants ask, "What do you want us to learn?" or "What do you want us to do?" Our answers to these oft-repeated questions are: "How do you feel?" "How do the rest of you feel?" "What might you do?" "What is happening here?" "How is what is happening relevant to your classroom?" or some such. Some participants accept our position and try to answer these questions or confront those who are opposed to these answers. Others reject the notion that questions are to be answered with questions. The staff, as experts, are being paid to provide answers. These participants especially reject the idea that feelings are relevant to the workshop (or the classroom). For many, exploring feelings is a job for therapists, churches, or homes, not the school, and certainly not for teachers of mathematics or geography.

Conflict and Confrontation

The issue is a crucial one and has led to considerable confusion, conflict, and confrontation in our meetings and workshop sessions among us and participants. We encourage such confrontations, as in the group with the can of worms. The strong feelings can hardly be denied. Insofar as we have violated the expectations of many, if not most, participants, and continue to provoke them, strong feelings are natural. The issue for many participants then becomes: "Can we violate another 'normal expectation' and value we tend to share as teachers and Americans, namely, the inappropriateness, even badness, of giving direct feedback, especially negative feedback, to people in public?" For many of us, it is just not acceptable to express strong feelings in the classroom or the in-service workshop, especially to authorities. Yet we continue to promote the feedback model, both positive and negative expressions of it. We even talk about ways of doing so effectively and usefully.

Over the span of the workshops, we have used several techniques for getting the feelings out into the open. Two have been especially helpful. One is an adaptation of Maier's Risk Technique (Maier, 1952), a method designed to help managers look at their feelings about using group decision techniques with their workers. The task is straightforward. Participants share, in small groups usually, the personal risks each one would take in giving and receiving feedback at the workshop. At times, the question is posed in terms of their classrooms. The lists are then discussed as well as the exercise itself and their feelings during it.

The second method includes a brief lecture on two general categories of functions of any group—the task and the maintenance (or socioemotional) functions. Then a t-group is defined, as earlier in this article, as a group whose tasks are to look at how it grows and functions and how the members see themselves and one another, essentially the socioemotional or maintenance functions. Given the definition, a "volunteer task-oriented t-group" is formed in the center of the room. Its tasks are (1) to share feelings about the workshop and staff and (2) to look at its own (the volunteer group's) functioning.

Currently we follow either activity by an explanation of the process to that point in the workshop. At times this explanation comes from participants, at other times from the staff, and includes, in brief form, the ideas about feelings and learning expressed in this paper and others (Lansky, 1969, 1972a, 1972b). The open confrontations directed at us are a benchmark in the workshops. In the jargon of sensitivity training, the "unfreezing" has been accomplished (Schein & Bennis, 1965). Although many participants continue to cope with their feelings about confrontation—and many will not do so at this point or ever in the program—most participants then begin to share more openly with one another how they feel, what they do well, and what they want to learn more about. They begin to see themselves, one another, and us as mutual resources and collaborators, rather than as competitors and "those responsible for my learning." Feelings about selves and relationships change. In addition, the participants begin to question their own previous stands vis-à-vis the workshop and their own classroom and schools. More than previously, they acknowledge that their behaviors at the workshop and at home represent choices that they have ceased to question. Indeed, rather than acknowledging their own decisions, they had tended, as we all do, to blame the "system" "the principal," or whatever. As the person who produced the last quote at the beginning of this article said so well, many are not too comfortable about their reawakening. The staff's response is essentially "Either way will hurt" (May, 1969, p. 176). We are surely all discontented with what we do and see in what passes for education; we also hurt when we see that the responsibility is partly ours and that we must take risks and struggle if there is to be change which we cannot guarantee. The choice is ours. We cannot escape it.

Collaboration and Choice

The confrontations of self and one another then change in quality. Instead of anger and irritation, there is a sense of mutual helpfulness and support. Feedback is to help both giver and receiver rather than to hurt or satisfy only one.

The late-middle and closing sessions of the workshops then focus on specific learnings. The entire atmosphere is very different from the beginning of the workshop and from most classrooms. There is an intensity and feeling of investment as well as a sense of joy in the relationships and thinking through issues, often using absurd, hostile examples to deal with the frustrations of difficult problems. The sense of freedom is reflected in the planning. Thus, a common closing activity, just before an evaluation of the program by staff and participants, is a workshop fair or cafeteria. Staff and participants brainstorm topics they would like to work on. Those with relevant skills set up stations where discussions, demonstrations, even lectures occur. The topics have included: more communication skills; specific curriculum materials and methods; evaluations without grades; designing new courses; dealing with "problem" students, fellow teachers, parents, and administrators; and laboratory techniques.

The workshop usually ends on notes of hope, despair, and specific plans: hope because of the sharing and opening up of choices; despair because of the scope of the task and the awareness that much more might be done if there were more time; the specific plans center around future workshops, programs at home, and continued contact among participants.

From the evidence to date, teachers have followed up their own classrooms and in working together to set up additional workshops. Several of the 20 or more programs came about because of teachers who had been participants. My hope is that the idea will be tried out in other fields and that more teachers will learn how to use these new techniques. Another hope is that confusion, conflict, confrontation, collaboration, and choice will become the norm rather than the exception in our schools.

REFERENCES

Borton, T. *Reach, touch, and teach: Student concerns and process education.* Cambridge, Mass.: McGraw-Hill, 1970.

Gage, N. L. *Handbook of research in teaching.* Chicago: Rand McNally, 1963.

Gage, N. L. *High school geography project: A course of study.* New York: Macmillan, 1971.

Lansky, L. M. Changing the classroom: Some psychological assumptions. In P. Runkel, R. Harrison, & M. Runkel (Eds.), *The changing college classroom.* San Francisco: Jossey-Bass, 1969, pp. 292-301.

Lansky, L. M. The content oriented workshop: Integrating sensitivity and in-service training for teachers. *Social Change: Ideas and Applications,* 1972, *2* (2), 4-6.

Lansky, L. M. A social psychologist's notes on the geography workshops: Developing a communications-content model. In N. Helburn (Ed.), *Challenge and change in college geography.* Boulder, Colo.: ERIC Clearing House for Social Studies/Social Science Education, 1972, pp. 89-102 (b).

Lansky, L. M. & Stafford, H. A. Manufacturing unit of the high school geography project. *Journal of Geography,* 1967, *66,* 175-179.

Maier, N. R. F. *Principles of human relations: Applications to management.* New York: Wiley, 1952.

May, R. *Love and will.* New York: W. W. Norton, 1969.

Mial, D. & Jacobson, S. *Ten interaction exercises for the classroom.* Washington, D.C.: National Training Laboratories Institute, 1970.

Nylen, D., Mitchell, J. & Stout, A. *Handbook of staff development and human relations training: Materials developed for use in Africa.* Washington, D. C.: National Training Laboratories, IABS, 1967.

Runkel, P., Harrison, R., & Runkel, M. (Eds.). *The changing college classroom.* San Francisco: Jossey-Bass, 1969.

Schein, E. H., & Bennis, W. G. *Personal and organizational change through group methods: The laboratory approach.* New York: Wiley, 1965.

The Counselor's Workshop: Teacher In-Service Workshops

Robert D. Myrick and Linda S. Moni

A DEVELOPMENTAL CONSULTATION APPROACH

Consultation is a relatively new development in the field of school counseling. Whereas consultation has not been a primary concern of many high school counselors, it is becoming an important function of elementary school counselors. In 1966, Smith and Eckerson reported that only 3 percent of the principals they surveyed indicated that their elementary school counselors spent "most time" with teachers, as compared to 77 percent who spent "most time" with students. They also reported that the consultant dealt primarily with socio-emotional problems in a crisis-oriented way. Now, less than a decade later, developments in the area of consultation have provided new directions in the field of counseling.

THREE CONSULTATION APPROACHES

Consultation can be described in three broad classifications. The first of these is called crisis consultation. In this case, the counselor as a consultant works with a teacher who is experiencing an urgent problem with a child's personal development or the learning process in the classroom. The anxious teacher in a crisis is often frustrated or confused and wants immediate assistance from the counselor-consultant. If, for example, two boys picked at each other in class and then one day a fight erupted, the teacher might ask the counselor for a solution to the problem. Or, if one of the boys' parents intends to meet with the teacher on short notice, the counselor might

Reprinted from *Elementary School Guidance and Counseling*, December 1972, Vol. 7, No. 2. Copyright 1972, American Personnel and Guidance Association. Reprinted with permission of the authors and publisher.

be consulted as to a plan of action. Situations like these place the counselor in a position of providing emergency first-aid. This type of consultation is the most difficult because of the extra psychological stress and defensiveness which is usually present in a crisis.

In preventive consultation the teacher is not experiencing a crisis, but it seems that he could be confronted with one. In this case, particular behaviors or events signal that a child or a group of children is headed toward some unusual difficulties and that something is desired as a means of intervening and preventing a crisis from occurring. In preventive consultation a teacher is usually less defensive and more open to constructive change because matters are perceived as potentially troublesome but not overwhelming. This kind of consultation allows for planned strategies which are developed jointly by the teacher and counselor.

The third approach is referred to as developmental consultation. This might also be viewed as preventive in nature but it tends to focus more on the desirable conditions of learning and positive growth rather than preventing something from happening. Developmental consultation is concerned with classroom and school learning climates and giving attention to the needs of all children. The counselor-consultant works as a human behavior and interpersonal relationship specialist, helping teachers to explore their own attitudes and interactions with children, as well as the facilitative conditions of learning.

IN-SERVICE WORKSHOPS: A DEVELOPMENTAL CONSULTATION APPROACH

In-service programs are a traditional part of most schools. Unfortunately, in-service work is too often viewed as a pre-school session when an outside speaker imparts "new" knowledge or ideas to teachers. Some administrators provide continuing in-service programs for teachers throughout a school year. In-service programs or workshops can be a valuable part of a guidance program, especially when they are carefully organized around effective guidelines.

Organizing in-service workshops, as a part of an elementary school counselor's function, has not received much attention in professional literature. While it may be debated that it is not the counselor's responsibility to assume leadership in this area, workshops can be an integral part of consultation. Most counselors realize that their time is limited and that they cannot reach all the children who could benefit from their services. Therefore, in-service workshops are an opportunity to promote more effective learning climates, to mobilize resources within a school, to help bring a faculty together as a team, and to provide a consultation readiness for more specific situations which may develop later.

Guidelines for Developing an In-Service Workshop

Here are a few simple guidelines that can be useful when developing an in-service workshop for teachers. Imagine that you are a teacher and that you have been asked to participate in a workshop. These questions must be answered to your satisfaction, just as every teacher wants them answered.

1. *What's it all about?* The objective or goals of the workshop should be carefully defined. The program should be tailored to meet the needs of teachers in your school. A "canned" program that directs attention to general ideas or theories tends to have only limited success. Be specific about behaviors and help the teachers work with one idea, one step at a time.

2. *How long will it take?* The place and time of a workshop can affect its outcomes. Teachers are busy people. There never seems to be enough time in a school day. An in-service workshop will take away planning time that teachers could use in their classrooms or with team members. Therefore, the counselor-consultant should use time wisely and provide a program that is short, well-organized, and to the point.

3. *What's in it for me?* Whatever the objectives may be, the information and experiences provided in the workshop must be relevant to teacher interests and needs. When a teacher can see how the workshop ideas are of immediate value to his classroom, then he is likely to be more motivated and willing to participate during the program. Therefore, whatever the program, it must have practical implications and be directly related to the work of the teacher.

4. *What do I do now that I'm here?* Almost everyone learns best through experiential learning. Most successful in-service workshops have at least one component in which the teachers are involved with the ideas or material that is presented. When someone talks *at* teachers they tend to tune out, letting their minds drift to the problems of yesterday or tomorrow. On the other hand, when teachers are personally involved in a discussion or an activity, they tend to remain tuned in to the present, which enhances the potential impact of the workshop.

5. *What does it mean to me?* Directly related to teacher involvement is the concept of personalizing ideas. That is, rather than having teachers involved with irrelevant textbook material or unfamiliar examples, they should think of personal examples or share some personal experiences. Personalizing the concepts makes them more meaningful to an individual and it also increases the probability that teachers will use the information and experiences from the workshop.

6. *Now what?* After the workshop, special steps are taken to follow up and support teachers in their efforts to experiment with the concepts from the workshop. A follow-up program provides the extra encouragement that many teachers need in order to try a new idea. A follow-up is also valuable in helping the counselor assess the outcomes of the workshop and to make future plans.

A COMMUNICATION WORKSHOP FOR TEACHERS

The following workshop is suggested as one way in which a counselor could help teachers to become more guidance oriented in their work. From systematic observation of classroom interactions, it appears that most teachers at this time respond to the feelings of children far too infrequently. Consequently, it is assumed that teachers can benefit from an in-service workshop which emphasizes the value and manner of responding to children's feelings.

Objectives. It is the purpose of this workshop to help teachers examine the general characteristics of a helping relationship and the behaviors that contribute to fostering a positive relationship. Specifically, teachers are introduced to six verbal responses and their general impact on relationships and communication in the classroom. Still more specifically, it is the goal of this workshop to increase the frequency of teacher responses to children's feelings in school.

Time and place. The one-day workshop could be a special faculty meeting. All members should be present because it offers an opportunity for the teachers to learn more about one another as well as effective ways of communication. A large room that is furnished with moveable chairs is desired. A minimum of one hour is needed.

Relevancy. During the first part of the meeting (approximately 20 to 25 minutes) the counselor-consultant introduces the focus of the workshop. Some counselors begin by drawing attention to the current demand for humanistic education and posing the question: What does it mean in terms of what we do? Using an overhead projector or perhaps a brief hand out, teachers are presented a continuum of facilitative responses that includes: reflecting feelings, clarifying, questioning, reassuring and supporting, interpreting, and advising and evaluating. The intent of each response, with specific classroom examples, is provided in order for teachers to differentiate the responses. The following material could be used in a handout or mini-lecture.

The Facilitating Responses

The responses below are used frequently by teachers and counselors when they respond to children. Research suggests that some responses tend to be perceived by the receiver as more empathic, caring, warm, and person-centered. Consequently, these responses have a higher probability than others in creating a helping relationship. A continuum of response leads is listed below from the least to the most facilitative. It should be remembered, however, that at the appropriate time and place, all of these responses could be facilitative.

1. *Advising or evaluating* indicates a judgment of relative goodness, appropriateness, effectiveness, or rightness within the teacher's own value structure. It implies what the child *might or ought to do*. ("If I were you, I'd study more and worry less.")

2. *Analyzing or interpreting* indicates an intent to teach, to impart insight, and show meaning by explaining or connecting ideas and events. It implies what the child *might or ought to think*. ("When you threw that eraser, you thought everyone would give you attention for being tough.")

3. *Reassuring or supporting* indicates an intent to reduce the apparent anxiety or intense feeling in the child, perhaps to pacify. It is implied that the child *need not feel as he does*. ("Don't worry, everyone feels like that sometimes.")

4. *Questioning* indicates an intent to seek additional information or provoke further discussion. It implies that the child *should develop a point further*. Questions that keep the focus on the child are more facilitative than those which lead to a generalized topic. Open-ended questions are more effective than closed questions. (Closed: "Do you get along with your other teachers?" Open: "What can you tell me about your other teachers?")

5. *Summarizing or clarifying* indicates an intent to understand correctly what the child is saying or to identify the most significant ideas or feelings which seem to be emerging from what is being said. It implies doubt or eagerness *to check out what has been heard* in order to be "with" the person. ("I think you're telling me that you think cheating and not getting caught is okay.")

6. *Understanding or reflecting of feelings* conveys to the child that the teacher *understands or is "reading" how the child is feeling*. In a sense it involves a reflecting kind of feedback that communicates accurately that this is how the child's world appears to him. ("You're angry with Harold." "Alice, you're confused right now.")

In some instances, teachers have responded with paper and pencil to cases which might occur in a school setting. Teachers select a favored response from a choice of six. The six choices, of course, represent the range of the six facilitative responses. For example,

> A teacher has been pointing to some errors in homework within a small group of children. One child, Mary, reacts by saying, "Everything I do is wrong." (Eyes water a little.) "I just don't do anything right. All the other kids hear you talk about me and they joke about it. Because of you, nobody likes me . . . I'm dumb, and you, you . . . always find *my* mistakes—and tell everybody!" (Tears come to eyes.)
>
> _____ (a) It seems, Mary, that you don't like the way I talk with you about your school work. (Clarifying)
>
> _____ (b) Mary, it's difficult for you to look at your mistakes because you think we will like you less because of them. (Interpreting)

_____ (c) There's nothing wrong with making a mistake, Mary. Most of us make mistakes now and then. (Reassuring)

_____ (d) Some time you're going to have to learn to be more objective, and not so sensitive, Mary. (Advising)

_____ (e) You're embarrassed and hurt because of what I said, Mary. (Reflecting)

_____ (f) What would have been a better way to talk with you about your work? (Open-ended question)

With a presentation and discussion of similar cases, teachers learn how some responses are more effective than others in opening communication, in creating a helping relationship, and in increasing the chances that a student will perceive the teacher as a warm, caring, respecting, and understanding person. See selected references (Dinkmeyer & Caldwell, 1970; Johnson, 1972; Wittmer & Myrick, in press) for additional material in this area.

TEACHER INVOLVEMENT (TRIADS)

It is time for teachers to get involved. Below is a procedure that can help teachers practice the helping responses associated with the concepts and provide them some feedback on their communication habits.

Teachers are divided into groups of three. Try to have them meet with people they know the least. Have each triad number off 1, 2, and 3. Let person #1 be the talker, #2 the listener or facilitator, and #3 the observer. The talker (#1) talks to the facilitator (#2) for three minutes, regarding one of the most dissatisfying things about teaching. (Other talker assignments could be: Something about my teaching that I want to improve upon; a criticism which students might have of me; or a disappointing experience with a student.) It is the task of the facilitator (#2) to assist the talker (without advising, praising, judging, or interpreting) to continue talking about himself. The facilitator should reflect in fresh words the ideas and feelings that the talker is expressing, using his sensitivity to hear the person. During the three minutes, the observer (#3) observes the facilitator and makes notes of his listening skills.

After three minutes, the observer feeds back his observations to the facilitator for about two minutes. Then the same talker (#1) takes another three minutes to talk about the positive aspects of the assignment given above (e.g., something about my teaching that pleases or satisfies me). The assignments for the others remain the same. Roles are switched in a second and third round (with the same talking assignment) until all three have been in each part. The three rounds will take approximately 30 to 35 minutes if the counselor serves as timer and leader. The triads are then assembled in a large group for final comments, observations, conclusions, and implications.

Personalizing. The choice of topic for the triad activity can personalize the experience and give it additional meaning. Teachers are directly involved in practicing facilitative behaviors and learning more about themselves and their fellow teachers in the process. This experience tends to foster faculty cohesiveness as teachers share pleasant and unpleasant feelings about their work, their students, and themselves. In addition, teachers will have learned and practiced a procedure (the triads) which could be used, with modifications, in their classrooms or in future faculty meetings.

Follow-up. This workshop is concluded with teachers agreeing to identify at least one student with whom they would like to improve their communication and relationship. During the next week each teacher consciously and deliberately increases his facilitative responses (reflecting and clarifying) to that child's feelings and notes the impact. At the next faculty meeting, one half hour might be used for teachers to share their case studies with other teachers, usually in small groups or triads. In addition, teachers might be tested with pre and post measures similar to the written case cited above, or a tape recording of children's voices might be used as a stimulus to assess teachers' facilitative responses before and after the workshop.

This workshop is informative and fun. It provides a base for times when more specific consultation, perhaps in a crisis, calls for an intervention strategy that features an increase of responding to a child's feelings and ideas. It alerts the faculty to the value and impact of feelings in the learning process. It often brings faculties together as a more cohesive unit because it provides an opportunity for teachers to disclose more of themselves, as well as their successes and failures with children. The counselor who uses developmental consultation concepts in an in-service workshop increases his visibility, value, and impact with teachers and children.

REFERENCES

Dinkmeyer, D., & Caldwell, E. *Developmental counseling and guidance.* New York: McGraw-Hill, 1970, Chapter 6.

Johnson, D. W. *Reaching out.* Englewood Cliffs, N.J.: Prentice-Hall, 1972, Chapter 7.

Smith, H., & Eckerson, L. *Guidance services in the elementary school.* U.S. Department of Health, Education, and Welfare, 1966.

Wittmer, J., & Myrick, R. D. *The facilitative teacher: Expanding human awareness.* Pacific Palisades, Calif.: Goodyear, in press.

The Laboratory for Transactional Analysis in the Classroom: A Model of Humanistic, Competency-Based, Teacher Education at Governors State University

David Crispin

The purpose of this paper is to offer a strategy for "maximizing the humane in competency-based teacher education." That strategy is a module, designed and conducted by the writer, in the College of Human Learning and Development at new, experimental, competency-based, Governors State University, Park Forest South, Illinois.

Established in July, 1969, by the State of Illinois as "an innovative and experimenting institution that is efficient, humane and open—to be future oriented, service minded and seeking qualitative excellence with special emphasis upon the educational needs of low income and minority students," Governors State opened to students on September 13, 1971. Including four distinct, unique and yet united colleges along an open, 1,137-foot long "academic street," the university's development is guided by four action objectives: (1) job efficiency; (2) functional citizenship; (3) intra- and interpersonal relationships; and (4) cultural expansion.

From the beginning, "grades," "marks," "pass/fail," "incomplete" and such traditional methods of recording student achievement have *not* been used. Instead, the entire university has employed competency-based (or performance-based) instruction. The professors, often with the help or input of the students, prepare competency statements which comprise a program—in Urban Teacher Education, for example—and then design

This paper was prepared for presentation at the National Conference, Humanizing Education Through C.B.T.E., at Wayne State University, Detroit, Michigan, May 20, 1974. Printed with permission of the author.

learning experiences, called "modules," in which students can learn and demonstrate the competencies. When the student has achieved the competency, that competency statement is placed on the student's transcript which, then, is a rather detailed (often many pages) record of the student's actual competence or skill mastered at the university. Self-instructional materials, alternative learning environments and independent projects allow students to begin modules at any time, go at their own pace, and end whenever they can demonstrate the competency. Most modules, and most students, begin at regularly scheduled sessions, meet (usually weekly) at regularly scheduled times and end at the end of the sessions, or soon after.

The module offered here as an example of humanistic, competency-based teacher education is listed in the catalog as follows:

Title:	Transactional Analysis in the Classroom
Coordinator:	Crispin
Time, Place:	6:30-10:20, Thursday, Room C3224
Competencies:	In this module, the student can achieve core competencies of the Urban Teacher Education Program in *Advanced Psychology* and/or *Communications* and *Human Relations*
Credits:	The student may earn 1 or 2 units of credit as follows:

I. *1 Unit:* The competencies, when satisfactorily achieved, shall appear on the student's transcript as follows:

A. "The student has written a paper accurately and adequately defining and giving (original) *examples* of:

- OK Critical Parent, Not-OK Critical Parent, OK Nurturing Parent, Not-OK Nurturing Parent, Free (Natural) Child, OK Adapted Child, Not-OK Adapted Child, OK Little Professor, Not-OK Little Professor, Authentic Adult, Ethical Adult, Logical Adult.
- Crossed Transactions—Complimentary Transactions—Ulterior Transactions
- Psychological Positions (What this means)
  I'm OK, You're OK—I'm OK, You're Not OK—I'm Not OK, You're OK—I'm Not OK, You're Not OK.
- Strokes—Time Structuring.
- Games (What this means)
  Three elements found in all games
  First Degree Games—Second Degree Games—Third Degree Games
- Scripts (What this means)
  Cultural Scripts—Subcultural Scripts—Family Scripts—Persecutor—Victim—Rescuer.

The student has been informed by lectures and discussions during the module and by reading *Born to Win* by James & Jongeward and *TA for Kids*, by Freed."

Learning activities toward achieving competencies for #A: The student shall read the two books (above) and learn the concepts listed. Also, most of the sessions will be designed to give time for lecturettes and printed materials and questions and answer periods to help the student master the concepts.

B. The competencies, when satisfactorily achieved, shall appear on the student's transcript as follows:

"The student has internalized the ego state behaviors and analyzed and reported his/her own personal growth toward autonomy, along the path of awareness, spontaneity and intimacy, by:

   1. Participating, here-and-now, in eight, three-hour sessions, in a TA lab, through trust building, encounter, self-disclosure and giving and receiving feedback, and

   2. By reporting, to the group weekly, his new awareness and analysis of his transactions with a child (his own, or a child in the class he teaches).

   3. By teaching a child or youth basic TA concepts."

Learning activities toward achieving competencies for #B: We shall meet from 6:30 until 10:20 at the prescribed place each week on Thursday evenings. Beginning with the second session, those who want to experience meditation-relaxation may arrive early between 6:10-6:30, take off their shoes, enter silently, find a place to lie down on the carpet, close their eyes and rest. No talking no smoking (during meditation-relaxation). All should dress casually for lounging on the floor. Women should wear slacks. Bring a pillow if you like. Through ceremonies and structured activities we shall create a humanistic classroom environment of trust and potential caring in which we can become aware of and share our own ego state behaviors and begin to grow toward autonomy.

During one session, the seventh session only, you are expected to bring a child (one), your own, if possible, between the ages of eight and eighteen. During this session, we will experience our own ego states with children and youth, observe and experience their ego states; and each student shall have the experience of teaching a child or youth the basic concepts of TA. Thirty minutes will be provided for this teaching. Concepts to be taught are: the twelve ego state behaviors and the four psychological positions.

Students are expected to attend all sessions of the lab and to arrive on time. The trust-building necessary to achieve our purposes cannot occur if students arrive late or leave early. If a student misses a session because of an emergency, he/she shall report the reason to the group. If he/she misses two or more sessions, he/she will not achieve competency #1.

II. *1 Unit:* The competencies, when satisfactorily achieved, shall appear as follows on the student's transcript:

   A. "The student has demonstrated mastery (70% or better reliability of a system for recording and analyzing teacher-student interactions in twelve categories of ego state behaviors as these behaviors occur—live, in the classroom, or from audio or video tapes.

   B. The student has done a transactional analysis of his/her own interactions with the children-youth he/she teaches (or, if not a teacher, with three or more children) by recording thirty minutes or more of interaction (audio or video), tallying from the tape, and presenting the coordinator the raw data (form) and an appropriately written analysis of the data. The analysis shall include the effects of the teacher's ego state behaviors upon the children's (youth's) ego state behaviors, and the effects of the children's (youth's) ego state behaviors upon the ego state behaviors of the teacher."

   (If the student cannot obtain an audio or video tape recording, he/she may arrange to interact with children (in school, or elsewhere) and have one of his/her classmates tally the live interactions, and base his/her report on that data.)

   Learning activities toward achieving the competencies for #II: The coordinator will explain and demonstrate the system—live —in class, and help the students master it. Students may practice in school, or at home, or anywhere they might observe teachers (adults) interacting with children or youth.

Let us examine this module to see how it satisfies generally accepted criteria for being both *humanistic* and *competency based.* Here is the contention that *what we learn—the theory and concepts* of transactional analysis—and *our own interactions with each other* as we internalize these concepts—*are humanistic:* that the *method for demonstrating understanding* of—and personal "ownership" of—the concepts is *competency-based.*

HUMANISTIC PSYCHOLOGY

A comprehensive review of the literature, especially the *Journal of Humanistic Psychology,* and particularly a synthesis of the basic tenets of Rogers, Adler, Berne, Bugental and Maslow, establishes the following as the minimum basis of the humanistic view of man:

Responsibility: Each of us is the most responsible agent for his own life. To accept that responsibility (to stop blaming others for one's hurts, problems, failures, etc.) is the essential first step toward self-actualization (Maslow), authenticity (Rogers), or autonomy (Berne).

Awareness: The simplest definition of neurosis is "lack of awareness," i.e., one doesn't know what one is feeling, one's motives or needs, or why one is doing what one is doing. All "craziness," neurosis, "mental illness" can be explained as distortion or denial of one's inner life, one's needs, motives and/or feelings.

Intimacy: After the basic needs of survival are met, to be wholly human each of us must experience intimacy—the close, warm and caring, trusting, potentially hurtful (and therefore scary) sharing openly of ourselves with another; Buber's "I—thou" relationship.

Mental Illness—Mental Health Model: Humanistic psychologists reject the illness-medical-model view of human psychological suffering or difficulty: they do not speak of "treatment" or "cure." Rather, human distress is seen as symptomatic of the "illnesses," neuroses, contradictions, confusions, etc., of the society—the social milieu—in which we live. A good social environment—a happy, responsible, intimate, *family*—produces autonomous children; a confused, bitter, distrusting, irresponsible family climate produces children who suffer fear, anger, alienation, apathy, etc. Maslow says (on a training tape we use), "The simplest formula I know for being mentally healthy is to be with people who are mentally healthy."

Implications for "Humanistic Teacher Education" of the Basic Tenets of Humanistic Psychology

Responsibility: Teacher education should aim at the personal growth of the teacher; should encourage the teacher to accept the responsibility for his/her own life, for growing and becoming. The Laboratory in Transactional Analysis in the Classroom encourages the teachers to take and own that responsibility. It is a personal growth experience based on Berne's stated value that "achieving autonomy is the ultimate goal in transactional analysis" (James & Jongeward, 1971). In this lab we establish that as our goal and begin the personal growth each of us needs toward that end.

Awareness: Teacher education should aim to develop in teachers the ability to be aware of their feelings, needs and motives, especially here-and-now. In our lab, achievement of a competency requires teachers to self-disclose their "inner lives," here-and-now, in the group, and also to recall significant interactions during the week, especially in school with children, in which their ego state behaviors were "hooked," i.e., Parent, Adult, Child, OK and Not OK.

Intimacy: Teacher education should aim at encouraging teachers to open themselves to, and take the risks of moving toward, intimacy. In our lab, the entire climate and specifically designed events encourage caring, nurturance, helping and sharing. Many abiding friendships occur. A generalized feeling of trust and belonging develops. Many cry, to say goodbye, at our last session. To care about each other—and to care about children— is clearly accepted (and *experienced!*) as OK. And children and youth actively participate with the teachers in this lab (often their own parents) and experience this caring and authentic sharing with us.

Mental Illness—Mental Health Model: Within the theory, concepts and rubric of transactional analysis, and in the presence of children and youth, teachers in this lab learn a specific methodology for "growing kids" toward autonomy; they are trained to recognize the destructive ego state behaviors of themselves and their students: The Not-OK Nurturing Parent, Not-OK Critical Parent, Not-OK Adapted Child, and the Not-OK Little Professor. They are taught to be aware of their own, and recognize their students', nurturing and constructive ego state behaviors: the OK Nurturing Parent, the OK Critical Parent, the Authentic Adult, the Ethical Adult, the Logical Adult, the Natural Child, and the OK Little Professor. And they learn a system for recording and analyzing these behaviors, objectively and reliably, to "scientifically" chart their own personal growth, the growth of their students, and their effects upon each other!

Clearly, then, the Laboratory in Transactional Analysis in the Classroom is humanistic in *content* (theory and concepts), in the commitment to the expressed *value* of autonomy, and in *practice* (the ways we behave with, and feel about, each other).

And, it is competency-based. At Governors State University—and generally, wherever competency-based methods are used—the minimum criterion for competency-based instruction is the use of *behavioral objectives* having the following properties:

1. Objectives are stated as *behavior:* specific, observable, in some way measurable (or quantifiable) behavioral acts.

2. Objectives include the criteria of performance—the *standard* (almost always a single standard) of acceptance: how well it should be done—the extent of the skill. Usually stated here also is the method of evaluation— how the behavioral performance shall be judged.

3. Wherever appropriate, objectives must include clear and complete explanations or descriptions of the conditions or limitations under which the behavior is to be demonstrated. This should also include the equipment or material, etc., required.

The competency is the broad, brief statement for the student's transcript. The behavioral objective is the more specific, detailed statement, taught and demonstrated within the module.

In this case:

Competency (Cognitive Domain): "The student has mastered the system, Classroom Transactional Analysis."

Behavioral Objective (Cognitive Domain): "Given a video-taped sequence of 500 spontaneous, teacher-student interactions in a classroom, the learner is able to categorize behaviors—by placing a 'tally' in the appropriate box of the PAC Form (enclosed)—with 70% reliability, or better, as compared with the tallies of the coordinator. The learner is able to tally a '1' for teacher behaviors; an 'O' for student-to-teacher behaviors; and an 'Ө' for student-to-student behaviors. Only verbal behaviors will be tallied. Tallies will be recorded every three seconds for on-going behavior, or as fast as behaviors occur in cases of change in behavior or speaker. The learner is able to work alone from memory, unaided by others or by any printed material (except the PAC Form)."

Competency (Affective Domain): "The Student has demonstrated the ability to take responsibility for his/her own personal growth by identifying his/her own growth issues and by reporting his/her progress along the path, awareness, spontaneity, intimacy, toward autonomy."

Behavioral Objective (Affective Domain): "The student has made this statement to the group: 'I hereby take responsibility for my life, for growing myself, and for the consequences of my behavior.'

The student has demonstrated *awareness* through *self-disclosure*, live, in the group, of his/her own ego state behaviors and has received feedback from the group, here-and-now, on those behaviors.

The student has demonstrated the ability to risk intimacy by his/her spontaneous expression of here-and-now feelings toward others, including anger, jealousy, caring, empathy, sympathy, like, love, guilt, resentment and sexuality.

The student has self-disclosed regularly in a small group his/her own assessment of his/her own progress in awareness, spontaneity, intimacy and autonomy and has received the group's feedback on these issues."

There is no intention to explain here the basic theories and concepts of transactional analysis. The single, most readable source for a complete coverage of TA is probably *Born to Win,* by James and Jongeward, the basic resource for this module. Figure 1 is a sample of the form, "Classroom Transactional Analysis," on which we learn to tally the behaviors of teachers and students as these behaviors occur, live, and/or on audio or video tapes. And this form has built in it a simple, quick method for the teacher to plot and check her/his personal growth and the growth of her/his students.

Autonomy, seen as ego state behaviors, includes OK Nurturing Parent, OK Critical Parent, Authentic Adult, Ethical Adult, Logical Adult, Natural Child, and OK Little Professor. An "unfree," frozen, unliberated, irresponsible and/or neurotic set includes all of the "Not-OK" ego state behaviors of Parent and Child. And so, if the teacher does Classroom Transactional Analysis at regular intervals throughout the year, she/he can see growth or the lack of growth. The movement on the form should be upward. As the teacher grows and as she/he "grows the kids," the boxes at the top will have increasingly more tallies than the boxes at the bottom.

Also, the complete system, including categories and types (see Figure 2), includes clear data about the "Therapeutic Triad." In his article, "A Populist's View of Psychotherapeutic Deprofessionalization," Thomas Oden (1974) reviews the relevant research and concludes, with Truax and Carkhuff, that the basic, necessary, minimum—and most therapeutic—helping skills are: (1) *accurate empathy,* (2) *nonpossessive warmth,* and (3) *genuineness* (or authenticity). These behaviors are "typed" and can be tallied in the Classroom Transactional Analysis system; note the types under OK Nurturing Parent, empathy and caring—and all of Authentic Adult would reflect genuineness. A check of these areas will tell the teacher quickly the degree to which he/she is practicing good psychology.

Finally, Dreikurs et al. (1971) declare that "encouragement is the first principle of pedagogy." Our system allows the teacher to check out his/her affectiveness here by noticing the relative number of tallies in the area called "strokes."

In this paper I have described briefly the mandate, philosophy and methodology of Governors State University, and have used as an example of humanistic, competency-based teacher education the module, Laboratory for Transactional Analysis in the Classroom, which I coordinate in the College of Human Learning and Development. I have demonstrated that this strategy is both humanistic and competency-based and holds great promise for "maximizing the humane in competency-based teacher education."

REFERENCES

1. Dreikurs, R., Grunwald, B., & Pepper, F. *Maintaining sanity in the classroom.* New York: Harper and Row, 1971, p. 65.

2. James, M., & Jongeward, D. *Born to win.* Reading, Mass.: Addison Wesley, 1971, p. 168.

3. Oden, T. A populist's view of psychotherapeutic deprofessionalization. *Journal of Humanistic Psychology,* Spring, 1974, p. 10.

Classroom Transactional Analysis

Teacher ego state behaviors are tallied with a vertical mark: "1." Student-to-teacher ego state behaviors are tallied with an "O." Student-to-student ego state behaviors are tallied with an "⊖." Tallies are placed in the appropriate box in the following form every three seconds, or faster in case of change of speaker or change of behavior.

Free Child	Authentic Adult	Ethical Adult	Logical Adult
⊦⊦⊦ 11000 011 ⊖⊖⊖	11000 ⊖⊖	011	⊦⊦⊦ ⊦⊦⊦ ⊦⊦⊦ ⊦⊦⊦ 00000 000001010 100110⊖⊖0 0⊖
OK Nurturing Parent 110	OK Critical Parent ⊦⊦⊦ 00 ⊖⊖ 11011	OK Adapted Child 0000⊖⊖⊖ ⊖⊖0111⊖0	OK Little Professor 001
Not-OK Nurturing Parent 101110	Not-OK Critical Parent 10110 ⊖⊖	Not-OK Adapted Child ⊖⊖⊖ ⊖⊖ ⊖⊖⊖⊖	Not-OK Little Professor ⊖⊖1⊖⊖11 0010⊖⊖

Classroom Transactional Analysis System:
Categories and Types of Ego State Behavior

OK Nurturing Parent

    Ask for Feelings
    Active Listening
    Empathy
    Protect
    Restrain
    Stroke: Encourage
               Hug
               Kiss
               Reward
               Praise
               Take Care of
               Touch
    Other

Not-OK Nurturing Parent

    Rescue (Unnecessarily)
    Tease
    Other

OK Critical (Prejudicial) Parent

    Criticize (Objectively) (Role
       Function)
    Direct-Command (Role
       Function)
    Express Beliefs
    Express Morals
    Judge (Role Function)
    Orient (Role Function)
    Other

Not-OK Critical Parent

    Blame
    Boss (Order)
    Criticize (The Person)
          Name Call
          Put-Down
          Moralize

Defend Own Authority
Moralize
Mystify
Pre-Judge
Punish
Threaten (Warn)
Other

Authentic Adult

Encounter:
    Give Feedback
    Receive Feedback
    Self-Disclose:
        Feelings (For Other)
        Inner States (With
            Other)
Self-Disclose:
    Feelings:
        Here-and-Now
        There-and-Then
    Inner States:
        Here-and-Now
        There-and-Then
Other

Ethical Adult

Accept Responsibility for Own
  Behavior
Behave Responsibly (Enforce
  Agreed upon Rules, etc.)
Decide
Persuade
Plan
State Opinion
Other

Logical Adult

Clarify
Collect Data
Demonstrate
Explain
Lecture
Present Evidence
State Fact
Other

Free (Natural) Child

Anger
Cry
Curious
Fear
Happy
Hurt (Not Cry)
Laugh (Giggle)
Groan (Moan)
Play
Sad
Sensuous
Shout (Scream)
Sigh
Sympathy
Other

OK Adapted Child

Cooperate
Give
Share
Stand Up for Own Rights
Take Turns
Other

Not-OK Adapted Child

Act-Out
Argue
Bicker
Bid for Attention
Bid for Power
Bully
Comply
Deny:
    Behavior
    Feelings
Give Up
Procrastinate
Pout
Revenge
Rebel
Selfishness
Strike:
    Person
    Object

Swear
Withdraw
Other

OK Little Professor

Believe in Magic
Create:
    Art
    Idea
    Problem Solution
Daydream
Fantasize
Intuit
Hunch (Guess)
Other

Not-OK Little Professor

Cheat
Intellectualize
Lie
Manipulate:
    Exploit
    Deceive
    Flatter
    Seduce
    Other
Pretend to Know
Steal
Show Off
Other

Selected Bibliography

Bach, G. R., & Goldberg, H. *Creative aggression.* New York: Doubleday, 1974.

Borton, T. *Reach, touch, and teach.* New York: McGraw-Hill, 1970.

Brown, G. I. *Human teaching for human learning.* New York: The Viking Press, 1971.

Brown, G. I., Yeomans, T., & Grizzard, L. *The live classroom.* New York: The Viking Press, 1975.

Castillo, G. A. *Left-handed teaching.* New York: Praeger, 1974.

Chase, L. *The other side of the report card.* Pacific Palisades, Calif.: Goodyear, 1975.

Clark, T., Bock, D., & Cornett, M. *Is that you out there?* Columbus, Ohio: Charles E. Merrill, 1973.

Corey, G. F. *Teachers can make a difference.* Columbus, Ohio: Charles E. Merrill, 1973.

Cratty, B. J. *Active learning.* Englewood Cliffs, N. J.: Prentice-Hall, 1971.

Curwin, R. L., & Curwin, G. *Developing individual values in the classroom.* Palo Alto, Calif.: Learning Handbooks, 1974.

Curwin, R. L., & Fuhrmann, B. S. *Discovering your teaching self.* Englewood Cliffs, N. J.: Prentice-Hall, 1975.

deMille, R. *Put your mother on the ceiling.* New York: The Viking Press, 1973.

Dillon, J. T. *Personal teaching.* Columbus, Ohio: Charles E. Merrill, 1971.

Gillies, J. *My needs, your needs, our needs.* New York: Doubleday, 1974.

Greenberg, H. M. *Teaching with feeling.* New York: Macmillan, 1969.

Greer, M., & Rubinstein, B. *Will the real teacher please stand up?* Pacific Palisades, Calif.: Goodyear, 1972.

Gunther, B. *Sense relaxation.* New York: Pocket Books, 1969.

Harmin, M., Kirschenbaum, H., & Simon, S. B. *Clarifying values through subject matter.* Minneapolis: Winston, 1973.

Hawley, R. C., & Hawley, I. L. *Human values in the classroom.* New York: Hart, 1975.

Hunter, E. *Encounter in the classroom.* New York: Holt, Rinehart and Winston, 1972.

James, M. M. *Born to love.* Reading, Mass.: Addison-Wesley, 1973.

James M., & Jongeward, D. *Born to win.* Reading, Mass.: Addison-Wesley, 1971.

Johnson, D. W. *Reaching out.* Englewood Cliffs, N.J.: Prentice-Hall, 1972.

Jones, R. M. *Fantasy and feeling in education.* New York: New York University Press, 1968.

Kline, L. W. *Education and the personal quest.* Columbus, Ohio: Charles E. Merrill, 1971.

Lederman, J. *Anger and the rocking chair.* New York: The Viking Press, 1969.

Leonard, G. *Education and ecstasy.* New York: Dell, 1970.

Lewis, H. R., & Streitfield, H. S. *Growth games.* New York: Harcourt Brace Jovanovich, 1970.

Lyon, H. C. *Learning to feel, feeling to learn.* Columbus, Ohio: Charles E. Merrill, 1971.

Mann, J. *Learning to be.* New York: Free Press, 1972.

Morgan, H. *The learning community.* Columbus, Ohio: Charles E. Merrill, 1973.

Olson, K. *The art of hanging loose.* Phoenix: O'Sullivan, Woodside and Co., 1974.

Otto, H. A. *Fantasy encounter games.* New York: Harper & Row, 1972.

Otto, H. A. *A guide to developing your potential.* N. Hollywood, Calif.: Wilshire, 1967.

Otto, H. A., & Mann, J. *Ways of growth.* New York: Pocket Books, 1968.

Pfeiffer, J. W., & Jones, J. E. (Eds). *A handbook of structured experiences for human relations training* (Vols. I, II, III, IV, & V). La Jolla, Calif.: University Associates, 1969-1975.

Pfeiffer, J. W., & Jones, J. E. (Eds). *The annual handbook for group facilitators.* La Jolla, Calif.: University Associates, 1972-1976.

Reichert, R. *Self-awareness through group dynamics.* Dayton, Ohio: Pflaum/Standard, 1970.

Romey, W. D. *Risk-trust-love: Learning in a humane environment.* Columbus, Ohio: Charles E. Merrill, 1972.

Saulnier, L., & Simard, T. *Personal growth and interpersonal relations.* Englewood Cliffs, N.J.: Prentice-Hall, 1973.

Sax, S., & Hollander, S. *Reality games.* Toronto: Popular Library, 1972.

Schrank, J. *Teaching human beings.* Boston: Beacon Press, 1972.

Schutz, W. C. *Joy: Expanding human awareness.* New York: Grove Press, 1967.

Seaberg, D. I. *The four faces of teaching.* Pacific Palisades, Calif.: Goodyear, 1974.

Shannon, R. L. *Where the truth comes out.* Columbus, Ohio: Charles E. Merrill, 1971.

Simon, S. B., Howe, L. W., & Kirschenbaum, H. *Values clarification.* New York: Hart, 1972.

Smith, G. W., & Phillips, A. I. *Couple therapy.* New York: Collier, 1971.

Stanford, G., & Roark, A. E. *Human interaction in education.* Boston: Allyn & Bacon, 1974.

Stevens, J. O. *Awareness.* New York: Bantam, 1971.

Way, B. *Development through drama.* New York: Humanities Press, 1967.

Weinstein, G., & Fantini, M. D. *Toward humanistic education.* New York: Praeger, 1970.

Wittmer, J., & Myrick, R. D. *Facilitative teaching.* Pacific Palisades, Calif.: Goodyear, 1974.

Zahorik, J., & Brubaker, D. *Toward more humanistic instruction.* Dubuque, Iowa: William C. Brown, 1972.